*Literary Lives*

Founding Editor: **Richard Dutton**, Professor of English, Lancaster University

This series offers stimulating accounts of the literary careers of the most admired and influential English-language authors. Volumes follow the outline of the writers' working lives, not in the spirit of traditional biography, but aiming to trace the professional, publishing and social contexts which shaped their writing.

*Published titles include*:

| | |
|---|---|
| *Angela Smith* <br> KATHERINE MANSFIELD | *Tony Sharpe* <br> WALLACE STEVENS |
| *Lisa Hopkins* <br> CHRISTOPHER MARLOWE | *Joseph McMinn* <br> JONATHAN SWIFT |
| *Cedric C. Brown* <br> JOHN MILTON | *William Christie* <br> SAMUEL TAYLOR COLERIDGE |
| *Peter Davison* <br> GEORGE ORWELL | *Leonée Ormond* <br> ALFRED TENNYSON |
| *Linda Wagner-Martin* <br> SYLVIA PLATH | *Peter Shillingsburg* <br> WILLIAM MAKEPEACE THACKERAY |
| *Felicity Rosslyn* <br> ALEXANDER POPE | *David Wykes* <br> EVELYN WAUGH |
| *Ira B. Nadel* <br> EZRA POUND | *Caroline Franklin* <br> MARY WOLLSTONECRAFT |
| *Richard Dutton* <br> WILLIAM SHAKESPEARE | *John Mepham* <br> VIRGINIA WOOLF |
| *John Williams* <br> MARY SHELLEY | *John Williams* <br> WILLIAM WORDSWORTH |
| *Michael O'Neill* <br> PERCY BYSSHE SHELLEY | *Alasdair D. F. Macrae* <br> W. B. YEATS |
| *Gary Waller* <br> EDMUND SPENSER | |

Literary Lives
Series Standing Order ISBN 0–333–71486–5 hardcover
Series Standing Order ISBN 0–333–80334–5 paperback
(outside North America only)

You can receive future titles in this series as they are published by placing a standing order. Please contact your bookseller or, in case of difficulty, write to us at the address below with your name and address, the title of the series and one of the ISBNs quoted above.

Customer Services Department, Macmillan Distribution Ltd, Houndmills, Basingstoke, Hampshire RG21 6XS, England

# Ted Hughes

## A Literary Life

Neil Roberts

First published in 2007 by
PALGRAVE MACMILLAN
Houndmills, Basingstoke, Hampshire RG21 6XS and
175 Fifth Avenue, New York, N.Y. 10010
Companies and representatives throughout the world.

PALGRAVE MACMILLAN is the global academic imprint of the Palgrave Macmillan division of St. Martin's Press, LLC and of Palgrave Macmillan Ltd. Macmillan® is a registered trademark in the United States, United Kingdom and other countries. Palgrave is a registered trademark in the European Union and other countries.

ISBN-13: 978–1–4039–3605–9 hardback
ISBN-10: 1–4039–3605–6 hardback

This book is printed on paper suitable for recycling and made from fully managed and sustained forest sources.

A catalogue record for this book is available from the British Library.

Library of Congress Cataloging-in-Publication Data
Roberts, Neil, 1946–
    Ted Hughes : a literary life / Neil Roberts.
        p. cm.
    Includes bibliographical references and index.
    ISBN 1–4039–3605–6
        1. Hughes, Ted, 1930–1998. 2. Poets, English – 20th century –
Biography. 3. Authors, English – 20th century – Biography. I. Title.
PR6058.U37Z82 2007
821'.914—dc22                                        2006049434
[B]

10  9  8  7  6  5  4  3  2  1
16  15  14  13  12  11  10  09  08  07

Transferred to Digital Printing 2007

*To Malcolm*

# Contents

# Acknowledgements

Excerpts from 'Two,' 'Mayday on Holderness,' 'Waving Goodbye, from your Banked Hospital Bed' and '1952–1977' ('A Nation's a Soul') from *Collected Poems* by Ted Hughes. Copyright © 2003 by The Estate of Ted Hughes. Reprinted by permission of Faber and Faber Ltd and Farrar, Straus and Giroux, LLC. Excerpts from unpublished writings by Ted Hughes, Copyright © The Estate of Ted Hughes. Reprinted by permission of the Estate of Ted Hughes.

Material from Chapters 3 and 5 appeared in 'The Common Text of Sylvia Plath and Ted Hughes', *Symbiosis*, vol. 7 no. 1, April 2003. An earlier version of Chapter 12 was published as 'Hughes, the Laureateship and National Identity', *Q/W/E/R/T/Y: Littératures et Civilisations des Pays Anglophones* (Université de Pau), 9, October 1999.

Warmest thanks to the staff of the Manuscript, Archives and Rare Book Library, Emory University, especially Steven Ennis, Kathy Shoemaker, Naomi Jacobs and Susan Macdonald, for being so welcoming and helpful, and making my visits there so pleasurable as well as rewarding. Thanks also to the staff of the British Library Manuscripts Room, especially Katherine Baxter, and the Special Collections staff at Exeter and Sheffield University Libraries.

I am also grateful to the following for help of various kinds: Andy Armitage, Carol Bere, Fran Brearton, Janne Stige Drangsholdt, Gavin Drummond, Terry Gifford, John Haffenden, Carol Hughes, Claas Kazzer, Melissa Maday, Diane Middlebrook, Joanny Moulin, Sylvia Paul, Keith Sagar, Ann Skea, Sue Vice, Daniel Weissbort.

# List of Abbreviations

| | |
|---|---|
| A | *Alcestis* |
| CB | *Cave-Birds* |
| CP | *Collected Poems* |
| D | *The Dreamfighter* |
| DB | *Difficulties of a Bridegroom* |
| EO | *The Earth-Owl and Other Moon-People* |
| FVB | *Ffangs the Vampire Bat and the Kiss of Truth* |
| G | *Gaudete* |
| M | *Moortown* |
| MD | *Moortown Diary* |
| O | *The Oresteia* |
| P | *Phèdre* |
| PM | *Poetry in the Making* |
| RCD | *Rain-Charm for the Duchy* |
| SGCB | *Shakespeare and the Goddess of Complete Being* |
| SO | *Seneca's Oedipus* |
| TB | *Three Books* |
| TO | *Tales from Ovid* |
| W | *Wodwo* |
| WP | *Winter Pollen* |
| WW | *Wolfwatching* |

# Introduction

As a young man, Ted Hughes must have seemed blessed. He was extravagantly gifted, as his juvenile poetry shows, and was warmly encouraged by his family and teachers. From a socially and economically modest background in Yorkshire, he won a place at Cambridge, despite performing poorly in the entrance exam: his teacher persuaded the college to accept him because of his talent as a writer.[1] His literary and intellectual gifts were matched by a personal magnetism that enabled him to make a strong impression on his circle of friends at Cambridge without posing as a public schoolboy or metropolitan intellectual. Aged twenty-five, he married an equally talented poet with whom he shared a creative partnership, and who possessed the ambition and competence to launch him on a career as a professional writer. From the age of thirty, he never had to take a salaried job, and was able to support himself – eventually to grow wealthy – by his writing. For an English poet in the late twentieth century, this was almost unique: Hughes's only rival in popularity, Philip Larkin, worked all his life as a librarian. For much of his life – and again, after a comparative decline in reputation, at his death – he was widely regarded, and with good reason, as the greatest British poet of the second half of the twentieth century, and a peer of the giants of the earlier part of the century, Eliot and Yeats.

Yet, later in life, he often felt cursed. The most obvious, and personally painful, reason for this was, of course, the suicide of Sylvia Plath followed, six years later, by that of his partner Assia Wevill, who also killed their child. Not only did Hughes suffer grief and guilt, but from the early 1970s onward he was publicly demonised to the extent that he felt he had lost possession of the facts of his own life. He was driven into silence about his private life, broken only by the occasional anguished protest. This public pressure reinforced a temperamental inclination to

1

reticence, in making his work rigorously impersonal. Late in his life when he decided to complete and publish *Birthday Letters*, he felt that this impersonality had damaged his development as a writer. He died feeling that he had not achieved what he had been capable of. Most of his readers probably think that his work 'went off' at some point. The most severe date this decline from after his second book *Lupercal* (1960); Hughes himself felt for years that he had lost momentum after *Crow* (1970); even his warmest admirers are unlikely to think that he wrote much original poetry of note (leaving aside the special case of *Birthday Letters*) after *River* (1983). In the last fifteen years of his life he devoted most of his energies to what often seemed to himself 'displacement activities': public Laureate verse, the monumental *Shakespeare and the Goddess of Complete Being* and a series of translations, mostly for the theatre. However, his translations have already contributed to the revival of his reputation, and while the Laureate verses are unlikely ever to win many admirers, the Shakespeare book, though over-long and at times obsessive, is a work of extraordinary and original insight that will assuredly contribute to Hughes's long-term reputation as an all-round man of letters.

The tragedies of Sylvia Plath and Assia Wevill will always, in the public mind, be the 'main plot' of Hughes's life, and their significance for his work is indeed immeasurable. But there is another 'plot', more deeply buried, more far-reaching and possibly more central to Hughes's vocation as a poet, that would have made his literary life far from straightforward even if his personal life had been less tragic. Hughes was profoundly at odds with the secular, rational and materialistic culture in which he lived. His temperament was formed in his early years, when he lived in the Calder Valley, and was taken up on to the moors on shooting expeditions by his much older brother, Gerald. In these years which he later described as 'paradise',[2] he formed a profound and passionate attachment to the natural world. Hughes's paradise was lost when his family moved to a town in South Yorkshire, and his brother left home, eventually to emigrate permanently to Australia, though Hughes found a substitute in the countryside around his new home. The lost paradise, and associated idea of the Fall, became a template for Hughes's *Weltanschauung*, and especially his construction of the history of Western civilisation. He felt increasingly that he was living in times when humanity had catastrophically lost connection with the sacred. The material signs of this were everywhere to be seen in the ecological crisis that gathered intensity in his later years, but for Hughes this material crisis was inseparable from a fundamentally religious sense of his, and his fellow-humans', relationship to nature.

Similar to Ovid, as he portrays him in the Introduction to *Tales from Ovid*, Hughes lived in an age in which the 'obsolete paraphernalia of the old official religion were lying in heaps ... and new ones had not yet arrived. The mythic plane, so to speak, had been defrocked' (*TO* x–xi). Yet myth and religion, in some form, were essential to his mental and imaginative life. He was deeply suspicious of rational prose discourse, as the language of the secular ethos that had, as he saw it, brought the world to this plight. But there was no other publicly shared language to which he could assent. He became a kind of religious *bricoleur*, drawing on Robert Graves for the idea of the Goddess, the antagonist of the masculine intellect and patriarchal Puritanism, but also on a range of mystical, archaic and anti-rational discourses such as astrology, alchemy and cabbala. This was emphatically not in a spirit of 'New Age' faddishness, but a disciplined attempt to resist the seductions of the rational intellect (he himself had a formidable intellect), and keep open communications with an inner life, which was also the life of the natural creature in him. His dream of a burnt fox who told him to give up studying literature at Cambridge, his imperviousness to the external environment and imaginative focus on the English natural world when in America, the obscure 'single adventure' of *Wodwo*, the literary myths of *Crow, Orghast, Gaudete* and *Cave Birds*, the 'tragic formula' that was the key to his interpretation of Shakespeare, even his attachment to the monarchy as the spiritual unity of the nation, are all manifestations, at various levels of artistic form, of this religious commitment.

Nothing Hughes wrote, which was not to some degree a report from this inner life had any value for him, and he frequently complained about the secular demands of a professional writer's life, which constantly drew his mind back to the surface. He once expressed his ideal as 'a faculty that embraces both worlds simultaneously' and 'keeps faith, as Goethe says, with the world of things and the world of spirits equally' (*WP* 150). He had a strong sense of secular responsibility, which he exercised indefatigably through encouraging children's writing, ecological campaigning (much of it local, concerning the health of Devon's rivers) and the Laureateship. But such was his sense of the prevailing culture's hostility to the inner life, that his most intense loyalties were to that world. His 'literary life', therefore, remarkable though its outward form undoubtedly was, was to a considerable extent a matter of the intense cultivation of the inner life.

This is not a biography of Hughes, though I have drawn on published biographies as well as on archival documents. It is primarily a critical study of his work in the context of his life and literary career. The early chapters place a particularly strong emphasis on biographical context, specifically Hughes's childhood, education and early relationship with Sylvia Plath. The later chapters mostly focus on major collections of poetry, with reference to contextual aspects that I think are particularly illuminating, ranging from Hughes's residence in America when writing *Lupercal* to the aborted saga that was his original plan for *Crow*. The major exception is Chapter 7, which concentrates entirely on contextual matters, reflecting the profound importance to Hughes's development of the controversies surrounding his relations with Plath. The plan of the book is mostly chronological, but I have grouped Hughes's writing for children and translations in separate chapters because the significance of these parts of his oeuvre might be lost in brief comments scattered through the book. Writers who live as long as Hughes usually end their lives either as celebrated but known quantities or in sad neglect. The publication of *Birthday Letters* in his last year ensured that Hughes avoided both these fates. He died the subject of renewed interest, and in the midst of a wholesale reassessment both of his life and of his work. This book is another chapter in that reassessment.

# 1
# Paradise Lost: Formation and Juvenilia

Hughes's poem 'Two', collected in *Elmet*, describes two hunters who 'stepped down' from a paradisal world, carrying the bodies of grouse, snipe, hares and crows. There is a hint of violation about their activity – the hares are 'stolen embers' (recalling Prometheus, a figure later to be very important for Hughes) and the snipe have been 'robbed of their jewels' – but the prevailing impression is one of primal innocence:

> The stream spoke its oracle of unending,
> The sun spread a land at their feet.

This paradisal world is brought to an end by 'the war' and 'a sudden yelling' that 'Ricocheted among huddled roof-tops', as a result of which one of the two, 'the guide', 'flew up'. The consequence for the other is that

> The feather fell from his head.
> The drum stopped in his hand.
> The song died in his mouth.[1]

In an interview given in 1995 to the *Paris Review* Hughes spoke of expeditions with his much older brother Gerald, from the age of three, hunting 'over the hillsides and on the moor edge with a rifle.'[2] Gerald 'mythologised his hunting world as North American Indian – paleolithic' and the young Ted 'lived in his dream.' This explains at one level the last three lines of the poem, quoted above, though as we shall see they have a deeper significance.

Hughes has said that this poem is 'simply about my brother and myself. He was ten years older than me and made my early life a kind of paradise ... which was ended abruptly by the war. He joined the RAF... . The closing of Paradise is a big event.'[3] Hughes had spoken about these hunting expeditions much earlier in the radio talk 'Capturing Animals', collected in the book *Poetry in the Making* (1967) and later excerpted in *Winter Pollen*. Here he links the activity of hunting directly, but ambivalently, to writing poetry. 'Capturing animals' is a metaphor for poetic creation – the young listener to the programme is told that when she or he has written a poem she or he 'will have captured a spirit, a creature', but Hughes says that

> At about fifteen my life grew more complicated and my attitude to animals changed. I accused myself of disturbing their lives. I began to look at them, you see, from their own point of view.
> And about the same time I began to write poems. (*WP* 11)

In this account the poems are in part a rejection of the hunting life. Nevertheless Hughes believed that 'my poems might be partly a continuation of my earlier pursuit'. Such an idea is certainly congruent with Hughes's popular reputation. The positive connection between poetry and the life on the moors with Gerald is also supported by his radio programme 'The Poet Speaks', cited by Keith Sagar, in which he gives as his first experience of poetry a Native American war-song chanted to him by his brother.[4]

However, one must beware of self-mythologising. Those early expeditions with Gerald certainly shaped Hughes's imagination forever, and he was bereft when permanently separated by Gerald's emigration to Australia; but Diane Middlebrook has pointed out that as Hughes got older, the age at which he started going out with Gerald got younger.[5] It is equally and perhaps more straightforwardly true that Hughes was inspired to write poetry at school. The first to take an interest in his writing was Miss Mcleod, the form mistress in his first class at Mexborough Grammar. Later a teacher called Pauline Mayne told him the phrase 'with a frost-chilled snap', in a poem he had written about wildfowling, was poetry. This encouragement was continued by his sixth-form teacher, John Fisher.[6] These teachers became family friends, and their influence was reinforced by that of his elder sister Olwyn, later to be his agent, 'who had a marvellously precocious taste in poetry'. However, Hughes goes on to describe this apparently ideal climate for a young writer as an experience of being 'in that cooker from the age of about eleven – and totally confident that I belonged to it, so by 16 I had no thought of becoming anything but writer [*sic*] of some kind, certainly writing verse'.[7] The image of the cooker is jarringly dissonant with the moorland world that he had shared with Gerald, and the phrase, 'totally confident that I belonged to it' carries the hint that this confidence was misplaced. This feeling about education is congruent with his subsequent reaction to Cambridge, but there is an important difference between the two. In Cambridge, as we shall see in Chapter 2, it was poetry that was stifled by the educational environment. At school the opposite seems to have been the case: the aspiration to be a writer is actively fostered by an environment which, implicitly, is stifling something else. It may be relevant to this that Hughes wrote to Gerald, 'From the age of about 16–17 my life has been quite false.'[8] This assessment was prompted by the depression that he suffered after the deaths of his mother and, even more significantly, Assia Wevill and their daughter Shura, and we should be cautious about interpreting it as a settled view of his life. However, the evidence does suggest that a neat continuity between the unfettered life of the moor-wandering boy and the creative life of the poet is an oversimplification, and Hughes may have been haunted by alternative lives that poetry required him to forfeit. He wrote in the *Birthday Letters* poem 'Ouija' that if he had not fallen in with the ambition of Sylvia Plath and her mother, he would have been 'fishing off a rock / In Western Australia.'

An important aspect of Hughes's life in the 'cooker' is that his close relationship with his brother ended in 1938, when Ted was only eight years old: the family moved from Mytholmroyd to Mexborough in South Yorkshire and Gerald, instead of moving with them, took a job as a gamekeeper in Devon and subsequently joined the RAF. The brothers were never together again except for short visits, though at least until the mid-1970s Hughes dreamed about a reunion. At the risk of being too literal-minded, I suggest that these events lie behind the 'war' and the flight of the 'guide' in 'Two'. Keith Sagar is surely right to point out that they sealed off Hughes's early years 'as a dream of innocence', in a similar, though of course less traumatic way, to Sylvia Plath's loss of her father and move from Winthrop to Wellesley at a similar age.[9]

Among Hughes's unpublished juvenilia, written in 1949 and 1950, are two long 'Birthday Odes' for Gerald, and an 'Ode on the anniversary of your leaving for Australia'. One of these poems begins,

'The year's sweet cry climbs no more through the woods;
Clouds, wind, leaves starve, forsaken of that voice'

and includes the line, 'I meant to embrace our spirits in one image.' Another one of the birthday poems is gathered into a home-made booklet, perhaps by Gerald, with a picture of Ted on the front, and covers sixteen pages, forty-seven lines per page, consisting of an 'Invocation to the Nearest Muse', Overture, three movements and an 'Epithalamium'.[10] The 'Invocation to the Nearest Muse' is an early version of the poem published in *The Hawk in the Rain* as 'Song', the only pre-Cambridge poem that Hughes collected in his lifetime. The structure of this whole work strikingly anticipates that of some of his laureate poems.

Even allowing for the self-conscious hyperbole of Hughes's early style, these poems strongly convey the young man's grief at the loss of his brother. Before Hughes met Plath he planned to join Gerald in Australia,[11] and his subsequent letters repeatedly plead with his brother to return to England, and attempt to lure him back with plans for a life together on a farm.[12] He told Daniel Weissbort that this reunion with Gerald was an 'infantile' dream that had persisted until he was in his forties, and that when he finally realised that it would be unfulfilled, 'it knocked me absolutely off my perch'.[13] He later told Gerald that when the latter went to Australia he was 'orphaned'.[14] The significance of all this for Hughes's imaginative life is hinted at in a letter to Keith Sagar, in which he connects Gerald's 'paradisal' life as a gamekeeper in Devon with the early influence of Henry Williamson's *Tarka the Otter.* These combined with the landscape of Old Denaby in South Yorkshire to become his 'inner life', in part motivating his move to Devon in 1961.[15]

Sagar comments on the final lines of 'Two' that Gerald had been Ted's 'spirit guide into the unfallen animal world for the apprentice shaman'.[16] Hughes had reviewed Mircea Eliade's book *Shamanism* in 1964, and described shamanism as 'a technique for moving in a state of ecstasy among the various spirit realms, and for generally dealing with souls and spirits, in a practical way, in some practical crisis' (*WP* 56). Most notably this 'practical' function is one of healing. In the review Hughes mentions singing, drumming and dreams of flight as fundamental aspects of shamanic practice and experience. Shortly before writing *Remains of Elmet*, Hughes had composed a long narrative poem, *Gaudete*, which might be described as the story of a failed shaman. The most important thing about the review is Hughes's assertion that the experiences which characterise the shaman are 'the basic experience of the poetic temperament we call "romantic" ', and he goes on to cite poems by Shakespeare, Keats, Yeats and Eliot as examples (*WP* 58). This is an idiosyncratic and obviously not 'academic' illustration of the concept of the 'romantic'. These poets are all, not surprisingly, included in what Hughes later called his 'sacred canon'.[17] There can be little doubt that it is a company in which he included himself, in aspiration if not in claims to achievement.

It seems to me that there is at least a tension between Hughes's career as a poet and the satisfactions he enjoyed on the moors as a boy and subsequently craved all his life. The one does not completely subsume the other. Certainly when he told Gerald, 'all I want to do is write',[18] he was expressing a permanent, or at least recurring, sentiment. But he also wrote to his brother, not long after, that being 'a writer – and nothing else' is a 'meaningless existence' unless 'it's helping you to form and give meaning to the rest of your life, the spontaneous part'.[19] Like many poets Hughes had a healthy scepticism about language. On the sleeve of a recording of *Crow* he described the God of that book as having the same relation to the Creator as ordinary English has to reality,[20] and several poems in that volume articulate this scepticism ('Crow Goes Hunting', 'The Battle of Osfrontalis', 'A Disaster'). Hughes praised the Hungarian poet János Pilinszky for saying, 'I would like to write as if I had remained silent' (*WP* 232). In an interview about *Orghast*, his theatrical experiment with Peter Brook, he said that the most important element in language is 'animal music', in which the 'real virtuosi' are 'certain animals and birds – though their ranges are pretty limited. When they speak the spirits listen. Not many human voices can make the spirits listen'.[21] It is perhaps significant that many of his best later poems are about fishing, an activity which he pursued passionately and has obvious links with his early hunting expeditions. In *Poetry in the Making* he drew an analogy between fishing and writing poetry (*WP* 18–19). One of his most memorable fishing poems, however, 'Go Fishing', begins thus:

> Join water, wade in underbeing
> Let brain mist into moist earth
> Ghost loosen away downstream
> Gulp river and gravity
>
> Lose words
> Cease
> Be assumed into the womb of lymph

'You must shamanize or die' (*WP* 58), Hughes writes of those who are 'called by the spirits' to this activity. There is no doubt that he thought he must write poetry or die; he wrote to Peter Redgrove, 'it's fatal – nearly literally – to stop writing'.[22] One of his more idiosyncratic beliefs was that verse reinforced the immune system and that his fatal illness was caused by writing too much prose.[23] Against this, 'Two' seems to narrate a loss of shamanic power resulting from the loss of the hunting life with Gerald, and I have been arguing that there are enough hints elsewhere to suggest that this feeling remained a counter-pressure in Hughes's life.

There is one further text, in my view the most affecting of all, that relates to this crucial aspect of Hughes's early formation. In 1994 he published a story, 'The Deadfall', collected the following year in *Difficulties of a Bridegroom*. It consists of three separate anecdotes about the narrator's childhood, whose links are experiential rather than narrative. Hughes has written that he wrote it in response to a request for a ghost story, and that 'an early experience of my own filled the requirements, and I wrote it out, with a few adjustments to what I remember' (*DB* ix). We must be cautious about the biographical value of this text, both because of those 'few adjustments' and because it was written nearly sixty years after the experience on which it is based. In the Emory archive there is a draft of the story which represents it as an experience of the narrator's father who, like Hughes's father, was a veteran of the First World War,[24] and in a letter to Gerald recalling the episode on which it is clearly based, Hughes makes no reference to the central incidents of the story.[25] However, whether considered as autobiography or as fiction, the story connects with and extends some of the central motifs in Hughes's work in extremely intriguing ways.

The first section of the story narrates the mediumistic experiences of the narrator's mother. On the night of the D-Day landings she has a vision of 'flashing crosses' filling the sky. She has vivid premonitions, once in the form of a ghost, of the deaths of close relatives. After her favourite sister's death at the age of eighteen her ghost visits the narrator's mother whenever a family member is about to die. (This is also the subject of one of Hughes's most moving late poems, 'Anniversary'.) Although the word is not used in the story, there can be little doubt that Hughes regarded her as an example of the shamanic 'temperament'. The second section of the story concerns the attempts of the narrator and his elder brother, inspired by their mother's experiences, to raise the ghost of an 'ancient Briton' supposedly buried under a great slab of stone in a wood on the hillside above Mytholmroyd. They go to the stone at night, light a fire and pour wine over it, and the elder brother intones an improvised chant including the words, 'Rise up, O ancient Briton, and quench your ancient thirst', which gives the narrator 'the sensation of my hair freezing solid' (*DB* 4). Although the narrator's fear is very effectively evoked, there is something slightly comic about this episode. We are made humorously aware of the youth of the protagonists, and in the end nothing happens.

In the light of the third, longest and most important section of the story, the implication seems to be that ghosts do not appear to those who deliberately seek them, but choose their own time, place and person. The brothers spend a weekend camping in a remote valley. Throughout the Saturday the elder brother goes hunting with a rifle, but is unable to shoot anything. They meet a farmer and his aged mother, and try unsuccessfully to shoot a rat for him. During the day the brother points out to the narrator a gamekeeper's deadfall, a heavy slab of stone held up at an angle by a flimsy support of sticks, and baited with a freshly killed wood pigeon. In the evening the trap is still unsprung. On the second night in the tent the narrator hears a voice whispering his name. Going out of the tent he sees an old woman who tells him there has been an accident. He assumes she must be the farmer's mother and that the farmer is the victim. But she takes him to the deadfall where a fox cub has its paw and tail caught under the stone. The boy manages to lift the stone and the cub darts away. When the boy looks for the old woman she has disappeared. In the morning the brothers return to the deadfall and find an adult fox dead under it. The elder brother digs a hole to bury the fox, and in the hole the narrator finds a tiny ivory fox which he conceals from his brother and keeps throughout his life. He makes unconvincing rational explanations to himself of the old woman's appearance and disappearance, but the elder brother suggests to him that she was the fox's ghost.

In this story the elder brother is a false guide. It is the narrator, not he, who is the inheritor of their mother's shamanic abilities: the brother is not able to bring a ghost to him, but one comes of its own choosing and picks him out by name. The prominence of the fox in this story links it with several other crucial texts in Hughes's *oeuvre*, which I shall be discussing at length in later chapters. As far as I know Hughes has, surprisingly, never made an explicit link between this story and the one published in *Winter Pollen* in which an eponymous 'burnt fox' appears to him in a dream, and tells him that he is 'destroying us' by studying English literature (*WP* 8–9). This story (which unlike 'The Deadfall' is a direct personal reminiscence) is implicitly linked to the claim Hughes has made that academic literary study was destructive of his poetic abilities, and Hughes explicitly linked it, at readings, with 'The Thought-Fox', the poem he identified as the first fruit of his poetic recovery. Another, much later poem that 'The Deadfall' illuminates is 'Epiphany' in *Birthday Letters*, in which Hughes, living with Plath and their baby child in a flat in London, refuses the offer of a fox cub in the street, and 'walked on / As if out of my own life.' Mysteriously the poem asserts that 'whatever comes with a fox / Is what tests a marriage and proves it a marriage', and that he had failed this test. 'The Deadfall' and 'The Burnt Fox' were both published in 1994, during a period in which Hughes probably wrote many of the *Birthday Letters* poems: he may have been consciously tracing this continuity.

In Chapter 2, I describe 'The Burnt Fox' as 'the founding myth of Hughes's poetic career'. If the fox in 'The Deadfall' is part of the autobiographical basis, however, the Cambridge dream was not the first episode in the myth. Hughes must have made a connection between the two foxes, one of which he saved, the other of which accuses him of destroying it. The first fox, or its ghost, is the 'spirit' who has 'chosen' him as a shaman. He obeyed the call of this spirit and rescued the cub; he also obeyed the second fox and gave up English at university. These stories help to explain the feeling of failure in 'Epiphany': on this third occasion he refuses the call. But what does this signify? It is certainly not a failure to commit himself to poetry: Hughes and Plath's common commitment to poetry, and its possible dangers, is a theme throughout *Birthday Letters*. In the poem 'Flounders' Hughes narrates a day spent unsuccessfully fishing off Cape Cod, becoming cut off from shore by the tide, rescued, and then discovering a channel in which flounders abound. This 'head-glitter day of emptiness' with its 'brilliant, arduous morning', 'wind-hammered perilous afternoon' and 'storm-gold evening' is like an adult version of the paradisal world of 'Two'. This, I suggest, is an example of 'what comes with a fox': 'a toy miniature / Of the life that might have bonded us/ Into a single animal, a single soul'. The poem ends,

> It was a visit from the goddess, the beauty
> Who was poetry's sister – she had come
> To tell poetry she was spoiling us.
> Poetry listened, maybe, but we heard nothing
> And poetry did not tell us. And we
> Only did what poetry told us to do.

Once again Hughes suggests that there was something more important than poetry, which poetry itself robbed him of.

Although Hughes seems to have had a happy childhood, his feeling about Mytholmroyd itself, the valley bottom in which the village is situated, is extremely negative. In a 1963 memoir, 'The Rock', he repeatedly refers to the feeling of being 'trapped', and writes that 'I can never lose the impression that the whole region is in mourning for the first world war'. The return to the valley from the moors he describes as 'a descent into the pit, and after each visit I must have returned less and less of myself into the valley. This was where the division of body and soul began.'[26] This statement not only reinforces the importance of his youthful experiences on the moors, but links these experiences anti- thetically with an often noted aspect of his childhood: the influence on his imagination, via his traumatised father, of the First World War.

William Hughes was one of only seventeen survivors of his regiment at Gallipoli. He rarely spoke of his war experience but would sometimes cry out at night in his sleep. Hughes writes about the First World War in poems throughout his career, most importantly in *The Hawk in the Rain*, *Wodwo* and *Wolfwatching*. I will discuss these poems in the appropriate chapters; here I just want to emphasise the importance of this inherited traumatic memory for his formation, or at least for his own representa- tion of his childhood. In poems written twenty years apart he describes himself as his father's 'luckless double' ('Out', *W*) and 'supplementary convalescent' ('Dust As We Are', *WW*). His father's trauma seems to have epitomised and perhaps conditioned his sense of Mytholmroyd as a bleak and oppressive place – though there is broader historical basis for this, in the history of industrial labour, its subsequent decline, and the heavy fatalities that the region suffered in the War. The most inter- esting piece of writing in Hughes's Laureate volume, *Rain-Charm for the Duchy*, is a prose 'note' in which he reflects on the symbolic importance of the Queen Mother from this personal and historical perspective (*RCD* 58–60; I will be discussing this in my chapter on 'The Poet Laureate').

More generally, the strong duality of Hughes's representation of his childhood, and particularly the weight of the past on the present felt through his father, may have influenced two characteristics of his work. One is the Manichaean element, felt most strongly in *Crow*. This is not to say that Hughes's mind rested in a dualistic or Manichaean world view – on the contrary, as 'Go Fishing' quoted above testifies, he strove above all to achieve and articulate a state of oneness with the cosmos, and to identify the spiritual with the natural. However, as he wrote in 'The Rock', 'This was where the division of body and soul began' – a fate imposed by experience and environment, not an innate condition, but a fate nevertheless that he had to contend with. The second characteris- tic that may be traceable to the weight of the past on his childhood is the element of determinism in his work. This is particularly strong in *Birthday Letters*, in which he represents Plath's life as determined by the trauma of her father's death.

The last factor that I want to emphasise in registering the importance of Hughes's early formation is his linguistic heritage. He was not a dialect or even, except incidentally, a regional poet. Nevertheless he said to Ekbert Faas,

> I grew up in West Yorkshire. They have a very distinctive dialect there. Whatever other speech you grow into, presumably your dialect stays alive in a sort of inner freedom, a separate little self.... . Without it, I doubt if I would ever have written verse.[27]

The most important single fact about this linguistic formation is that it is non-metropolitan. Whatever the overt ideological bearings of the poetry, the language exerts a pressure away from the metropolitan 'centre'. More specifically, it is a form of English that is more influenced by Danish morphology and phonology than more southern forms, and less by Norman French. This element in Hughes's background is explicit in poems such as 'Thistles' and 'The Warriors of the North' (both *W*). As a conscious verbal artist, and a highly educated man, Hughes is of course not at the mercy of these elements, and commands the full range of English. Nevertheless the influence of northern speech on his poetry is unmistakable, and there is evidence that he consciously cultivated it. In 1959 he wrote to his Cambridge friend Lucas Myers that he wanted to break the taboo against dialect.[28] Although Hughes normally spoke standard English, in a transcript by Ann Skea of an Australian radio interview he appears to use the northern dialect form 'tret' for 'treated'.[29] This is reinforced by the children's poem 'The Dracula Vine' (*EO*), which has the rhyme, 'So this is a useful pet / And loyal if well-treat.' In an unpublished manuscript fragment about the Laureateship he writes that there is 'Nowt to be sorry at' in accepting this post, and that 'The summit's / Summat.'[30] As well as the unquestionable non-metropolitan character that I have mentioned, these elements also bear certain associations of class (the common people) and gender (rugged masculinity) that are commonly detected in Hughes's poetry. The earliest archived piece of writing by Hughes is a couplet written on a school photo dated 1940: 'Twice armed is he who has his quarrel just. Thrice armed is he who gets his blow in fust.' This may not be original, but it displays a relish of dialect, and an association of dialect with a feeling of robust masculine independence.[31]

Hughes began writing poetry in his early teens. Between the ages of fifteen and nineteen he published six poems in the Mexborough Grammar School magazine *Don and Dearne*. These poems are notable for their variety and, not surprisingly, for their almost uniformly high level of accomplish-ment. Hughes said to Ekbert Faas that his early poems about the Wild West and African tribal warfare were 'in imitation of Kipling', but those that survive suggest that a more immediate influence was 'the Canadian Kipling', Robert Service. Service's most famous poem, 'The Shooting of Dan McGrew', is included in Hughes and Heaney's anthology, *The Rattle Bag*.

> Then I ducked my head, and the lights went out, and two guns blazed
>     in the dark;
> And a woman screamed, and the lights went up, and two men lay
>     stiff and stark.
> Pitched on his head, and pumped full of lead, was Dangerous Dan
>     McGrew,
> While the man from the creeks lay clutched to the breast of the lady
>     that's known as Lou.

Hughes's earliest extant poem, 'Wild West', is clearly an attempt at this kind of ballad narrative, though the seriousness of the attempt is a little undermined by joky references to a teacher and 'Two-gun Ted'.

> Then like a flash the two men went,
> And Carson McReared the Terrible sent
> A leaden slug weighing 200 grains
> Slap into Kinkaid's squirming brains.
> Then turning to his hoss he strode,
> Leaving Kincaid the Marshal dead in the road.

Hughes has not directly imitated Service's metre, but has adapted the method of regular stressed syllables with varying number of unstressed, in a form that anticipates his mature attraction to alliterative metre. It is also noteworthy that his earliest influence is a mode of *popular* poetry.

Hughes was still writing in this mode in 'Too Bad for Hell', a poem about pirates, three years later, but his range was by now considerably wider. His promise as a poet is most remarkably evident in 'The Recluse', which begins,

> O lean dry man with your thin withered feet,
> Feet like old rain-worn weasels, like old roots
> Frost-warped and shrunken on the cold sea beach,
> You have a sad world here:
> Only the bitter windy rain and bareness of wet rock glistening;
> Only the sand-choked marram, only their dead

Throats whispering always in despair:
Only the wild high phantom-drifting of the gulls ...[32]

The distinctive sense of the bleak beauty of the natural world, and the place of humanity in it, above all in the line about the gulls and the superb simile 'like old rain-worn weasels', would not be out of place in a poem written at the height of Hughes's powers, where observation is transformed into vision. The command of rhythm shows a subtlety far beyond the comparatively simple accentual metre of the poems influenced by Kipling and Service. Few poems in *The Hawk in the Rain* achieve these qualities. In an essay on his early development Hughes has written that in Yeats's *The Wanderings of Oisin* he found a 'wilder and more hauntingly varied' metre than in Kipling, in trying to imitate which he 'fell, without knowing it, into Virgil's hexameter' (*WP* 6) – an example of which is the fifth line above. The title, alluding to Wordsworth's unfinished long philosophical poem, suggests that Hughes is already, at the age of seventeen, emulating and even challenging the great Romantics.

The two other poems published in this issue of *Don and Dearne* are less impressive, though they contribute to one's sense of the variety of Hughes's verse at this period. 'Initiation', a melodramatic description of a dance, is like a parody of his mature work, heavily dependent on the repetition of words such as 'frenzy', 'crazed', 'barbaric', 'insanity' and 'Demon'. 'Here in the Green and Glimmering Gloom' is a highly proficient but unoriginal imitation of early Yeats, enlivened with a dash of Ariel's songs from *The Tempest*. In addition to these published and, now, collected early poems there are also a number in the archives lodged at Emory University by Gerald Hughes and Edna Wholey, an early friend of Hughes. These poems vary between the facetious and the highly ambitious; sometimes they are occasional (anticipating, as I have said, Hughes's Laureate poetry); often they are long and written in elevated, occasionally bombastic diction. Even in his teens, Hughes is not using poetry as a means of emotional indulgence or therapy, but experimenting with the public, oracular voice of the poet as bard, or spokesman of his tribe.

Another contribution of Mexborough Grammar School to Hughes's creative development was the gift by a teacher of Robert Graves's *The White Goddess*. This book was to be a profound influence on Hughes's work and thought, perhaps the most important single text, excluding poetry and the Bible, that he read. He has said that the reading he did for the Archaeology and Anthropology tripos at Cambridge was 'an infinitely extended appendix' to Graves's book.[33] Graves's central contention is that poetry is a distinct mode of thought, which is destroyed if subjected to the disciplines of prose and rationality. We shall see the influence of this idea on Hughes in the next chapter. Much of the book consists of an elaborate argument about Celtic poetic symbolism, in particular the symbolic use of alphabet systems. The most important aspect of the book for Hughes, however, is Graves's metaphysical take on poetry, to which gender is central. Poetic thought is dependent on the matriarchal world-view out of which, according to him, it developed. 'The male intellect trying to make itself spiritually self-sufficient'[34] is destructive of poetry. The true poet is a devotee of the Muse, who is identified with the 'triple goddess' in the form of maiden, mother and crone. Graves draws a logical, if in the real world absurd, conclusion from this apotheosis of gender, that 'woman is not a poet: she is either a Muse or she is nothing' (though he immediately backtracks by denying that he means 'a woman should refrain from writing poems', rather that 'she should write as a woman, not as if she were an honorary man').[35] It is clear from Hughes's relationship with Plath that he did not entertain the absurd idea that 'woman is not a poet'. It is likely however that another belief of Graves's may have put a strain on their relationship, namely that 'The White Goddess is anti-domestic; she is the perpetual "other woman".'[36]

More certainly, Hughes's mythicised view of history, epitomised in his book on Shakespeare, derives directly from Graves. In this view, Judaic monotheism, Greek rationalism, the Protestant reformation and the scientific revolution are stages in a progressively more disastrous usurpation of the goddess by a patriarchal system of thought in which 'man tells himself lies about his own completeness'.[37] Hughes's creative response to this idea was to reach its peak in the mythological works of the late 1960s and 70s, especially *Crow*, *Gaudete* and *Cave Birds*.

The earliest poem he chose to collect – the earliest by five or six years according to him[38] – already shows evidence of an affinity with Graves. 'Song' is a love poem; hyperbolic praise of the beloved, and comparisons of her to nature, are commonplace, but the poem is particularly marked by imagery that is reminiscent of *The White Goddess*. The beloved is blessed by the moon, caressed by the sea and kissed by the wind; the stars swim in her eyes. Her power is such that the poet is in her shadow, and when she turns away, her shadow turns to ice. She 'will not die, nor come home'. Above all, there is a complete absence of contingent detail that could link the 'lady' of the poem to any actual woman or girl the young Hughes might have known. Her combination of desirability and destructiveness is exactly that of Graves's goddess, in other words of the

Muse, and the success of the poem is that it lends itself to reading both as a conventional love poem and as an address to the Muse. As we have seen, he included it in a Birthday Ode to Gerald with the title 'Invocation to the Nearest Muse'. Remarkably, Hughes almost certainly wrote this poem before reading *The White Goddess*,[39] but in it Hughes is declaring himself as a 'Muse poet', in other words a true poet according to Graves, and his decision to collect it, alone among his juvenile work, in *The Hawk in the Rain* and every version of his selected poems (even placing it first in the joint collection with Thom Gunn) repeats that declaration.

# 2
# 'The Thought-Fox':
# Hughes and Cambridge

In 1951, at the age of twenty-one, Hughes went up to read English at Pembroke College, Cambridge. He later described this period as 'the years of devastation', and 'total confusion,' during which he wrote no poetry that he saved.[1] One reason for this may have been what he described as 'social rancour'.[2] Probably more important, as we shall see, was an aversion to the academic study of literature.

However, Brian Cox, who was an undergraduate and postgraduate student at Pembroke throughout Hughes's time there, and knew him well for the rest of his life, was 'convinced that Ted was happy at Pembroke',[3] and Elaine Feinstein, after reviewing the memoirs of this period, asks, 'Exactly where then lay the "devastation" of those university years?' without offering a confident answer.[4] In 1952, near the end of his first year, he wrote to his sister that he sometimes thought Cambridge 'wonderful', at other times, 'a ditch ... where all the frogs have died'. There was something in the air that made people 'very awake'. He admired the lectures of George Rylands and A.P. Rossiter.[5]

It is possible that at least to some degree Hughes's negative experience is retrospective, and I shall be arguing in particular that the values of Cambridge English were much closer to his poetic practice, as it emerged in the years immediately following his graduation, than his dismissive comments suggest.

From at least as early as the mid-1970s Hughes told a story that might be regarded as the founding myth of his poetic career. He eventually published a version of it in *Winter Pollen* (*WP*) in 1994. In this story he describes the resistance that he felt to writing academic essays, which became stronger as he overcame 'the initial culture shock of University life ... in other words as I became happier' (suggesting that it was deeper than and independent of 'social rancour'). On one particular occasion,

19

after an evening struggling to write an essay, he left it barely started on his desk and went to bed. He dreamed that he was back at his desk trying to write the essay, and was visited by a large fox-like creature that walked erect on its hind legs but was 'roasted, smouldering, black-charred, split and bleeding'. This creature placed a hand (which was like a human hand) on Hughes's essay and said, 'Stop this – you are destroying us.' When it removed the hand it left a bloody print on the paper (*WP* 8–9). Hughes changed from the English to the Archaeology and Anthropology tripos.[6] In Brian Cox's version of this story the dream recurred and 'the fox nodded its head approvingly'.[7] In 1958 Hughes wrote a letter to Lucas Myers which implied that 'my fox' was a regular visitor to his dreams, and a critic of his writing.[8] His resistance at Cambridge to writing critical essays is an early sign of a profound hostility to discursive prose as the agent of the rational intellect that is the enemy of poetry and, one might go so far as to say, of life. This is an important element in Hughes's unusually extreme and persistent hostility to literary criticism. In a later letter to Keith Sagar, Hughes referred to writing prose as 'burning the foxes',[9] and in another letter to Myers he asserted that 'all discoursive [*sic*] prose vocabulary' is 'essentially false'.[10] In later life, however, he wrote in more temperate terms to Leonard Scigaj (admittedly himself a critic), saying that he did not know why he felt so hostile to literary study, but that he did feel a violent hostility, which he still did not understand. Does literary criticism, he wondered, really have a 'torturing destructive effect ... on some essential part of our psyche', or was it a peculiarity of his own?[11]

Despite the cultural interests that led Hughes to anthropology, and the (perhaps) personal experiences narrated in 'The Deadfall' (see Chapter 1), it is unlikely that at this time he knew much about shamanism.[12] There can be no doubt that later, however, he would have interpreted this dream as a shamanic experience. In his review of Mircea Eliade's *Shamanism*, written in 1964, he describes shamanism as 'a technique for moving in a state of ecstasy among the various spiritual realms', and writes that a man[13] is most commonly 'chosen' to be a shaman through a dream in which he is visited by the spirits, often in the form of an animal. Once this has happened, 'there is no other life for you, your must shamanize or die'. Most significantly of all, Hughes asserts that the initiation dreams and other shamanic experiences are also 'the basic experience of the poetic temperament we call "romantic" ' (*WP*, 56–8). As we have seen, his understanding of the word 'romantic' is eclectic: Shakespeare, Keats, Yeats and Eliot, all figures in what he later called his 'sacred canon'.[14]

Hughes used to tell the burnt fox story when introducing readings of 'The Thought-Fox', a poem which is, more explicitly than any other by Hughes, a representation of the process of poetic imagination. In 1994 he described it as the first poem that he saved after 'six years of total confusion' – the earliest poem, apart from 'Song', that he collected. This statement should be treated with caution, however.[15] Since 1972 'The Thought-Fox' has stood at the head of each version of his *Selected Poems*.

This fox is in a much healthier state – 'Brilliantly, concentratedly, / Coming about its own business' – but, like the fox in the Cambridge story, it visits a man sitting at a desk, trying to write, late at night. It comes not through the door but from somewhere that is both 'more near' and 'deeper within darkness' than a star: an inward depth, the source that for Hughes is paradoxically both intimately close and immeasurably distant – distant because the everyday self is alienated from it. At the beginning of the poem the persona inhabits a world that is defined by starlessness, the ticking of the clock, and the blankness of the page on which, nevertheless, his 'fingers move'. He is writing something, but the page remains blank. What he is writing is, however, presumably not an academic essay: the first line of the poem is 'I imagine this midnight moment's forest'; through this act of imagination the speaker becomes aware that 'Something else is alive', and as the poem progresses, this 'something', the fox, fills the starless, blank and lonely world of the first stanza, with its own life, and the poem is written. The words 'I imagine', however, represent the only activity in the poem attributed to the speaker. In the middle stanzas the fox takes over. The title, with its hyphen, means not a thought about a fox, or a fox that exists only in thought, but a thought that is a fox. Hughes does everything possible to suggest that the agency of creating the poem has passed from the speaker to the fox.

Hughes discussed this poem later in *Poetry in the Making*, in which he compares writing poetry to fishing with a float, an activity in which 'your imagination is alarming itself with the size of the thing slowly leaving the weeds and approaching your bait', whose purpose he describes as 'to bring up some lovely solid thing, like living metal, from a world where nothing exists but those inevitable facts which raise life out of nothing and return it to nothing' (*WP* 19). Again, the emphasis is on passivity, allowing something to happen rather than making it happen. Apart from a strained pun on the paw-prints of the fox and the printed page, which unfortunately determines the last line, the poem seems to me entirely successful. But Hughes's account of its production, implicitly in 'The Thought-Fox' itself and explicitly in *Poetry in the Making*, strikes me as disingenuous. I have no doubt that the trope of the living creature rising from the depths, evoked by a mental state approaching meditation, which recurs frequently in Hughes's work, represents a distinctive experience which is a profound psychological as well as creative necessity. But Hughes has nothing to say about how this experience becomes translated into words: *these* words, which are so instantly recognisable as a poem.

The first stanza of 'The Thought-Fox' evokes a scene that is very reminiscent of Coleridge's 'Frost at Midnight'. The phrase 'midnight moment's forest' is a reworking of Blake's 'forest of the night', and its alliteration perhaps carries an echo of Hopkins's 'morning's minion' – the 'Windhover' that Hughes would probably have regarded as Hopkins's shamanic spirit. These three poets are all members of Hughes's 'sacred canon', which he says was 'fixed' by the time he went to university. If his canon really was fixed by this time, it perhaps explains why the university had so little to offer him intellectually. The other members of the canon were Chaucer, Shakespeare, Marlowe, Wordsworth, Keats, Yeats and Eliot.[16] This is very similar to the canon of Cambridge English at the time. The main difference is that Hughes's canon is notably more exclusive – nothing between the early seventeenth and late eighteenth centuries.

Less obviously, but perhaps more notably, Hughes's early poetry at its best exemplifies the qualities that Eliot found in the poetry of Elizabethan drama. Eliot's essays on Elizabethan drama and Metaphysical poetry were perhaps the most powerful influence on Cambridge criticism in the early 1950s. In his essay on 'Philip Massinger' Eliot writes of a 'perpetual slight alteration of language, words perpetually juxtaposed in new and sudden combinations, ... which evidences a very high development of the senses'[17]. Consider these lines from Hughes's poem:

> warily a lame
> Shadow lags by stump and in hollow
> Of a body that is bold to come
> Across clearings ...

The poem does not *say* that the fox's shadow is distorted by the irregular terrain over which it passes. Rather that sense-impression is completely saturated by the figurative displacement of the fox's natural fear on to its shadow, leaving the fox itself free to represent a bold venturesomeness. The separation is reinforced by the literal separation of the shadow from the body and by the rhythm: the dragging, front-heavy stresses of the first complete line quoted, in contrast to the rapid anapaestic rhythm of the second, and the leap across the stanza-break. I am not suggesting that Hughes secretly learned how to do this by attending lectures in the Cambridge English faculty, but that when he obeyed the command of his spirit-fox the resulting poetry was great in ways that an intelligent member of that faculty should have had no difficulty recognising.

The image of the poet, or his persona, embodying a 'wise passiveness' that allows his creative power – often in animal form – to express itself, recurs many times in Hughes's best poetry. It may be related to the more problematic kind of passivity that he attributes to himself in *Birthday Letters*. 'The Thought-Fox', however, is with 'The Horses' one of only two poems in *The Hawk in the Rain* that have this quality and, though possibly the best poem in the volume, is therefore untypical of it. More characteristically, the personae have one of two more disturbing relations to what he later called 'the elemental power-circuit of the Universe':[18] they are threatened by it, or they embody it in a violence of their own. This last kind of poem – the only kind that might justify the more lurid aspects of Hughes's reputation – is rare, even in *The Hawk in the Rain*, and never appears in later volumes. An example is 'Law in the Country of the Cats', which narrates and celebrates a motiveless and elemental violence between men, and concludes with one man defiantly claiming responsibility for the other's death: 'I did it, I.' Its inferiority to 'The Thought-Fox' is epitomised by the cliché-ridden line, possibly the worst Hughes ever published, 'Then a flash of violent incredible action.' This kind of poem, which as I have said disappears from Hughes's later work, perhaps corresponds to his Pembroke contemporary D.D. Bradley's account of him 'masquerading as a wild man'[19] when an undergraduate, a description that is confirmed by a boast in a letter to his brother that he 'set the college on fire'.[20] It looks back to the worst poem Hughes published as an adolescent, 'Initiation' (see Chapter 1).

The other kind of poem, in which the human protagonist is threatened or diminished by natural energy, remains much more characteristic throughout Hughes's oeuvre, and accounts for most of the best poems in *The Hawk in the Rain*: the title poem, 'Wind', 'Jaguar', 'Meeting', 'October Dawn'. The opening stanza of 'Wind' exemplifies this kind of writing at its best:

This house has been far out at sea all night,
The woods crashing through darkness, the booming hills,
Winds stampeding the fields under the window
Floundering black astride and blinding wet
Till day rose ...

The threat posed by the elements to the human order, explicit later in the poem in images of the house's vulnerability, is already present in the disruption of the linguistic order, though the poetry makes such a vivid impression that this can easily be overlooked. Agency passes from the house to the woods, to the hills and to the wind, and the metaphor shifts from one of storm at sea to animals stampeding on land before the fourth line confusedly combines the two. The animal metaphor in the third line retrospectively colours the 'woods crashing though darkness' but is confusedly extended in the fourth line where 'astride' suggests a rider rather than an animal, and 'blinding wet' seems in terms of the image to suggest that the wind is blinded, whereas a naturalistic interpretation of the scene would take the 'blinding' to be inflicted by the wind on someone or something else. These lines may echo Macbeth's famous lines:

> And pity, like a naked newborn babe
> Striding the blast, or heaven's cherubin horsed
> Upon the sightless couriers of the air,
> Shall blow the horrid deed in every eye,
> That tears shall drown the wind.[21]

I am not suggesting that Hughes's poetry is of the same order as Shakespeare's, which uses images of natural turmoil to represent a mind racked with anticipatory guilt and fear of divine retribution – a dimension wholly lacking in 'Wind'. But the relation to language is very similar. The image of pity is famously so condensed as to defy visualisation and bring the very term 'image' into question. The verb 'blow' grammatically has 'pity' and 'cherubin' as subjects, but a reader (and even more a theatre audience) would surely more naturally link it with 'blast'. The Cambridge editor glosses 'sightless' as 'invisible', which makes sense, but the meaning 'blind' was longer established than 'invisible' (which *OED* first records only in 1589) and likely to be more familiar to Shakespeare's audience – at least to suggest itself long enough to confuse the blindness of the 'couriers' with the implied blindness caused by the 'tears' which startlingly drown not the person shedding them but the 'wind' that caused them.

Elaine Feinstein quotes these lines from 'Wind' and comments, 'It is as if years of Leavis have been overthrown in a moment.'[22] This seriously misrepresents Hughes's relation to the models of thought about poetic language that were or might have been available to him at Cambridge. Hughes might have had many reasons for resisting the influence of

F.R. Leavis, not least that Leavis showed no interest in new poets after the early 1930s. But Feinstein represents Leavis as if he were a neo-classical critic rigidly policing such solecisms as mixed metaphor: as if, indeed, he were Dr Johnson. But in arguing against Johnson and claiming that the neo-classical principles of 'correctness', 'clarity' and 'logic'[23] made an achievement such as Shakespeare's impossible, Leavis invokes precisely the passage from *Macbeth* that, I have argued, uses language in a way similar to the opening of 'Wind'. His description of another Shakespeare passage as 'a complex play of diverse and shifting analogy'[24] is precisely applicable to Hughes.

Leavis was also hostile to the tradition of English versification inaugurated by Spenser, Pembroke College's other great poet, whom D.D. Bradley rightly sees as Hughes's polar opposite, both because he 'originated the mythic image of Protestant Man', against which Hughes vehemently polemicised (*The Iron Man* might be considered his riposte to *The Faerie Queene*), and because he 'restored to English poetry the grace of Chaucer's versification', while Hughes was more drawn to 'the strong stress patterns of native Anglo-Saxon poetry'.[25] Both these judgements seem to me broadly true, but the word 'native' plays into a dangerous myth whose most extreme manifestation has unfortunately been endorsed by one of Hughes's foremost critics and most eloquent champions, Keith Sagar. In his second study of Hughes, *The Laughter of Foxes*, Sagar quotes the following passage from 'an unpublished essay by A.S. Crehan', implying that it speaks for him:

It is a return to an alliterative poetry that, pounding, brutal and earthbound, challenges the Latinate politeness of artificial society with ruthless energy and cunning, and so drags the Latinate words into its unruly, self-ruling world, that even *they* come to sound northern and Germanic. The pummelling trochees and lead-weighted, bludgeoning spondees have a mesmeric effect, beating and rooting out of us those once apparently safe underlying rhythms of rhetorical and philosophical discourse, mental scene-painting and nostalgic or evocative reflection, with which the iambic pentameter is so closely associated. Quite literally, by asserting the naked, deeper rhythms of our Germanic (and also onomatopoeic) heritage, Ted Hughes is taking the English language back to its roots.[26]

What concerns me about this passage is not so much its political subtext (though that is hair-raising enough) as its crudity and inaccuracy as an account of Hughes's verse, even at this early stage of his career. It is quite true that Hughes prefers, and writes more effectively in, the alliterative than the iambic form. This may be connected to the 'social rancour' and resentment of 'the tabu on dialect as a language proper for literate men',[27] since medieval alliterative poetry is written in non-metropolitan forms of English. Antony Easthope has argued that iambic pentameter is a 'hegemonic form' that 'includes and excludes, sanctions and denigrates ... discriminates the "properly" poetic from the "improperly" poetic', the latter represented by the various forms of accentual metre found in nursery rhymes, industrial folk songs and football chants.[28] However, as I shall argue in a moment, Hughes's attachment to the Germanic elements in English is neither exclusive nor aggressive.

Hughes has himself encouraged the corrosive myth that permeates A.S. Crehan's commentary, in a 1964 review that he reprinted in *Winter Pollen*: comparing Greek-Roman and Anglo-Saxon-Norse-Celtic mythologies, 'there's no doubt which of these alternatives belongs to our blood' (*WP* 41). 'Whose blood?' Hughes might have asked himself, at least when reprinting this review in 1994. Fortunately (as Sagar himself recognises elsewhere in his book) there is far more to Hughes's relation to his linguistic heritage than a fascistic 'bludgeoning' nostalgia for monoglossic linguistic 'roots'.

The contrast between the predominantly consonantal and more often monosyllabic Anglo-Saxon and Norse elements in modern English, and the more polysyllabic and lightly stressed Norman-French elements has complex ideological bearings. In the nineteenth century it was an important element in a new ideology of Englishness, subtly analysed by George Meredith in the first chapter of *One of Our Conquerors*. Anglo-Saxon is also associated with the common man, as Walter Scott demonstrates in the first chapter of *Ivanhoe*. Furthermore, there is a persistent tendency to gender aspects of (nationally specific) language, notable for example in many commentaries on Seamus Heaney: 'the displacement of the feminine Gaelic vowel by the hard consonantal language of English'.[29] At the same time, the persisting evidence of the hybridity of the English language is a genuine resource for poets, and one that Hughes uses in various ways. I shall be returning to this in my fourth chapter, with reference to 'Hawk Roosting' and 'View of a Pig', but here I just want to comment on 'The Hawk in the Rain'. The poem opens with one of Hughes's most effortful evocations of the enmired creatureliness of man:

> I drown in the drumming ploughland, I drag up
> Heel after heel from the swallowing of the earth's mouth,

From clay that clutches my each step to the ankle
With the habit of the dogged grave.

From this earthly prison the speaker admires the hawk whose

Wings hold all creation in a weightless quiet
Steady as a hallucination in the streaming air.

I do not want myself to fetishise etymology, but in the first stanza, every word apart from 'habit' is of German or Scandinavian origin, whereas most of the key-words in the lines describing the hawk – creation, quiet, hallucination, air – come from French. More to the point, the monosyllabic diction with its 'bludgeoning spondees' belongs to the poem's negative pole, while the mastery of the hawk to which the speaker aspires ('master / Fulcrum of violence', indeed: every substantive word from French or Latin) is represented in a more polysyllabic, much less heavily accented diction. There may be a subliminal allusion to the Norman-French language of falconry. It is true that the poem ends anticipating the hawk's 'heart's blood' being mixed with 'the mire of the land', but what the poem *values* is not at all identified with heavily accented Anglo-Saxon diction.

The only foreign poet Hughes mentions as having been important to him in his youth is Rilke: 'I had one or two collections with me through my national service. I could see the huge worlds of other possibilities opening in there. But I couldn't see how to get into them.'[30] The Rilke that is most enduringly significant for Hughes is probably the *Duino Elegies*, whose 'schrecklich'[31] (terrible) angels are surely a presence in such *Wodwo* poems as 'Pibroch' ('This is where the staring angels go through') and 'Ghost Crabs' ('We cannot see them or turn our minds from them ... . They are the powers of this world'). But one of Hughes's best early poems, 'The Jaguar', is clearly both a tribute and a riposte to 'Der Panther', from Rilke's *New Poems* of 1907. Both poems are meditations on the caged energy of an animal in a zoo. In Rilke's panther the vitality ('a great will stands numbed') and more importantly the inner vision ('It seems to him there are a thousand bars/ and behind a thousand bars no world')[32] are radically diminished. Hughes's poem is clearly indebted to Rilke. In its first published version it included the line 'Swivelling the ball of his heel on the polished spot',[33] an image of constrained energy that perhaps echoes Rilke's 'The supple pace of powerful soft strides, / Turning in the very smallest circle'. Hughes removed this line in revision, to use it later in 'Second Glance at a Jaguar'. But

Hughes's jaguar's energy is undiminished: in one of his most effective early uses of sprung rhythm 'The world rolls under the long thrust of his heel'. And the most significant contrast is that for Hughes this sustained energy is associated with vision: in marked contrast to the panther for whom there is no world behind the bars, for the jaguar 'there's no cage to him / / More than to the visionary his cell' and 'Over the cage floor the horizons come'. In Rilke's poem there is no reference to a human observer. In Hughes's the jaguar is explicitly seen through the eyes of the crowd which 'stands, stares mesmerized / Like a child at a dream.' The crowd thus stands in for the reader of the poem. The original version ended with a banal reversal by which it is the crowd who 'like life-prisoners ... through bars stare out.' Hughes was surely right to make the change, since the original ending both undercuts the reader's identification with the 'mesmerized' crowd and draws attention away from the jaguar to make a cheap point. In its place we have the superb evocation with which the poem now ends: 'The world rolls under the long thrust of his heel, / Over the cage floor the horizons come.'

I have so far concentrated on a small number of poems that seem to me the best in *The Hawk in the Rain*, and to belong with many of the best poems in *Lupercal* and *Wodwo*. To them might be added 'Meeting' and 'October Dawn', though I think that the use of terza rima in one and couplets in the other imposes an unhelpful formal constraint in which one might suspect the influence of the early Plath (the influence of the later Plath on poems from *Wodwo* on is another matter). As I have said, 'The Thought-Fox' is almost in a category of its own , but all these poems are imaginative explorations of the central theme or event in Hughes's poetry: the usurpation or invasion of the world that the rational intellect has constructed, by a power that is represented as greater and ultimately more real. This is fundamentally a religious theme, though it is not until some time later that Hughes begins to present it in explicitly religious terms (this may be the 'huge worlds of other possibilities' that he saw in Rilke but 'couldn't see how to get into'). In these most successful early poems the usurping power is represented as an overt natural force. Hughes's marvellous gift for vivid representation of the natural world, combined with the fact that this had been his most abiding passion and most intense experience until this point in his life, sufficiently account for this success. But those early critics who called him a 'zoo laureate' and asked what he would do when he ran out of animals, missed the point entirely. In the critical terminology of Hughes's Cambridge, the fox, hawk, wind and jaguar are objective correlatives, 'a set of objects, a situation, a chain of events which shall be the formula of that *particular* emotion.'[34] There is also a group of relatively successful poems about war, and two others about violent death, of which this might be said, and a larger number from which it is lacking.

There are a number of love poems in the volume that attempt to address the central theme by representing sexual relations as a desperate elemental struggle. In 'Billet-Doux', for example, the speaker portrays himself as 'dispropertied ... .By the constellations staring me to less/ Than what cold, rain and wind neglect'. The effect of this is of a romantic and rhetorical self-projection that owes too much to its literary antecedents in *King Lear*'s Edgar. It is perhaps an expression of the Hughes who 'delighted to play Heathcliff.'[35] Several poems that deal with the central theme in a more discursive way similarly lack an adequate 'formula'. 'Egghead' for example attempts a direct statement of the theme:

> Long the eggshell head's
> Fragility rounds and resists receiving the flash
> Of the sun, the bolt of the earth.

Here Hughes is reduced to a kind of rhetorical shorthand: single words such as 'flash' and 'bolt' are called on to do the work of whole stanzas in 'Wind' or 'The Jaguar'.

In the war poems Hughes is more successful in working out his theme through the imagined experience of others. As has often been noted, most of the images of war in his poetry are of the First World War, almost certainly because of the influence of his father's trauma. In 'Bayonet Charge' he memorably portrays the suspended sense of temporality in a man going through an extreme crisis – something that he achieves with equal effect later in *Gaudete*:

> He was running
> Like a man who has jumped up in the dark and runs
> Listening between his footfalls for the reason
> Of his still running, and his foot hung like
> Statuary in mid-stride.

This gives more substance to the conventional sentiment that

> King, honour, human dignity, etcetera
> Dropped like luxuries in a yelling alarm.

Several of the poems that were to make Hughes's reputation – certainly 'The Jaguar' and probably 'The Thought-Fox' and 'Wind' – had been written before Hughes met Sylvia Plath in February 1956. It is doubtful, however, whether Hughes would have had the literary career that he had without Plath's influence. The first stage of their literary relationship is the subject of my next chapter.

# 3
# The Encounter with Sylvia Plath

Hughes's relationship with Sylvia Plath was undoubtedly the most profoundly important event of his adult life, in its effect on the life itself, and on his work. The relationship has been conscripted by many commentators into a narrative of gender conflict, often with consequent distortion. I shall be returning to aspects of the relationship in various chapters of this study, and my main theme will be the extent to which – however calamitously their personal relationship ended – their writing life was a common endeavour. Their mutual influence is obvious, and it would even be true, if a partial truth, to say that they created a common text, in which many important motifs cannot be straightforwardly assigned to one or the other writer/protagonist. Many critics have invoked the word 'myth' to describe the way Plath's work, in particular, and her relationship with Hughes, have been publicly mediated. Much of this myth, however, is the work of the poets themselves. In this chapter, I will be focussing on the immediate aftermath of their meeting. The dynamics of the intertextual relationship change in Plath's final months, when she is bitterly hostile to Hughes, but in those final months, and beyond, in Hughes's writing it remains a crucial element in the work of both poets.

After graduating in June 1954, Hughes took a series of jobs in London as a security guard (where he told his brother that he spent the whole time writing[1]), gardener, dishwasher at the zoo, and reader for J. Arthur Rank, film producers.[2] He also began, immediately on graduation, publishing poems for the first time since 1950, in the student magazines *Granta*, *Chequer* and *Delta*. This combination suggests that he was dedicating himself to the life of a poet, but not to making a professional literary career for himself. An informant of Elaine Feinstein reports that Hughes was 'seriously considering emigration to Australia',[3] which suggests a persistent longing for reunion with his brother.

During the two years between graduation and his marriage to Sylvia Plath, Hughes's life in London is much less well-documented than his occasional visits to Cambridge to stay with old friends such as David Ross and Daniel Weissbort, and new ones such as the American Lucas Myers. The most substantial memoir of the period is Myers's *Crow Steered, Bergs Appeared: A Memoir of Ted Hughes and Sylvia Plath*; Philip Hobsbaum, then editor of *Delta* and founder of 'The Group', the pioneering poetry workshop which Hughes later occasionally attended, has written a slightly less fond memoir,[4] and Elaine Feinstein has interviewed or corresponded with David Ross, Daniel Weissbort and Michael Boddy. These reminiscences all focus on Cambridge.

Hughes's first two published poems after graduating appeared under pseudonyms, Daniel Hearing and Peter Crew. Late in life he wondered 'if it wouldn't be a good idea to write under a few pseudonyms' because '[t]he moment you publish your own name you lose freedom' – the freedom to 'do anything new' because '[t]here's an unanimous reaction to keep you as you were'.[5] After these two early poems, however, he never again used this device. The name 'Peter Crew' does not have any obvious significance (unless it is an indirect allusion to Peter's denial of Jesus), but 'Daniel Hearing' might be interpreted as an announcement of Hughes's aspiration to be a shaman-poet. 'Daniel' might have been borrowed from his friends Daniel Weissbort and Daniel Huws, but probably alludes, at least in part, to the prophet Daniel who 'had understanding in all visions and dreams'.[6] Once, when Daniel is so overwhelmed by the vision of the angel that 'there remained no strength in me', 'Yet I heard the voice of his words' and Gabriel says to him, 'understand the words that I speak to thee, and stand upright.'[7] The pseudonymous surname implies that the poet listens to voices to which the average person is deaf.

Hughes did not collect either of these poems, but in the next issue of *Chequer* he published 'The Jaguar' and 'The Casualty', which made it not only into *The Hawk in the Rain* but also into the 1994 *New Selected Poems*, and in February 1956 he published another four poems that were destined to be collected. These appeared in the first and only issue of *St Botolph's Review*, published by Hughes himself and his friends, including Lucas Myers, Daniel Weissbort and Daniel Huws. On 26 February a party was thrown to celebrate the launch and the magazine was sold in the streets of Cambridge during the day. One person who bought it and read it that day was Sylvia Plath. She went to the party with the intention of meeting Myers and Hughes, whose poetry she admired, and Daniel Huws, who had written a scathing review of her own poetry.

When Hughes and Plath met, an occasion that has become legendary since the partial publication of Plath's journals in 1982, she had not only read the four poems published in *St Botolph's Review* ('Soliloquy', 'Secretary', 'Law in the Country of the Cats' and 'Fallgrief's Girlfriends', though only the last had a title), but almost certainly also 'The Casualty' and 'The Jaguar', since she records herself quoting from the former at their meeting. He had certainly read two of hers, published in the most recent issue of *Chequer*: 'Epitaph in Three Parts' and the ominously titled ' "Three Caryatids without a Portico" by Hugo Robus. A Study in Sculptural Dimensions'.[8]

Of Hughes's *St Botolph's Review* poems, at least three are characterised by the most macho posturing to be found anywhere in his *oeuvre*:

> When two men at first meeting hate each other ...
> There will be that moment's horrible pause
> As each looks into the gulf in the eye of the other,
> Then a flash of violent incredible action.
> Then one man letting his brains gently into the gutter,
> And one man bursting into the police station
> Crying: 'Let justice be done. I did it. I.'
> ('*Law in the Country of the Cats*')

Two of these poems are also among his most misogynistic:

> If I should touch her she would shriek and weeping
> Crawl off to nurse the terrible wound.

('Secretary')

The speaker of 'Soliloquy' looks forward to the grave:

> To be lying beside women who grimace
> Under the commitments of their flesh,
> And not out of spite or vanity.[9]

'Fallgrief's Girlfriends' has the merit of appearing, at least, to treat such attitudes with some distance and irony.

The two poets' respective attitudes to each other's works were very different. Though (unlike Myers, with whom she classes him at this stage) Hughes's name does not appear in Plath's *Journals* before this meeting, it was evidently already one to conjure with, as her first mention of him makes clear:

> Then the worst happened, that big, dark, hunky boy, the only one there huge enough for me, who had been hunching around over women, and whose name I had asked the minute I had come into the room, but no-one told me, came over and was looking hard into my eyes and it was Ted Hughes. I started yelling again about his poems [she had earlier been 'yelling' to Myers about his poems] and quoting: 'most dear unscratchable diamond' [from Hughes's 'The Casualty'].[10]

Hughes and his friends, however, despised Plath's poems, which they considered precious and formalist. Daniel Huws had recently written in their publication *Broadsheet*, 'Of the quaint and eclectic artfulness of Sylvia Plath's two poems my better half tells me "Fraud, fraud", but I will not say so; who am I to know how beautiful she may be.'[11] This may seem contemptible half a century later, but in her journal Plath ignored the gratuitous reference to her appearance and saw only a critical truth: 'The clever reviewer and writer who is an ally of the generous creative opposing forces, cries with deadly precision: "Fraud, fraud" '.[12] In her report of meeting Daniel Huws at the party her tone is sharper but her planned riposte is evidence that she has been stung by the review: 'me at last saying my immortal line of introduction which has been with me ever since his clever precocious slanted review: "Is this the better or worse half?" '[13] The review is also a topic of her first conversation with Ted Hughes: 'We shouted as if in a high wind, about the review, and he saying Dan knew I was beautiful, he wouldn't have written it about a cripple, and my yelling protest in which the words "sleep with the editor" occurred with startling frequency.'[14] This is a good example of something not often noted: that there is at least as much comedy as erotic melodrama in Plath's reconstruction of the meeting.

Whereas all six of the Hughes poems that Plath had read (out of only nine that he had published since his teens) were collected in *The Hawk in the Rain*, none of the poems Plath had written before the meeting made it into *The Colossus* and only two are included in the main section of her *Collected Poems* (edited by Hughes of course): all her other earlier work is relegated to a 'selection' of 'Juvenilia'. It is true that Plath herself made this judgement on her pre-1956 work but, as Jacqueline Rose has pointed out, it is a judgement that 'she repeated over and again, and in relation to different moments, throughout her career'.[15] Hughes's dating of the Plath canon from early 1956 remains a significant decision.

I shall be discussing Hughes's editing of Plath in Chapter 7. In this chapter I want to concentrate on how these early poems of Hughes are interwoven into texts of Plath. As I have said, Hughes is not named in the *Journals* before the meeting, but on that very day she had written an appreciation of Lucas Myers's poetry:

> His poetry is great, big, moving through technique and discipline to master it and bend it supple to his will. There is a brilliant joy, there, too, almost of an athlete, running, using all the divine flexions of his muscles in the act .... Luke is all tight and packed and supple and blazing. He will be great, greater than anyone of my generation whom I've read yet.[16]

The influence of the New Criticism is apparent in Plath's critical language, including the gendered character of its evaluative terms (still to be heard twenty years later in Seamus Heaney's essay on Hopkins: 'In the masculine mode ... the poetic effort has to do with conscious quelling and control of the materials ... athletic, capable, displaying the muscle of sense'[17]). There is often a disconcerting (homo)eroticism in this critical discourse, which in Plath's case breaks the bounds of textuality. '[U]sing all the divine flexions of his muscles in the act' and 'Luke is all tight and packed and supple and blazing' suggest that she was not only thinking about his poetry. There are many similar appreciations of male bodies in her early journals: for example, 'myron is a Hercules ... lean, hard and clean'.[18] One poem of Myers's that she had almost certainly read, because it was published with Hughes's 'The Casualty', is 'Dolphin Catch', whose style is exemplified by these lines:

> The fish is still
> Eyes fixed, baffled jaws agape, distended gills desperate
> Over his scales the changing light
> Shimmering blue green gold and bright
>
> The fishermen stand and talk and clean their lines
>
> Crescent spasming, flashing in the air
> The dolphin fiercely jumps and slaps the deck
> Thrashing wood sound echoes in the sun
> And is gone. [19]

The violent subject matter, concrete imagery and predominance of plain, Anglo-Saxon, monosyllabic language suggest a closeness of poetic aspiration to Hughes. At the same time the predominance of the descriptive mode, generating feeling by implication, and a certain detachment make the poem conform more closely than Hughes's to the New Critical norms Plath espouses at this stage.

When it comes to Hughes, the boundary between the poetry and the male person disappears in Plath's writing.

> I was stamping and he was stamping on the floor, and then he kissed me bang smash on the mouth and ripped my hairband off, my lovely red hairband scarf which has weathered the sun and much love, and whose like I shall never again find, and my favourite silver earrings: hah, I shall keep, he barked. And when he kissed my neck I bit him long and hard on the cheek, and when we came out of the room, blood was running down his face. His poem 'I did it, I.' Such violence, and I can see how women lie down for artists. The one man in the room who was as big as his poems, huge, with hulk and dynamic chunks of words; his poems are strong and blasting like a high wind in steel girders. And I screamed in myself, thinking: oh, to give myself crashing, fighting, to you. The one man since I've lived who could blast Richard [Sassoon].[20]

This is a passage that has often been quoted and commented on, mainly with reference to the fact that Hughes's theft of the hairband and earrings was cut from the 1982 edition. This was one of Hughes's most serious misjudgements in editing Plath, since even in the complete text it is evident that while she attaches the language of violence to him, it is she who commits the most violent action. Equally interesting is the constant slippage between Hughes's poetry and his person, and the way the poetry infiltrates Plath's own writing. 'Law in the Country of the Cats', which Plath quotes here, is a poem about irrational and unmotivated violence between men, a crude endorsement of 'their blood before / They are aware.' In Plath's exclamation 'Such violence, and I can see how women lie down for artists', there are several remarkable slippages. One is the lightning shift, which the quotation from Hughes's poem facilitates, between her act of violence against him and the masochistic image of the woman lying down; another is the appropriation of the poem's narrative of mutual violence between men for a heterosexual narrative in which the woman is submissive; yet another is the shift from 'violence' to 'lie down for artists', as if violence were the defining characteristic of art. All this anticipates 'Every woman adores a fascist' in 'Daddy'. Further on the word 'blast' migrates from the description of Hughes's poetry to his imagined effect as a lover: the most explicit possible elaboration of what was implicit in her appreciation of Myers's poetry. 'Huge, with hulk and dynamic chunks of words' does not directly echo any of the poems she had read, but it is a highly mimetic (and unintentionally parodic) representation of one of the most obvious features of the early Hughes, his use of heavily assonantal and consonantal patterns, as in 'The Hawk in the Rain': 'rain hacks my head to the bone, the hawk hangs ...' It was not long before this kind of language found its way into Plath's poetry, as in the 'Ode for Ted', written two months later, which is a tribute to its dedicatee in style as well as theme:

> Loam-humps, he says, moles shunt
> Up from delved worm-haunt;
> Blue fur, moles have; hefting chalk-hulled flint
> He with rock splits open
> Knobbed quartz.[21]

A further point of interest about Plath's narrative of the meeting is that she represents this highly articulate man as speaking like a stereotypical 'hulk' ('You like?' 'Hah, I shall keep'). Either he is acting a role, or she is casting him in it.

The day after her journal entry, two days after the meeting, Plath wrote a poem, 'Pursuit', that she described to her mother as 'a symbol of the terrible beauty of death' which 'includes the concept of love'[22], but in the *Journals* is 'about the dark forces of lust' and 'dedicated to Ted Hughes'.[23] She rightly considered that this was the best poem she had yet written. It is not only completely free from the archness and preciosity of such poems as 'Three Caryatids without a Portico' (see below); it is more assured and emotionally compelling than any of Hughes's *St Botolph's Review* poems. Plath noted in the letter to her mother that it was influenced by Blake's 'Tyger'. She might also have mentioned Tennyson, since she uses the stanza of *In Memoriam*, no doubt with the passage about 'Nature, red in tooth and claw'[24] in mind. Although 'Pursuit' is uneven, and at times its sexual content breaks through the symbolism in an ineptly obvious manner, the use of the heavily stressed tetrameter both to control and to emphasise emotionally violent subject matter is more reminiscent of Geoffrey Hill's precocious early poem 'Genesis' than of anything by Hughes.

> There is a panther stalks me down:
> One day I'll have my death of him;
> His greed has set the woods aflame,
> He prowls more lordly than the sun ... .

Insatiate, he ransacks the land
Condemned by our ancestral fault,
Crying: blood, let blood be spilt;
Meat must glut his mouth's raw wound.[25]

The image of the panther may well have been suggested, as Margaret Dickie Uroff has remarked,[26] by Hughes's 'Jaguar', which Plath had probably read because it was published with 'The Casualty'. The choice of a panther specifically is the first appearance of a motif of blackness associated with Hughes in her writing, that culminates, with an effect deadly to his reputation, in the 'man in black with a Meinkampf look' of 'Daddy'. Although, as I have said, the poem is not stylistically reminiscent of Hughes, rather drawing to good effect on her early obsessive formalism, the line 'Blood quickens, gonging in my ears' echoes 'By the bang of blood in the brain deaf the ear' of 'The Jaguar'. A few months later, the poem was accepted by *Atlantic Monthly*, 'one of her big breakthroughs as a poet.'[27]

The panther is a 'black marauder, hauled by love' with 'taut thighs' that are 'hungry, hungry'. Later when Plath learns that Hughes is in Cambridge again (an episode that figures prominently in *Birthday Letters*) she self-consciously quotes from the poem in her journal: 'Oh, he is here; my black marauder; oh hungry hungry, I am so hungry for a big smashing creative burgeoning burdened love.'[28] As when, in her journal entry about the meeting, she seems to locate the violence of her own action in him, via the medium of his poetry ('I did it. I'), so here the 'hungry, hungry', which in the poem characterises the feared and desired appetite of the 'marauder', when quoted becomes her own appetite for him.

These texts that I have been considering – the early Hughes poems, Plath's 'Pursuit' and her journal entries – combine to produce some of the most potent elements in the Hughes-Plath myth. It is extraordinary how much of that myth has already begun to take shape within a few days of their meeting: Hughes as violent sexual predator, the relationship doomed to end in her death, the apparent inextricability of personal and textual relationships. These texts undoubtedly contributed to the dissemination of the myth, especially in the 1980s after the publication of the 1982 edition of the *Journals* (in America only) and the *Collected Poems* in 1981. Their interest lies partly in how difficult it is to separate out two clearly defined protagonists, to attribute particular motifs and even particular textual elements to one or the other. The 'violence' that Plath quotes from Hughes's poem and seems to attribute to him while reporting her own act of violence against him, and the 'hungry, hungry' that shifts from the predator's desire for her to her desire for him, are the most striking instances of this. Another significant feature is the constant shifting between the poetry and the person, the erosion of the distinction between the textual and the physical.

To turn to Hughes's early reading of Plath: we know, as I have said, that he had read two poems of hers published in *Chequer*, and that Daniel Huws publicly called her a 'Fraud'. In *Birthday Letters* there are two poems relating to this, both focussing on 'Two Caryatids without a Portico'. Plath's poem, elaborately formal, archly impersonal in tone, with its classical imagery and attempt at subtle suggestiveness and (in Eliot's phrase) 'slight lyric grace' would have been unlikely to please the author of 'Law in the Country of the Cats'. For Hughes 'It was the only poem you ever wrote/ That I disliked through the eyes of a stranger.' He thought it 'thin and brittle ... / Like the theorem of a trap' ('Caryatids (I)'). For the Hughes of *Birthday Letters*, however, nothing that Plath wrote or did was insignificant. For this Hughes his earlier self missed the significance of the 'white, blindfolded, rigid faces' of the Caryatids and the 'massive, starless, mid-fall, falling / Heaven of granite'. These details are all supplied by Hughes's imaginative reading: none of them is literally present in Plath's text. They have been read back from later poems such as 'The Disquieting Muses', 'The Moon and the Yew Tree', 'Sheep in Fog' and 'Child'. This is not to say that he is inventing the significance however. The central idea of Plath's poem is the absence of a portico to complete the sculptural design: the caryatids are in the posture of supporting a burden, with no burden to support. The link between this and 'I am so hungry for a big smashing creative burgeoning burdened love' is not hard to see. The sculptural imagery, and particularly the phrase 'Greek serenity / of tranquil plaster', foreshadows what was possibly Plath's last poem, 'Edge' ('The illusion of a Greek necessity // Flows in the scrolls of her toga').

Whereas Plath's journals and poems such as 'Pursuit' and 'Ode for Ted' give us a contemporary textual response to her early relations with Hughes, nearly all of his published writings that explicitly refer to Plath are written considerably later, after her death and in the thick of the ideological warfare that ensued. One exception is a poem, 'Bawdry Embraced', first published in *Poetry* in August 1956. Plath wrote to her mother that the poem was 'dedicated to me',[29] and it can be read as a grotesque erotic narrative of their meeting. It is a comic variant of the narrative of the sexual 'marauder' that Plath had initiated in 'Pursuit'. The male protagonist, amusingly named 'Tailfever', features more prominently than the female, more dubiously named 'Sweety Undercut' ('picked out / Of promiscuity's butchery'). Tailfever is a 'Raging delicate beast' whose 'bared weapon blazed' and who deflowers virgins just by looking at them. 'Bawdry Embraced' is a high-spirited poem of triumphant sexual love, and in that respect very different from the obsessive and fearful craving of 'Pursuit'. The parallels, perhaps echoes, are therefore the more significant. Plath's panther is 'hauled by love'; Tailfever's weapon blazes 'As if a firedrake through the dark / Dragged him by the waist.' Plath asserts, 'One day I'll have my death of him'; Hughes's lovers, in one of his most Donne-like moments,

<blockquote>
Each became a lens<br>
So focussing creation's heat<br>
The other burst in flames
</blockquote>

and 'Died face to face'. These are common enough tropes, but the way they pass between the poets, and between poems so different in tone, is further evidence of the interfusion of their writing at this stage.

I shall be picking up this story of 'interfusion' again in my chapters on *Wodwo* and *Birthday Letters*. I want now to return to the remark I made at the start of this chapter, that between 1954 and 1956 Hughes appeared to be dedicating himself to the life of a poet but not doing anything to shape a professional literary career. Plath, by contrast, in the words of Linda Wagner-Martin, 'considered herself a professional writer beginning in 1950, when at the age of seventeen, she published nine pieces of writing in *Seventeen, The Christian Science Monitor*, and *The Boston Globe*, all for payment. In college, her publications appeared in *Harper's, The Atlantic*, the *[Christian Science] Monitor, Mademoiselle* and *Seventeen*, as well as campus magazines.'[30] This contrasts poignantly with the fact, remarked on above, that nothing Plath wrote before 1956 made it into her first collection, whereas Hughes had, according to Keith Sagar, already written about half the poems that were to be collected in *The Hawk in the Rain* by the time they met.[31] Philip Hobsbaum (perhaps with some retrospective exaggeration) describes the physical appearance of the first Hughes poems he saw (in Spring 1954) as 'greasy and typed in grey characters, as though the ribbon in the typewriter had been used a great many times over a period of years, and had never been changed'.[32] Plath changed all this, bringing to the development of his career the same professionalism that she practised on her own behalf. Lucas Myers has written that 'she always had Ted's poems, like her own, meticulously typed and out at English and American magazines'.[33] In the Emory archive there are many typescripts of Hughes's poems with the journals to which they have been submitted listed in Plath's hand. Through her efforts Hughes published a further twenty-three poems before the appearance of *The Hawk in the Rain* in September 1957, in periodicals such as *Poetry, The Nation, Atlantic Monthly, The Spectator, Harper's Magazine, The New Yorker, The Times Literary Supplement* and *The London Magazine*. All the typing up and sending off of these poems was done by Plath. More importantly still, it was Plath who got hold of a leaflet about the Harper Brothers and New York Young Men's Hebrew Association Poetry Centre's competition for a first volume, and submitted *The Hawk in the Rain*.[34] Myers comments, 'I don't think Ted would have heard of the Harper prize on his own.'[35] Hughes won the contest, which was judged by W.H. Auden, Stephen Spender and Marianne Moore, and his career as a professional writer was launched.

Many years later, in the *Birthday Letters* poem 'Ouija', Hughes wrote about the ouija sessions that he and Plath shared in their early married life, and about one occasion in particular, when he asked the ouija spirit if they would be famous. To Hughes's astonishment, Plath retorts angrily, 'fame will ruin everything.' Hughes reflects,

> I was stunned. I thought I had joined
> Your association of ambition
> To please you and your mother.
> To fulfil your mother's ambition
> That we be ambitious. Otherwise
> I'd be fishing off a rock
> In Western Australia.
>
> (*BS* 55–6)

This might be considered an ungracious piece of bad faith on Hughes's part. It is an example among many of the passivity that he attributes to himself throughout his relationship with Plath. It is however another reminder of the persistence of the dream of a free life, associated with his brother Gerald, that I discussed in my first chapter, and which was antipathetic to the professionalised writing life that Hughes was beginning to embark on: within a month of their becoming lovers, by 9 May 1956, Plath had dissuaded Hughes from carrying out his plan to go to Australia.[36]

Reviews of *The Hawk in the Rain* were, in the main, remarkably favourable. Given that this is an extremely uneven volume with a number of poems that it would be easy to mock, critics focussed mostly on what was distinctive, original and strong in the book. One favourable review that particularly pleased Hughes was by W.S. Merwin (though at this time he writes disparagingly of the poetry of Merwin, who was to become a close friend).[37] Merwin detects 'a capacity for incantation … combined with an ear, a sense of form and development, and a poetic intelligence, all of a high order'.[38] No other reviewer gave quite such comprehensive praise, though the *Times* praised Hughes's 'brilliance and variety', and Robin Skelton in the *Manchester Guardian* spoke of 'the emergence of a major poet'. Edwin Muir in the *New Statesman* compared 'The Jaguar' favourably with Rilke's 'Panther' and launched a word that was to haunt early criticism of Hughes by speaking of his 'admirable violence'.[39] Likewise John Press in the *Sunday Times* described Hughes as 'a genuine poet, whose smouldering emotional violence and brooding intellectual passion have an authentic ring'. Reviewers varied considerably in the poems they singled out for praise. The only one to focus on 'The Thought-Fox' was A. Alvarez, who commented on Hughes's 'deliberate, anti-poetical toughness' and claimed that Hughes 'writes in such a way that his feelings take on a physical inevitability'.[40] Ironically, in view of the importance Alvarez was soon to assume as a champion of his poetry, Hughes expressed contempt for this review, and described its author as a 'new critic' who 'writes the dullest, deadest poems imaginable'.[41] Robert Conquest wrote with tempered praise of Hughes's promise and 'strength and distinction of language' but interestingly did not seem to see Hughes (as he was soon to be widely seen, partly by the influence of Alvarez) as an antagonist of the Movement, of which Conquest's anthology *New Lines*, published a year earlier, was considered the flagship. The only review to portray Hughes in this light was also the only wholly hostile review, by Alan Brownjohn in *Listen*, the magazine of David and Jean Hartley, the publishers of Larkin's *The Less Deceived*. Brownjohn, however, was later to be a prominent admirer of *Crow*.

Hughes had a lifelong dislike of criticism, but it could not be attributed to the reception of his first book. Perhaps the reason why he was particularly pleased by Merwin's review was that it was published in the *New York Times Book Review*, and by the time it came out, Hughes and Plath were living in America.

# 4
# Dreaming from America: *Lupercal*

Hughes has often, and with good reason, been compared to D.H. Lawrence. The two writers' provincial non-conformist backgrounds contributed in both to a healthily independent outlook, and they were both of course remarkably responsive to the natural world. Lawrence's great animal poems such as 'Snake' and 'Fish' are the most obvious precursors of the poems that made Hughes famous. Comparison of Hughes's relationship to Sylvia Plath with Lawrence's to Frieda, is a recurring motif of Elaine Feinstein's biography, and they named their daughter after Frieda Lawrence.[1]

In one striking respect, however, Hughes is very different from Lawrence. Between June 1957 and December 1959 Hughes and Plath lived wholly in America. This was only a few months less than the time Lawrence spent on the American continent in the early 1920s, and Hughes's only extended residence abroad. Their creative responses to their American experiences could not have been more contrasting. Almost everything Lawrence wrote in the New World was directly and overtly inspired by his experience of the continent: this included the novel *The Plumed Serpent*, the travel book *Mornings in Mexico*, the stories 'St Mawr', 'The Princess' and 'The Woman Who Rode Away', and poems such as 'Eagle in New Mexico' 'The Red Wolf', 'Autumn in Taos', 'Blue Jay' and 'Mountain Lion'. Hughes's creative achievement while living in America was *Lupercal*.[2] This is a book that reveals no imaginative response whatever to the new country in which its author was living. On the contrary, it is a book that is saturated with English, and specifically Yorkshire, scenes, landscape and wildlife – more than any other volume of Hughes's apart from *Elmet*. Even the poem entitled 'Fourth of July' shows no evidence of American experience.[3]

There are some external reasons for this difference. Lawrence went to America specifically to write about it, and because he was disillusioned with Europe. Hughes went there because Plath had been offered an instructorship at her old college, Smith. The America Lawrence went to was the mountains, desert and Native American culture of New Mexico; for Hughes it was genteel New England, which he found stifling. Yet even when, in their last American summer, he and Plath went on a ten-week tour of the continent, taking in the Dakota Badlands, Yellowstone Park, the Mojave Desert, Grand Canyon and New Mexico, wild places that must have deeply impressed him, these experiences left no trace in Hughes's poetry. It is only years later, in *Birthday Letters*, and subordinated to his relationship with Plath, that any imaginative response to this American residence appears in his work. His letters at the time repeatedly give evidence of this: America is 'cellophane-wrapped', 'sterilised', his 'feelings are in hibernation'.[4]

Several poems in *Lupercal* – and some of the best – are written as if the English scene were literally present to the speaker: 'Mayday on Holderness' begins 'This evening'; 'Crow Hill' and 'Pennines in April' refer to 'these hills'; 'Strawberry Hill' to 'the lawns here'; in 'Dick Straightup' Heptonstall is 'this village'. This is of course a rhetorical device, but taken with the absence of American inspiration it implies something about Hughes's imagination, and especially about his famous 'eye'. Hughes uses the word 'imagination' far more than Lawrence. Lawrence habitually exposes himself to the outside world and is, to some extent, transformed by it: the development of his career is drastically affected by his movements around the world. With Hughes by contrast one has the impression of a writer intently preserving an inner resource: even in such an apparently extravert poem as 'Dick Straightup' the 'here' is an inward place, its scenes and creatures (as one might expect of the author of 'The Thought-Fox') spiritual as much as physical realities. This is not to say that Hughes is like Blake, whose 'Tyger' owed nothing to observation of nature. As Hughes is removed physically from the English scenes on which he imaginatively draws, so he seems to become more specific in his notation. In *The Hawk in the Rain* there is almost no regional character – only 'The Horses' and 'Wind' even implicitly draw on the landscape of Hughes's childhood. In *Lupercal* 'Mayday on Holderness', 'Crow Hill', 'Dick Straightup', 'Esther's Tomcat' and 'Pennines in April' all explicitly declare their Yorkshire allegiance, and many other poems do so implicitly.

A complementary feature of the book, which reinforces its inward nature, is the frequent recurrence of the word 'dream', which is used more than twice as often as in *The Hawk in the Rain*. Few of the poems are oneiric in form or atmosphere ('A Dream of Horses' is the obvious exception) and their visualisation is mostly clear and precise; but Hughes took dreams very seriously, and it is his achievement, in his best poems, to have carried the dream-work into poems that are far more coherent than actual dreams.

The use of memory, implicitly of childhood, is also important in *Lupercal*. Again, and perhaps surprisingly for a first collection, there are no instances of this in *The Hawk in the Rain*, whereas it is central to three of the finest *Lupercal* poems: 'Pike', 'View of a Pig' and 'The Bull Moses'. I will concentrate here on 'Pike', which combines to a particularly successful degree the main qualities that distinguish the volume as a whole.

There are two 'movements' in 'Pike': the first, seven stanzas long, is anecdotal, brilliantly visualised and predominantly abrupt in diction; the second, consisting of the last four stanzas, focuses on a single memory, in a style that is fluent and full of sound-echoes, from which visualisation has disappeared, replaced by darkness and tense anticipation. In the first movement the representation of the pike is characterised by a doubleness, summed up in the phrase, 'submarine delicacy and horror'. As in 'Thrushes' the predatory efficiency of the pike is celebrated, but as also in 'Thrushes', where the shark's mouth 'hungers down the blood-smell even to a leak of its own / Side and devouring of itself', the predatory instinct is both deterministic and self-destructive: 'A life subdued to its instrument. ... One jammed past its gills down the other's gullet.' But this is by no means the final or dominant note of the poem. The harsh, blunt observation of the last line quoted is the necessary condition of what the poem celebrates, creatures that 'move, stunned by their own grandeur, / Over a bed of emerald.' As in many of Hughes's poems, it is the creature's complete oneness with itself that compels the attention, a oneness that entails unconsciousness – here, 'stunned'. The pike maintains this integrity of being even in an act of suicidal cannibalism:

> The outside eye stares: as a vice locks –
> The same iron in this eye
> Though its film shrank in death.

Unlike 'Thrushes' ('With a man it is otherwise …') this poem does not moralise on the difference between animal and human existence. In the second 'movement', however, the human significance is all the more compelling. Here the speaker recollects fishing in a pond of 'legendary depth ... as deep as England', which held 'immense and old' pike, the thought of which terrified him. The depth signified by the pond is at once autochthonous, imaginative and temporal. This world, the realm of the immense pike, is one of mutually reinforcing dimensions of authenticity – an authenticity different from that of 'The jaws' hooked clamp and fangs / Not to be changed at this date' but, in Hughes's distinctive vision, related to it. Shortly after arriving in America Hughes complained to Lucas Myers about his inability to 'fasten some associations into this place'.[5] The multiple associations of the pond contrast forcefully with the imaginative barrenness of Hughes's actual environment. Its 'depth' becomes still more resonant in the final stanza when the pike that the young fisherman is fishing for in terror becomes

> The dream
> Darkness beneath night's darkness had freed
> That rose slowly towards me, watching.

The 'Darkness beneath night's darkness' echoes the 'deeper within darkness' of 'The Thought-Fox', the place where the fox enters the loneliness of the writer's world. Like the fox, the pike has become a psychic reality, something that is both within the mind of the speaker and other to it. The fox is both the creative spirit that makes the poem and a wild, predatory animal 'coming about its own business'. Despite its predatory nature it doesn't arouse fear in the poem's speaker. The unsatisfactorily neat conclusion of 'The Thought-Fox', 'The page is printed', betrays an evasion of the actual gulf between a fox and a fairly traditional, though excellent, poem. The conclusion of 'Pike', quoted above, is much more open. The poem ends on a present participle, an uncompleted action, and the speaker is threatened rather than fulfilled by the imagined predatory creature. Yet the pike, no less than the fox, is a manifestation of creative power. This is confirmed by *Poetry in the Making*, where Hughes illustrates his theme of 'Learning to Think' with 'View of a Pig' but compares the kind of thinking that produced the poem to fishing with a float, when 'your imagination is alarming itself with the size of the thing slowly leaving the weeds and approaching your bait' (*PM* 60). The pike's menacing ascent is reminiscent of a more grotesque and explicit image in 'Mayday on Holderness':

> What a length of gut is growing and breathing –
> This mute eater, biting through the mind's
> Nursery floor, with eel and hyena and vulture,
> ... entering its birthright.

The grotesqueness here comes from the otherness being imagined as part of the speaker's own body – his gut, which is aligned metaphorically with the predatory creatures that usually fulfil this role in Hughes's poetry. The image of something 'biting through the mind's / Nursery floor' provides one way of imagining what might be about to happen (or what the speaker fears is about to happen) in 'Pike': the violent breaching by the power of otherness (including the otherness within the self) of the mental defences designed to keep it at bay. In *Lupercal*, of course, this power is precisely the inner resource that the poet is desperate to preserve.

Hughes has himself given an account of the stylistic evolution of his poetry in *Lupercal*. He cites 'To Paint a Water Lily' as an example of the kind of style from which he was trying to liberate himself, which he describes as 'like writing through a long winding tube, like squeezing language out at the end of this long, remote process'.[6] Like 'October Dawn' this poem is written in rhyming couplets, presumably as an attempt to formally echo its vision of the duality of the plant's above-water and below-water existence. Its diction is marked by a formal, didactic rhetoric that Hughes possibly picked up from John Crowe Ransom: 'study / These, the two minds of this lady', 'Think what worse / Is the pond-bed's matter of course'. Hughes's reaction was to write 'View of a Pig', which he claims he wrote in one or two drafts. The difference between these poems may be what Hughes had in mind when he wrote to Lucas Myers that he wanted to break the tabu against dialect, and avoid 'gesture'.[7] As my quotations indicate, 'To Paint a Water-Lily' is a very gestural poem: the tone is almost arch. In 'View of a Pig' Hughes develops the exploitation of the tonal – and most importantly regional – connotations of etymology that he had earlier explored in 'The Hawk in the Rain':

> The pig lay on a barrow dead.
> It weighed, they said, as much as three men.
> Its eyes closed, pink white eyelashes.
> Its trotters stuck straight out.
>
> Such weight and thick pink bulk
> Set in death seemed not just dead.
> It was less than lifeless, further off.
> It was like a sack of wheat.

The lexis of these stanzas is predominantly Anglo Saxon / Norse. It is heavily characterised by monosyllables and short vowels flanked by

abrupt consonants, especially 'd', 'k' and 't'. But the effect is quite different from 'The Hawk in the Rain'. These are not aggressive 'bludgeoning
spondees'. The effect, rather, is quiet and measured: the speaker is not
forcing the reader's attention but speaking under a compulsion to pay
attention himself. Above all, while the language is not exactly dialect it
is colloquial ('stuck straight out') and, like its subject, 'deadly factual'. It
has no overt traces of education, in the form of Latinate diction. To this
reader, while I would find it hard to demonstrate conclusively, it is
unmistakably northern English. This corresponds well with the apparent element of childhood memory in the poem. In 1970 Hughes said,
'Whatever other speech you grow into, presumably your dialect stays
alive in a sort of inner freedom,' and that 'the West Yorkshire
dialect ... connects you directly and in your most intimate self to middle English poetry,'[8] by which he must have meant alliterative poetry,
since Chaucer was a Londoner. These lines from *Sir Gawain and the Green
Knight* might give an idea of what Hughes meant:

> Fro the swyre to the swange so sware and so thik,
> And his lyndes and his lymes so longe and so grete,
> Half etayn in erde I hope that he were,
> Bot mon most I algate mynn hym to bene,
> And that the myriest in his muckel that myght ride.[9]

This has something of the monosyllabic, consonantal and alliterative
character of 'View of a Pig', but Hughes is here aiming for something
simpler and more condensed than the art of a medieval chivalric poem,
however 'dialect', or indeed than his own most characteristic effects. In
the same interview in which he spoke of 'To Paint a Water Lily' and
'View of a Pig', Hughes said that he followed the latter up with 'Pike'
which, however, 'became much more charged with particular memories
and a specific obsession'. That 'obsession' may be what I have already
drawn attention to in 'Pike' – the identification of the predatory creature
with creative power – but what is immediately obvious about this poem
is that it doesn't confine itself to any particular etymological register.
Opening phrases such as 'Pike, three inches long' and 'Killers from the
egg' have some of the plain-speaking bluntness of 'View of a Pig', but by
the second stanza Hughes is writing like this:

> Or move, stunned by their own grandeur,
> Over a bed of emerald, silhouette
> Of submarine delicacy and horror.

These are poetic effects – effects of rhythm and musical pitch – that are not possible without drawing on the Norman-French element in Hughes's linguistic heritage. Here plain-speaking is not called for, but rather a sense of awe that demands a higher register. At the same time this language is not 'gestural' like that of 'To Paint a Water-Lily'. Hughes has just as much of an intimate feel for the precise tonality of emerald (rich in sound as well as connotation) and silhouette (a disturbing shadowiness enhanced by whispering phonetics and hints of artifice) as he has for 'thick pink bulk' and 'like a sack of wheat'.

'Pike' is one of two poems in *Lupercal* that would make it on to a shortlist of Hughes's best. The other is 'Hawk Roosting', which perhaps more than any other early Hughes poem epitomised what was disturbing about his imagination. In a 1970 interview Ekbert Faas raised the fact that some critics accused him of celebrating 'violence for its own sake',[10] and Hughes was still sufficiently annoyed by this accusation more than twenty years later that he composed a lengthy retrospective reply to the interviewer's question, in which he asserts that the hawk and the pike are '"at rest in the law" – obedient, law-abiding, and are as I say the law in creaturely form. If the Hawk and the Pike kill, they kill within the law and their killing is a sacrament in this sense' (*WP* 262).

Hughes's argument in this piece is very forceful. He writes compellingly about what he means by the law, and the ways in which it is violated by 'our customary social and humanitarian values' (the interviewer's phrase which Hughes repeats with increasingly vehement contempt). In doing so he reveals the political dimension of his poetry which is centred in ecological thought but extends (in commenting on the 'violence' of Yeats's poetry) to 'England's stranglehold policy on Ireland' (*WP* 265). What he does not address, however, is the language of these poems, and the ways in which that language might provoke the readerly revulsion that he is addressing. No sane person could morally or aesthetically object to the spectacle of a thrush dragging a worm out of the ground or a hawk seizing its prey, or to an empathetic literary representation of these things. However it is Hughes who, in 'Thrushes' (the poem that he most fully discusses in this essay), attaches the phrase 'bullet and automatic purpose' to the birds. The mechanistic associations – associations indeed of mechanistic modern warfare – don't sit easily with Hughes's account of the birds as 'the law in creaturely form'. The argument here is not that critics who berated Hughes for 'celebrations of violence' were right, but that the poem itself articulates a more conflicted feeling about its subject than the author's commentary. At the time when he was composing these poems, Hughes wrote very differently about their animal subjects. In a remarkable letter to his sister Olwyn he described the theme of *Lupercal* as 'God the devourer ... which is brainless & the whole of evil.' The only protection against this evil is love. What Hughes in this letter calls 'the lower animals' have no love, and consequently 'their world is entirely evil'.[11]

Questions of language are even more deeply embedded in the greater poem, 'Hawk Roosting' – a poem whose greatness hinges on the conflicts generated by its language. Consider these lines:

> I kill where I please because it is all mine.
> There is no sophistry in my body:
> My manners are tearing off heads.

The first line is compatible with the idea of a creature 'at rest in the law' because it is 'the law in creaturely form'. Appropriately, the language is at the plain, colloquial end of the Hughesian spectrum. One could argue that giving a reason at all, using the word 'because', is not the behaviour of a creature at rest in and identified with the law, but that might be captious. Not so the following line. There is no sophistry in the hawk's body but it knows what sophistry is. It is capable of articulating abstract concepts in order to reject them – 'sophistry' is in its head. This hawk is an intellectual. Still more sophisticated is the wonderful third line quoted. This line lures the reader into revulsion from the hawk's apparent thuggishness, while actually stating that if 'manners' means behaviour that is fitting, then it is a precisely appropriate word to describe its killing.

There are examples of this, one might call it, citational use of abstract language throughout the poem – in the phrase 'no falsifying dream' for example, or 'No arguments assert my right'. This is the only adult poem in the whole of Hughes's *oeuvre* in which an actual creature (as opposed to a mythological one as in *Crow* or *Cave Birds*) speaks. The poem runs up – to its immense imaginative advantage – against the question whether being 'at rest in the law' is compatible with occupying a subject position, being able to say 'I', in Lacanian terms being in the Symbolic order. Contrast this with these lines from a later poem, 'Skylarks':

> A towered bird, shot through the crested head
> With the command, Not die
>
> But climb
>
> Climb
>
> Sing
> Obedient as to death a dead thing.

To quote again from Hughes's self-defence, these birds 'are innocent, obedient, and their energy reaffirms the divine law that created them as they are' (*WP* 259). In a profound piece of metaphysical wit (but here the wit belongs to the poet, not the bird) the obedience to life is identical to the obedience to death – neither is compatible with possessing an *ego*. No reader could feel that the hawk is 'innocent' in the way these birds are, and not because the activity in question is killing rather than climbing and singing. The hawk plainly possesses an *ego* that relishes its own 'advantage' and its ability to make mocking use of the language of 'our customary social and humanitarian values'. The result is a hybrid creation, in which the concept of a splendid, innocent natural creature is shadowed by something more human and sinister.

'Hawk Roosting' is another poem that, like 'View of a Pig', Hughes claims he wrote almost without revision.[12] As Keith Sagar has shown in his analysis of the composition of a Hughes poem, however, this was by no means his normal practice.[13] What is important about these poems is their linguistic assurance and integrity. The language of each, as we have seen, is very different, but both are intently focussed on what I have called Hughes's 'inner resource', that sense of 'the law' that he is determined to protect, and if possible develop, against external distractions.

There is nothing showily or gratuitously 'poetic' about either of these poems, or about 'Pike' (whereas there perhaps is a little about 'To Paint a Water Lily'). They are, however, tidy and coherent poems that don't offer any formal challenge to the reader. In an unpublished essay on the transition from *Wodwo* to *Crow* Graham Bradshaw has proposed, as the epitome of the revolt against the style of 'To Paint a Water Lily', not any of the poems I have discussed so far but 'Mayday on Holderness', in which he sees Hughes 'moving towards a freer, more personal and improvisatory or, as he put it, "natural" style'.[14]

'Mayday on Holderness' may be a less successful poem than 'Hawk Roosting', 'View of a Pig' or 'Pike' – it is certainly less popular – but unlike them it anticipates the more radical styles that Hughes was to develop in the 1960s. It begins with what seems an evocation of benign nature: 'This evening, motherly summer moves in the pond.' This is however immediately followed by two lines that anticipate the uncomfortably autochthonous language of Geoffrey Hill's *Mercian Hymns*:[15] 'I look down into the decomposition of leaves – / The furnace door whirling with larvae.' The hint of trouble in relation to 'motherly summer' is intensified when the river is described:

> A loaded single vein, it drains
> The effort of the inert North – Sheffield's ores,
> Bog pools, dregs of toadstools, tributary
> Graves, dunghills, kitchens, hospitals

'A loaded single vein' might suggest Nature's plenty, but it also combines potentially painful bodily connotations with mineral and implicitly industrial ones. The phrase 'The effort of the inert North' can hardly be understood except in industrial and historical terms – condensing into one phrase the energy of the industrial past and post-industrial depression – an understanding that is reinforced by the name of one of northern England's most famous industrial cities. What seems to be happening here is a collapse between the categories of nature and history. This anticipates a later poem, 'Stealing Trout on a May Morning', which Hughes initially relegated to *Recklings* (a volume of rejects from *Wodwo*) but subsequently promoted to his *Selected Poems*:

> This headlong river is a rout
> Of tumbrils and gun-carriages, rags and metal,
> All the funeral woe-drag of some overnight disaster ...

The passage from 'Mayday on Holderness' is actually more radical, however, since the 'Stealing Trout' passage could be interpreted as a metaphor, whereas the earlier one cannot be recuperated in this way.

The speaker in 'Mayday on Holderness' is located with unusual precision, in relation to the city of Hull and the river Humber, 'melting eastward, my south skyline'. If this poem was indeed written in America, it is an extreme example of Hughes's imaginative resistance to his actual environment. It is perhaps more significant that the carefully established sense of a precisely located, individual human speaker becomes difficult to sustain:

> Birth-soils,
> The sea-salts, scoured me, cortex and intestine,
> To receive these remains.
> As the incinerator, as the sun
> As the spider, I had the whole world in my hands.
> Flowerlike, I loved nothing.

'I' here could be either a personification of the river, or the (autobiographical) speaker reflecting on his early life in the 'inert North', or
both. For a later reader, the word 'remains' suggests the title of Hughes's
1979 book about his birthplace, *Remains of Elmet*. But there seems to be
at least an identification of the speaker with the river, while 'I had the
whole world in my hands. / Flowerlike, I loved nothing' is reminiscent
of 'Hawk Roosting' and being 'at rest in the law'. The reference to the
traditional gospel song, popular in the 1950s, reinforces these religious
connotations, and the song title itself alludes to Job 12.10: Hughes
claimed in interview with Ekbert Faas that the hawk was 'some Creator
like the Jehovah in Job but more feminine.'[16] In the speaker's self-repre-
sentation, as in the description of the river, 'the law in creaturely form'
seems to collide with the burden of history (Bradshaw uses the term 'col-
lisional poems' of *Lupercal*). The word 'incinerator', echoing 'furnace' in
the third line, and even more jarring, may even hint at the Holocaust.
This passage is followed by the one I quoted earlier in this chapter, in
which a 'mute eater' bites through 'the mind's / Nursery floor'. I then
proposed it as an image of what the speaker fears at the end of 'Pike', but
it may be more complex than that: not only the revenge of 'the law'
against the rational intellect, but a rebuke to the (childish) illusion that
a comforting 'motherly' Nature is available as a simple cure for history,
industry and atrocity. Much later, the poem 'A Green Mother' in *Cave
Birds* is a more extended representation of this illusion.

'Mayday in Holderness' differs from other poems in *Lupercal* in its
apparent determination to dissolve boundaries. In this it might be seen to
anticipate the more assured 'Wodwo' and even the protagonist of *Crow*.

Returning to the theme with which I began this chapter – the essential inwardness of *Lupercal* despite its abundance of natural observation,
and its resistance to the external circumstances of its composition – it
might be argued that the spirit of the whole volume is epitomised by the
creature celebrated in the poem 'An Otter': especially the second part of
the poem. Late in his life, Hughes said that he wrote this poem in obedience to an ouija spirit: he wrote the first part 'dutifully', but hallucinated the text of the second part, and copied it down.[17] Hughes himself
thought the second part far superior, and indeed it is much more like
'Pike' and 'Hawk Roosting'. Hughes's otter is 'Attendant and withdrawn', and 'belongs / In double robbery and concealment'. When discovered he is 'Yanked above hounds' and reduced to 'this long pelt over
the back of a chair' – a premonition of how Hughes was later to feel
when he could no longer protect his inner life from the invasion of the
external world.

*Lupercal* was probably the best received of all Hughes's collections of poetry for adults, apart from the special case of *Birthday Letters*. Most critics saw it as an advance on *The Hawk in the Rain*.[18] Alvarez, now the most influential British poetry reviewer (at a time when that was not a contradiction in terms) announced that Hughes had 'emerged as a poet of the first importance'.[19] However, perhaps the most significant thing about the reviews is the way so many of the writers seem drawn to the word 'violence', even in order to reject it: Kenneth Young writes that the poems 'have been called violent, [but] are in fact genuinely powerful', while Norman McCaig asserts that they are 'not violent, which implies carelessness of aim and imprecision of feeling' (implicitly complimenting Hughes by borrowing a phrase from Eliot).[20] A few years later Hughes echoed McCaig in an interview: 'My poems are not about violence but vitality. Animals are not violent, they're so much more completely controlled than men.'[21]

As we have seen, Hughes felt America to be an imaginatively sterile environment for him. After the publication of *Lupercal* he called those years 'a barrenly spiritless time'. He thought that the book suffered from a consequent 'lack of the natural flow of spirit and feelings'.[22] This is an interesting comment on a book that many readers (though perhaps not Hughes's greatest admirers) still think to be his best. However, as we shall see, apart from the period of *Crow*, Hughes almost never felt satisfied with his creative conditions or with his work.

# 5
## Wodwo: the 'single adventure' and the death of Sylvia Plath

As we have seen, Hughes felt that America was hostile to his imaginative life, and that the poems of *Lupercal* bore traces of this. But when he returned to England in 1959, and he and Plath settled in London, he felt equally trammelled by his environment. Looking back at this period after his move to Devon late in 1961, he wrote to Ben Sonnenberg that he had written 'more or less nothing' for over a year, that he 'never had so many ideas, so many genuine inspirations, nor such utter debility of the faculties that could have made anything of them'.[1] He blamed life in London for this. This was the beginning of a period of six years that were to be the most traumatic of Hughes's life. At the end of this period he had only forty poems that he wanted to put into a major collection – the same number that he had written in half the time for each of his previous books – but these were to include some of the finest poems he ever wrote, and represented a crucial artistic advance.

We should not take 'more or less nothing' too literally. During the year before the move to Devon Hughes published over twenty new poems. He also had a radio play, 'The House of Aries', broadcast: writing plays for radio and, more speculatively, the theatre, took up a great deal of his creative energy in the early 1960s. Three other plays for adults were broadcast in the early 1960s: 'The Wound' (1962), 'Difficulties of a Bridegroom' (1963) and 'Dogs: A Scherzo' (1964).[2] Peter Hall, the young artistic director of the newly established Royal Shakespeare Company, encouraged Hughes to submit a play, but the two that Hughes offered, 'The Calm' and a revised version of 'Difficulties of a Bridegroom', were rejected. Hall judged that the latter 'wasn't *theatre*. The scenes were static, the characters mere vehicles carrying the allegorical freight.'[3] Hughes aspired to find theatrical expression for an inward, shamanistic drama. Evidently he failed. It was not until his translation of Seneca's

*Oedipus* for Peter Brook in 1968, when the dramatic structure was already provided, that his gift for theatrical writing emerged (see Chapter 14).

This was also the period during which Hughes established himself as a writer for children: his first four children's books were published between 1961 and 1964 (see Chapter 13). These books were printed in larger runs than his adult poetry books and must have contributed significantly to his ability to live independently by his writing. He also did a lot of reviewing in this period, mainly of poetry, children's literature and anthropology. Between 1960 and 1965 he wrote thirty reviews, and only a handful outside this period. Another significant source of income and public recognition was the BBC. Between 1960 and 1965 Sagar and Tabor's bibliography lists fifty-two broadcasts. These included talks by Hughes, readings of his poems and stories by himself and others, plays for adults and children, interviews and readings by Hughes of others' poetry. Especially significant were the schools' broadcasts that he did, for the series 'Listening and Writing', 'The Living Language' and others. These commissions brought forth his classic poetry primer *Poetry in the Making* (1967; *Poetry Is* 1970 in America) and the plays collected as *The Coming of the Kings and Other Plays* (*The Tiger's Bones and Other Plays for Children* in America, 1970).

But he was dissatisfied with what he wrote, at least for adults. He was repeatedly critical of his adult plays, and he wrote to Lucas Myers in Winter/Spring 1961 that he had written nothing 'or complete confusion' in the previous year, singling out only 'Pibroch' and an unidentified poem called 'Eucharist' ('Theology'?) as 'main-line': the rest are 'marginal'.[4]

Hughes's sense of the difference between his stronger and weaker poems is unusually strong and persistent during the period, 1960–6, of the composition of *Wodwo*. In another letter written in 1961 he mentions 'Sugar Loaf', 'Gog' (Part One) and 'Wino', all eventually published in *Wodwo*, as 'very marginal exercises, thin'.[5] In 1966 he announced to Lucas Myers his intention to publish 'a big book of second-rate poems, a thin book of better ones'. This might seem to point to the actual publication of the limited edition *Recklings* (meaning runts of the litter) alongside *Wodwo*, with some exaggeration of the proportions – there being thirty poems in *Recklings* and forty in *Wodwo*. However, in the same letter he outlines a book containing five stories, 'The Wound', sixty poems that he describes with a series of derogatory epithets and 'about 25 power-pieces',[6] which sounds like a hugely expanded version of *Wodwo* including all the *Recklings* poems and others that were never collected.

The eventual structure of *Wodwo*, and especially the author's note which tells the reader that the book is to be read as a 'single adventure', have caused problems for readers ever since it was published. This is partly because of a natural if illegitimate inclination of readers to look for the biographical narrative of the death of Sylvia Plath, which happened in 1963. In fact only one poem refers directly to Plath's death: 'Ballad from a Fairy Tale', which Hughes considered weak[7] and omitted from all versions of his *Selected Poems*. But even without this distraction, readers would find it difficult to identify the 'adventure', because it is intensely private and imposed on the book retrospectively.

Hughes described the 'single adventure' in two letters written at the time of the book's publication, to Ben Sonnenberg and János Csokits. The central event (of the book and, Hughes says, of his life from 1961–2 onwards) is the 'invitation or importuning of a subjective world' which he (Hughes explicitly identifies the protagonist of the 'adventure' as himself) refuses, the consequence of which is 'mental collapse into the condition of an animal'. To make sense of this account, we need to understand what Hughes meant by subjectivity and objectivity. In his 1976 essay, 'Myth and Education', he wrote:

> Sharpness, clarity and scope of the mental eye are all-important in our dealings with the outer world, and that is plenty ... . But the outer world is only one of the worlds we live in. For better or worse we have another, and that is the inner world of our bodies and everything pertaining.

He goes on to say that the inner world of the body cannot be seen as 'an extension of the outer world', that the 'sharp, clear, objective eye of the mind' is inadequate to comprehend it, and that the word '"subjective" was invented for a good reason – but under that vaguest of terms lies the most important half of our experience' (*WP* 144–5). The inner world is part of the material world but because it is within us, and constitutive of us, we have a completely different relationship to it than to the material world outside of us. The refusal of the invitation to 'subjectivity', then, may be interpreted as a failure to make that world fully human – hence the 'mental collapse into the condition of an animal'.

'The Rain Horse' narrates the refusal of the invitation, and 'The Harvesting', in which a man turns into a hare the moment he shoots it, represents the collapse. The poems in the first part belong to the period before the event, when he had 'an undisturbed relationship with the outside natural world', the stories are 'episodes of the event', and the poems in the third part are after the event. This arrangement, however, does not at all correspond to the chronology of the poems' composition. Some of the poems in Part III – for example, 'Theology', 'Pibroch' and 'Wodwo' – are among the earliest in the volume, while Part I poems such as 'Second Glance at a Jaguar', 'Logos' and 'The Bear' were almost certainly written much later. Moreover, the stories 'Snow', 'Sunday', 'The Rain Horse' and 'The Harvesting' were all published in 1960, and when he reprinted them in *Difficulties of a Bridegroom*, Hughes wrote that they were composed between 1956 and 1959 (*DG* vii): of the Part II pieces, only the radio play 'The Wound' and the story 'The Suitor' belong to the *Wodwo* period, or to the period of the 'event'. Hughes says explicitly that the 'adventure' is a retrospective construction, and that none of the pieces in the book were written with it in mind. He hoped that, arranged in this way, the book would operate on himself as a mental cure and (in a remarkable statement that I do not think is paralleled anywhere else in his writing) allow himself to return to 'the objective world where my talent really belongs'.[8] Hughes's usual attitude to objectivity divorced from the subjective is epitomised by 'Myth and Education', where he writes, 'The exclusiveness of our objective eye, the very strength and brilliance of our objective intelligence, suddenly turns into stupidity – of the most rigid and suicidal kind' (*WP* 146). The statement in the letter to Janos Csokits is the only instance I know of, where Hughes seems to be saying that his 'talent' does not answer to his most pressing human needs.

Soon after *Wodwo* was published Daniel Hoffman wrote a remarkably perceptive essay about it, in which he recognised the 'adventure' as the call to the shamanic life, and 'The Wound' as a version of the *Tibetan Book of the Dead* (*Bardo Thödol*), which Hughes had interpreted as a shamanic narrative (*WP* 56).[9] As Hoffman points out, 'The Wound' was written two years before Hughes read Mircea Eliade's *Shamanism* in 1964 (though not before he had read the *Bardo Thödol*), which may partly explain why the 'adventure' is retrospective: it may have been suggested to him by the idea he got from Eliade that once 'chosen by the spirits ... there is no other life for you, you must shamanize or die' (*WP* 58). In Hughes's account of the 'adventure' we can see a dim foreshadowing of his most overtly shamanic work, *Gaudete*, especially in his use, in both letters, of the word 'abduct', which he uses to describe what happened to himself after his refusal of the invitation, and repeats in the 'Argument' to the first edition of *Gaudete*, where it refers to the carrying off of the original vicar to the spirit world. The first version of *Gaudete*, a seventy-one page film scenario, dated 1964–5, has Lumb 'drumming on a Siberian shaman's drum'.[10] The 'adventure' also has a bearing on the *Birthday Letters* poem 'Epiphany', about an incident that must have taken place in 1960 or 61, when Hughes's refusal of the offer of a fox-cub in a London street is represented as a failure of 'the test' and of his marriage.

The attempt to relate *Wodwo*, and the 'single adventure', to that other narrative, of Sylvia Plath's death, is difficult and potentially impertinent. Hughes encourages some such link, however, by saying that, in the story 'The Suitor', the narrator is himself, the girl is Sylvia and the stranger is death: he describes the story, written in January 1962, as a prophecy.[11] The lure of the biographical narrative is so great that Ekbert Faas, in *Ted Hughes: The Unaccommodated Universe*, completely identifies the two, on the manifestly false assumption that all the poems were written after Plath's death. Diane Middlebrook, a much more careful scholar, nevertheless also errs when she says that all the poems were written before the move to Devon in August 1961, apart from 'Song of a Rat', 'Heptonstall', 'Ballad from a Fairy Tale', 'Mountains', 'Pibroch' and 'The Howling of Wolves', and that these last are 'funerary poems for Sylvia Plath'.[12] ('Mountains' and 'Pibroch' had both been published before Plath's death.) Hughes himself has written that he wrote almost all of *Wodwo* before Plath's death in February 1963, mentioning only 'Song of a Rat', 'The Howling of Wolves', 'Skylarks' and (doubtfully) 'Gnat-Psalm' as exceptions, but as we have seen Hughes is not a reliable informant about the dating of his works.[13]

The 'single adventure' is of more obvious interpretive value in relation to the stories and the play than to the poems. Three of the stories narrate violent encounters between human beings and animals, and in four of them the human protagonist is portrayed in a way that suggests alienation from the natural world and attachment to a world of social values. The young man in 'The Rain Horse' is wearing a suit that he is anxious to keep clean, and he plans a walk along 'pleasantly-remembered tarmac lanes' but has turned 'dreamily' into the ploughland where he encounters the horse (*W* 45). The boy in 'Sunday' is wearing a school uniform 'loaded with honours and privilege' (*W* 56). Mr Grooby in 'The Harvesting' wears a trilby that ineffectively protects him against the sun (*W* 85) and adopts a 'managerial air' (*W* 87) when speaking to the farm workers. The narrator of 'The Suitor' is wearing thin-soled dancing shoes in the rain because he wants to 'feel smart' (*W* 93). At the end of each story the protagonist's world, or even his self, has been undermined: in 'The Rain Horse' he sits 'staring at the ground, as if some important part had been cut out of his brain' (*W* 55); in 'Sunday' Michael is unable to speak and runs blindly away from the bestial scene he has witnessed (*W* 70); in

'The Harvesting' Mr Grooby turns into the hare he has just shot; and the Suitor is grotesquely transformed: 'I writhe up my features again, stretching my mouth wide, making my eyes bulge ...' (*W* 103). All five stories take place in extreme weather conditions (torrential rain in two, overwhelming heat in two, and a blizzard in one) that their protagonists are ill-equipped to withstand.

'The Rain Horse' is the story that, according to Hughes, directly narrates the central event of invitation and refusal, and this is the only story that really fits the scheme without forcing: the young man is 'dreamily' lured off the safe tarmac where he has planned to walk (*W* 45); the horse has an uncanny quality, 'running on its toes like a cat', silhouetted against the sky 'like a nightmarish leopard' (*W* 46), and is the only animal in the stories that doesn't behave in a purely 'natural' way, pursuing the young man with mysterious intent. It involves no strain to interpret this horse as a shamanic spirit, and the young man's violent avoidance of it as a refusal for which he will pay a heavy spiritual price.

However, the significance of 'The Rain Horse' does not, without prompting, seem greatly different from that of many poems by Hughes in the mid-to-late 1950s (the period of its own composition), featuring uncanny encounters with animals, such as 'The Thought-Fox', 'Meeting', 'Pike' and 'The Bull Moses'. It clearly belongs to the inspiration that produced the most memorable poems of *The Hawk in the Rain* and *Lupercal*, and it is difficult to see it as prophetic of a spiritual crisis specific to the early 1960s.

'The Wound', which derives from a dream that Hughes had twice in one night (*DB* viii), is by contrast very different from anything in the first two volumes. Hughes often made use of dreams in his writing, but this is perhaps his most elaborate oneiric text. Daniel Hoffman reported that he found it 'really *scary*; the terror is not that of its Gothic conventions but, as Poe said, "of the soul" '.[14] The situation in which the protagonist, Ripley, finds himself, being driven on relentlessly and irrationally by the Sergeant to '[k]eep going' (*W* 104), his arrival at a ruined 'chateau' that seems to be a brothel, the mocking and menacing behaviour of the women there, the scenes of cannibalism and the eruptions into his consciousness of his real situation, lying on his back with a hole in his head, is like being trapped in a nightmare. But the dream effect is not random or gratuitously bizarre. What makes it appropriate to describe 'The Wound' as 'shamanic' and to compare it with a text such as the *Bardo Thödol*, is that it powerfully and unnervingly suggests what it is like to die, the struggles of consciousness overwhelmed by the brute destiny of the body: as Hughes told Janos Csokits, 'it all takes place in a few seconds when the protagonist's heart stops.'[15]

'The Wound' looks forward to the 'other world' texts *Gaudete* and *Cave Birds*, but neither it, nor the 'single adventure' which it may well have prompted, provides in any simple or obvious way an interpretive key to the poems, which have a life of their own, independent of the scheme. Hughes's construction of this 'adventure', making it such an internal event, and so elusively related to the external events of his life, might be interpreted as an evasion of the biographical narrative, an example of the resistance to the 'confessional', to the direct use of autobiography in poetry, that he maintained until *Birthday Letters* and, as we shall see, came to regret. It may also be a symptom of his insecurity about the quality of the poems – though most critics would place at least 'Thistles', 'Skylarks', 'Pibroch', 'Gnat-Psalm', 'Full Moon and Little Frieda' and 'Wodwo' among his finest work, and it is notable that in *The Epic Poise*, a volume in which admirers of Hughes are invited to choose a poem to write about, more choose from *Wodwo* than from any other collection.[16]

The retrospective emphasis of the narrative, and Hughes's description of some of the poems as prophetic,[17] does however point to one curious aspect of the *Wodwo* poems: the fact that very early in the period of their composition he came up with poems that seem to point beyond *Wodwo* to the work of Hughes's most creatively happy period, *Crow*. The most obvious of these is 'Theology', in which Hughes suddenly seems to come up with the form, tone, attitude and idiom of the Garden of Eden poems in *Crow*. An otherwise uninformed reader would assume that this was composed close in time to poems such as 'Snake Hymn' and 'Apple Tragedy', but it was written before March 1961 and, apart from the comparatively laboured 'Reveille', there is nothing else like it in the *Wodwo* period.

A less obvious but perhaps more deeply significant example is the title poem. This was published in September 1961, but Hughes places it last in the volume: the most striking example of his notion that some of the poems are prophetic. This decision might be connected with the idea that the protagonist of the 'single adventure' suffers 'a mental collapse into the condition of an animal'. Hughes took the name Wodwo from the medieval poem *Sir Gawain and the Green Knight*. This choice is significant both because of his sense of the connection between his native dialect and Middle English, discussed in Chapter 1, and for the quest motif that underlies Hughes's personal mythology. In the medieval poem the Green Knight enters Arthur's court and calls for a volunteer to exchange blows: to strike a blow at the Green Knight himself there and then, and to meet to receive one in return a year later. Gawain accepts the challenge. It is a sophisticated chivalric tale, but nevertheless the Green Knight is plainly the Green Man of pagan iconography, familiar from many medieval churches, an autochthonous spirit, 'the archetype of our oneness with the earth' as William Anderson calls him.[18] It is therefore not too outlandish to see a connection between the Green Knight's challenge and Hughes's 'single adventure', especially if we think of the rain horse's 'importuning' of the young man. But Hughes, unlike Sir Gawain, refused the invitation, and consequently he identifies himself not with the questing knight but with a creature that the poem mentions only in passing, a 'satyr' or 'troll of the forest' according to the Tolkien and Gordon edition that Hughes would almost certainly have read.

Hughes told Alvarez that the name derived from the Old English wudu-wasa, meaning 'one of the early aboriginals who took to the woods when the decent citizens came', and that it 'degenerated' to its Middle English meaning.[19] The Old English meaning is one with which Hughes might well have ideologically identified, while the actual wodwo of Middle English is closer to the 'mental collapse into the condition of an animal' of the 'single adventure'. This would be one way of interpreting Hughes's decision to place this poem at the end of the volume. However, as more generally with the 'single adventure', it is not an interpretation that is likely to occur to a reader unprompted. Rather than 'collapse', the wodwo seems to represent a *developing* consciousness, curious about the world and determined to 'go on looking'. In one of the most perceptive reviews of the book, Eavan Boland wrote that whereas in *Gawain* the wodwos are simply reminders of a transcended savagery, in Hughes it signifies 'the struggle for survival and identity'.[20]

I called 'Wodwo' 'prophetic' because it seems such a stylistic and conceptual leap from *Lupercal*, and to be much closer in spirit to *Crow*. Hughes abandons the vestiges of stanzaic structure and formal syntax in *Lupercal* and writes a poem whose second half is entirely unpunctuated, making radical use of enjambement and requiring ideally to be read with a single breath. Hughes never wrote quite like this again (it is also his only poem in which the initial letters of the lines aren't capitalised) but it does broadly anticipate the much greater formal and stylistic freedom of the later *Wodwo* poems and of *Crow*. Along with 'Gog', 'Wodwo' is the first instance of Hughes taking a mythological or folkloric creature as the speaker of a poem – another anticipation of *Crow*.

Conceptually, it is very revealing to compare 'Wodwo' to that other Hughesian 'dramatic monologue', 'Hawk Roosting'. The condition of being 'at rest in the law' means that the hawk is completely incurious about the world. It knows everything that it needs to know, most importantly that 'I kill where I please because it is all mine' and that 'I hold Creation in my foot'. It is this complete blindness to the possibility that the world may exist for others, rather than the hawk's supposed violence, that makes it seem so sinister if considered as a human consciousness. In contrast to the hawk, the wodwo asks,

> Do these weeds
> know me and name me to each other have they
> seen me before, do I fit in their world?

The wodwo says 'I suppose I am the exact centre' but immediately adds, 'but there's all this'. Whereas the hawk's consciousness is one that is incapable of asking a question (because it doesn't need to), 'Wodwo' consists almost entirely of questions, including the most fundamental question of all, 'What am I?' The awareness that the world may exist for others suggests the beginnings of an ethical consciousness and therefore of humanity. However, this emerging humanity also brings handicaps: the wodwo appears to have no intuitive sense of its own being, to be a consciousness out of touch with its instinctive life, so that it does not even know when it is eating:

> Why do I find
> this frog so interesting as I inspect its most secret
> interior and make it my own?

It does not know why it is picking bits of bark off a rotten stump and, in a line that both brilliantly condenses a philosophical question and sums up a familiar experience, remarks, 'me and doing that have coincided very queerly'.

It is customary, encouraged by the title of the book, to interpret the wodwo as a figure for the poet's own imagination. Keith Sagar writes that 'Hughes is a wodwo in all his poems, asking these same questions of the world in which he finds himself',[21] and helpfully compares the poem with Hughes's commentary on Eastern European poets in his essay 'Vasko Popa': 'Their poetic themes revolve around the living suffering spirit, capable of happiness, much deluded, too frail, with doubtful and provisional senses ... continuing to explore' (WP 222–3). In this essay Hughes contrasts Popa, Miroslav Holub, Zbigniew Herbert and Yehuda Amichai with Beckett, saying that while their world resembles Beckett's, theirs is more human, since their standpoint is that of participants, whereas his is that of a detached observer. It may be an accident that 'Wodwo' recalls Beckett's novel *The Unnameable*, both structurally, in the gradual abandonment of punctuation, and in its concluding assertion, 'I'll go on looking', which echoes Beckett's conclusion, 'you must go on, I can't go on, I'll go on.'[22] Whether it is accidental or not, the echo reinforces the sense that, as in the Popa essay, the poem is more positive in spirit, actively looking outward, in contrast to the stoical endurance of Beckett's speaker.

On the other hand, as we have seen, the wodwo is almost freakishly out of touch with its inner life, which Hughes consistently identifies with the body: 'we come to regard our body as no more than a somewhat stupid vehicle. All the urgent information coming towards us from that inner world sounds to us like a blank ...' (*WP* 146). This is the 'subjective world' into which Hughes is invited in the 'single adventure'. We have already seen that the 'single adventure' is retrospective, and quite possibly it caused Hughes to reinterpret many of his own poems. This should encourage readers to feel comfortable about entertaining conflicting perspectives on the poem – indeed, the possibility of doing so accounts for a large part of its fascination.

The narrative of Sylvia Plath's death seems most obviously relevant to the poems that Hughes has said he wrote in its immediate aftermath, 'Song of a Rat' and 'The Howling of Wolves'. These are the earliest poems about animals in *Wodwo*,[23] and they are radically different both thematically and stylistically from Hughes's previous animal poetry. Hughes has said that after them he wrote nothing until 'Skylarks' two years later,[24] but as usual we should not take this too literally. When he says he has written nothing he often means nothing that pleases him, and between 1963 and 1965 he certainly wrote the play *Eat Crow* and the 71-page prose film scenario that was the first version of *Gaudete*. Diane Middlebrook suggests that Hughes's creative revival in 1966 may partly have been stimulated by the award of a five-year fellowship by the University of Vienna, worth two-thirds of a professor's salary, to be used entirely to support his creative work.[25]

Comment on the significance of Plath's death for this change can only be speculative, but there is an intriguing intertextual link. In August 1962, the month after she discovered Hughes's relationship with Assia Wevill, Plath wrote only one poem: 'Burning the Letters'. Unlike every subsequent poem it was omitted from *Ariel, Winter Trees, Crossing the Water* and Plath's own projected *Ariel* collection. Lynda K. Bundtzen, who has written most interestingly about this poem, describes it as 'halting in its rhythms, enervated in its tone, and misshapen on the page'.[26] The poem is related biographically to an incident, following her discovery of Hughes's affair with Assia, in which Plath is reported to have burned papers from his study.[27] One of the drafts is written on the verso of a typescript of 'The Thought-Fox'. Hughes and Plath both habitually used old typescripts and manuscripts of their own and each other's work for new drafts, but Susan Van Dyne may nevertheless be right in describing this particular use as an 'emotionally laden gesture'.[28] The fox, as we have seen, was Hughes's totem animal or shamanic spirit, and 'The Thought-Fox' had a special place in his canon. The impression it gives, that the fox actually writes the poem, has perhaps done more than anything else to identify Hughes with his animal subjects in the minds of his readers.

'Burning the Letters' concludes:

> The dogs are tearing a fox. This is what it is like –
> A red burst and a cry
> That splits from its ripped bag and does not stop
> With the dead eye
> And the stuffed expression, but goes on
> Dyeing the air,
> Telling the particles of the clouds, the leaves, the water
> What immortality is. That it is immortal.

Bundtzen describes this as 'an anti-thought fox', a rejection of 'poetic lyricism' and 'literary convention' in favour of 'the poetic efficacy of shrieks … . Something crude and sensational.'[29] Van Dyne sees Plath's fox as 'Hughes's poetic agency' which is 'set upon and devoured by his own deception': 'In quarrelling with Hughes's telling of the fox's story, Plath contests his prior claims to immortality.'[30] This refers to Hughes's statement in *Poetry in the Making*, 'I suppose that long after I am gone, as long as a copy of the poem exists, everytime (*sic*) anyone reads it the fox will get up somewhere out in the darkness and come walking towards them' (*WP* 15). One might dissent from Bundtzen's description of 'The Thought-Fox' as 'one of those tricky little self-reflexive pieces about the process of creating the poem's writing of itself'[31] – one may consider it one of the finest poetic achievements of the decade – and still feel that Plath's raw evocation of the fox's death addresses something troubling about the facility with which Hughes appropriates the fox with puns on 'sets neat prints into the snow' and 'The page is printed', and his confidence that the poem is immortal.

At the time when he wrote 'The Thought-Fox', Hughes was much less trapped by 'literary convention' than Plath. Nevertheless it is a neatly constructed poem, arranged in four-line stanzas, with lines of roughly equal length and varying patterns of half-rhyme. 'Burning the Letters' by contrast is written in an extremely loose form of free verse that Plath had only recently developed, and that characterises most of the poems of *Ariel*. It is thus both thematically and stylistically in dialogue with the poem on the other side of the paper. The tearing of the fox can be read both as a textual assault on Hughes, particularly in the image of the predatory 'marauder' that both 'The Thought-Fox' and her own 'Pursuit' had erected, and as a challenge to his investment in the animal world, his identification with creatures such as 'The Thought-Fox', 'The Jaguar', 'Hawk Roosting', 'Thrushes', that seem to rise above death and suffering.

It is precisely in this respect that 'Song of a Rat' and 'The Howling of Wolves' differ from Hughes's earlier animal poems. The former is written from the point of view of a rat caught in a trap:

> Iron jaws, strong as the whole earth
>
> Are stealing its backbone
> For a crumpling of the Universe with screechings.
>
> For supplanting every human body inside its skull with a
>   rat-body that knots and unknots,
> A rat that goes on screeching …

The wolf has

> eyes that never learn how it has come about
> That they must live like this,
>
> That they must live
>
> Innocence crept into minerals … .
>
> It goes to and fro, trailing its haunches and whimpering
>   horribly.

It would be banal to say that these creatures are objective correlatives for the pain Hughes was feeling when he wrote them, though it is noteworthy that an early draft of 'Song of a Rat' is titled 'Refuse Comfort', and written on the verso of a draft letter about the need to sell his house because of his wife's death.[32] These poems are not only expressions of pain; they testify to a loss of the faith exemplified by poems such as 'Hawk Roosting'. This loss is temporary – it was after all much later that Hughes declared the hawk to be 'at rest in the law' – but the change of emphasis from the animal as predator to the animal as suffering victim has a lasting influence on Hughes's poetry: it is one of the strengths of the farming poems in *Moortown*, for example. The change of emphasis is especially significant in 'The Howling of Wolves', where the need to eat and the predatory instinct itself are portrayed as burdens suffered by the wolves. Both in feeling and in style these poems resemble 'Burning the Letters' much more closely than 'The Thought-Fox'. It would be rash to assert that Hughes had taken note of the rebuke to himself in 'Burning the Letters', and that in 'Song of a Rat' and 'The Howling of Wolves' he is not only mourning Plath but paying poetic tribute to her. Nevertheless, the resemblance of the 'enervated' tone, the 'misshapen' appearance, the supplanting of 'poetic lyricism' with 'something crude and sensational', is striking.

Most of the earlier *Wodwo* poems, such as 'Thistles', 'Still Life', 'Her Husband' and 'Pibroch', still look neat on the page, with regular stanzas like most of their predecessors. It is true that, as we have seen, the title poem looks like a sudden leap forward stylistically, and that in an earlier poem such as 'Full Moon and Little Frieda' Hughes makes use of drastically varied line-length. But 'Full Moon and Little Frieda' is the most 'lyrical' poem in *Wodwo*, and its long lines such as 'Cows are going home in the lane there, looping the hedges with their warm wreaths of breath' have an obvious mimetic rhythmic function that contributes to the lyricism. They don't present the kind of aesthetic challenge that lines like 'It goes to and fro, trailing its haunches and whimpering horribly' do. In these poems written after Plath's death we can see for the first time the emergence of an aesthetic of ugliness, a challenge to poetic norms, that is to become much more conscious and systematic a few years later in *Crow*.

But 'ugliness' is not an end in itself, and the same freedom that made the *Crow* poems possible also enabled Hughes, between the 1963 poems and *Crow*, to write two of his most radiant celebrations of the natural world, 'Skylarks' and 'Gnat-Psalm'.[33] These are also, I suggest, poems that illuminate what Hughes meant by 'subjectivity'.

Daniel Hoffman wrote that in *Wodwo*, Hughes 'abandons stanzaic and metrical conventions for line-breaks and the spacing of bursts of lines which try to capture the shape of the experience'.[34] This is outstandingly exemplified in these lines from 'Skylarks:

A towered bird, shot through the crested head
With the command, not die

But climb

Climb

Sing

Obedient as to death a dead thing.

Here the formal freedom is combined with great sensitivity to rhythm and intonation. The lineation of the short lines creates pauses which map them rhythmically on to the longer line that follows. At the same time the rising pitch of 'Climb ... Sing' enacts both the literal rise and the transformation of effort into musical utterance, while the rhyme 'Sing / thing' creates an unsettling double effect, echoing the utterance while reducing the lark to an object.

In its early drafts this poem was called 'Against Larks' and 'Ode to Indolence', and featured a much more prominent persona, who grumpily declares that he doesn't like larks and someone else will have to write poems about them. He is like the persona of 'The Hawk in the Rain', staggering and floundering in mud with 'leaden legs'. A trace of him remains in 'My idleness curdles' and 'All the dreary Sunday morning'. Perhaps the most revealing lines of the early drafts are 'Everything your eye has winced or dodged from/ Screams in your ear', suggesting an unsettling of the 'objective' point of view.[35]

The persona in the published poem represents the larks as mad, 'Squealing and gibbering and cursing', and as alienly material, 'The larks carry their tongues to the last atom / ... With long cutting screams buckling like razors.' This language alternates with a reassuring anthropomorphism: 'the earth gives them the O.K.', and at the end of the poem as published in *Wodwo* they perch on a wall 'Conscience perfect'.[36] I see this not as a conflict between the subjective and the objective, but as a stress within Hughes's concept of subjectivity. What Hughes calls the subjective world, 'this inner world of the body', is almost inaccessible to the mind:

> After all, what exactly is going on in there? It is quite frightening, how little we know about it. We can't say there's nothing – that 'nothing' is merely the shutness of the shut door. (*WP* 144)

What is normally thought of as the 'subject' – as in Lacanian psychoanalysis for example – is represented by Hughes's 'we'. But 'we' are in this discourse excluded from 'our' subjectivity, which sounds more like the Lacanian Real, 'outside language and unassimilable to symbolisation.'[37] Sometimes Hughes sounds as if he shares this view of language, as in the poem 'Crow Goes Hunting', where Crow 'Decided to try words' to catch a hare but, after much shape-changing on the part of the hare, Crow ends up 'Speechless with admiration'; or in his statement on the sleeve of a recording of *Crow*, that the God of *Crow* has as much relation to the Creator as 'ordinary English has to reality.'[38] However, the phrase 'ordinary English' is the key, and when Hughes writes more positively about language we can see that his work, like that of many poets, represents a challenge to the notion of an impermeable boundary between the symbolic and the real: 'the deeper into language one goes, the more dominated it becomes by purely musical modes, and the more dramatic it becomes – the more unified with total states of being and with the expressiveness of physical action.'[39]

'Gnat-Psalm' is a notably more relaxed poem than 'Skylarks'. It begins 'When the gnats dance at evening' and seems as if it is going to be one long sentence with the main clause deferred while it accumulates adjectival and adverbial phrases evocative of the gnats' dance. Long before the end, however, such a linear structure is forgotten, and the accumulating phrases and clauses relate to each other in a free-form way that mimics the movement of the gnats 'brimming over / At large in the nothing'. But the stylistic achievement of the poem is not just a matter of freedom from syntactical constraint. It ranges from the precise diction of 'frail eyes and crepuscular temperaments' to the high spirits of 'Everybody everybody else's yoyo'. It is epitomised by the conclusion:

> O little Hasids
> Ridden to death by your own bodies
> Riding your bodies to death
> You are the angels of the only heaven!
>
> And God is an Almighty Gnat!
> You are the greatest of all the galaxies!
> My hands fly up in the air, they are follies
> My tongue hangs up in the leaves
> My thoughts have crept into crannies
>
> Your dancing
>
> Your dancing
>
> Rolls my staring skull slowly away into outer space.

The image of 'little Hasids' exemplifies the poem's combination of humorous observation and transcendent exaltation, referring back both to the description of the gnat-swarm as a 'dumb Cabala' and to the observation of their 'little bearded faces'. The poem's humorous but completely unironic quality of religious affirmation is condensed in the lines, 'You are the angels of the only heaven! // And God is an Almighty Gnat!' The following lines bear traces of Hughes's affinity with the alliterative tradition, but the alliterative form is much more lightly used than in 'The Hawk in the Rain', and the repetition of 'dancing' is suggested as much by the poem's movement as by the image of the gnats. The loss of self in these final lines, the suggestion, part humorous and part hyperbolic, that the speaker has become a gnat, might seem superficially to be another example of 'mental collapse into the condition of an animal'. Actually it is the antithesis of the relationship to the animal world in 'The Rain Horse'. By identifying with the gnats the speaker escapes from isolating objectivity and joins the 'dance' which is also his own inner life. To suggest that this poem evokes what Hughes means by 'subjectivity' might seem extremely odd, but we must remember that for Hughes a genuine encounter with the animal world is an objective correlative for communicating with the inner life, and 'staring' ('the mental eye') is an index of objectivity. It is the objective consciousness that is dissolved at the end of the poem, and if 'Skylarks' concludes by rendering the birds in human terms, 'Gnat-Psalm' does the opposite.

The reception of *Wodwo* suggested that Hughes was by now widely accepted as a major poet. Eavan Boland takes this status for granted; C.B. Cox calls it 'undoubtedly one of the great books of the 1960s' and Michael Baldwin affirms that it 'marks the emergence of Ted Hughes as a poet of major stature.' But the divisions of critical opinion, which in earlier reviews had been more nuanced and often juggled within the same review, began to be more polarised. The *Times Literary Supplement*, in particular, which was to become one of Hughes's most powerful enemies, found much of it 'unintentionally comic'.[40] While this betrays a blindness to how much *intentional* comedy there is even at Hughes's grimmest moments (for example, the wonderfully straight-faced line 'This will be serious for the hill' in 'Sugar Loaf') it anticipates the highly polarised response to *Crow*.

# 6
# The Making of *Crow*

In October 1970 Hughes published *Crow: From the Life and Songs of the Crow*, a book that attracted more publicity and attention than any other with the exception of *Birthday Letters*. Hughes himself described these poems as 'songs with no music whatsoever, in a super-simple and a super-ugly language which would in a way shed everything except just what [Crow] wanted to say'.[1] Although, as we have seen, there are anticipations of this aesthetic of ugliness in *Wodwo*, the concentration of poems in this style, in a volume which appeared to take an unremittingly grim view of existence, was a shocking experience. Critical response to Hughes became more polarised than ever: while Eavan Boland found them to be 'poems in the fullest, richest, most assured sense' and Douglas Dunn wrote that 'they may be the fiercest poems in the language, but they are not inhuman', Richard Holmes in *The Times* complained of a 'brutish metamorphosis coming over Hughes's linguistic skill' and a lack of 'life-enhancement', while in the *TLS* Ian Hamilton, in what was perhaps the most hostile review Hughes ever received, sneered at *Crow* as 'a cosy, unperplexing wallow'.[2] Hughes anticipated these negative responses by asserting that *Crow* was in the tradition of 'the primitive literatures', which was his 'own tradition',[3] and later claimed that the style deliberately excluded everything that 'the average Pavlovian critic' knew how to respond to.[4]

*Crow* was the result of the only period of Hughes's life, from 1965 to 1969, when his work seems to have completely satisfied him. He described it as his 'masterpiece'[5] and repeatedly lamented his inability to return to the creative point he had reached with it.[6] However, he later said that publishing the book was a mistake, and that publication 'aborts the gestation process'.[7] Picking up this metaphor, one of Hughes's most respected and enthusiastic commentators, Keith Sagar, has written that

'*The Life and Songs of the Crow* would undoubtedly have been one of Hughes's greatest works had that project not been aborted in 1969' and that its incompleteness caused it to be 'widely misinterpreted'.[8] The dust jacket of the first edition described the book as 'the passages of verse from about the first two-thirds of what was to have been an epic folk-tale'. The form it eventually took is at least partly the result of the second tragedy in his life, when Assia Wevill killed herself and took with her their daughter Shura. Hughes said that the last poem to be written, 'A Horrible Religious Error', was composed on 20 March 1969, five days before Assia's death, and there is no sense that the project had come to a conclusion.[9] As with many of Hughes's statements about the dating of his writing, we should treat this information with caution. Even at the time he sent contradictory messages. In July 1969 he told Leonard Baskin that he was 'pushing on' with *Crow*,[10] but four months later wrote to Ben Sonnenberg that 'Crow no longer says anything to me,' and the following March, a year after Assia's death, told same correspondent that he had written nothing in that period.[11] As late as 1984, however, he wrote to Leonard Baskin that he had written 'two books – or booklength chapters – of what was once Crow'.[12] That last phrase, however, is revealing. Hughes always regarded the period of *Crow* as one of extraordinary inspiration, of access to inner resources that he craved to recover: 'what was once Crow' might signify a return of that inspiration, rather than something recognisable as the original project.

It seems reasonable to assume that at least the poems collected in the volume were all written before Assia's death. The only poems identified by Hughes as belonging to *Crow* that he definitely wrote after this are 'The Lovepet' (first published January 1971) and 'Bride and Groom Lie Hidden for Three Days' (1975), both of which Hughes said he wrote 'against terrific odds' in an attempt to continue the project.[13]

There is, then, the book *Crow*, and a number of other texts and rumours that surround it and potentially destabilise a reading of it. Some of these texts, the Crow poems that were not included in the volume, are unproblematic, because it was Hughes's choice not to collect them.[14] The 'epic folk-tale' or framing narrative, however, and especially the suggestion that the book corresponds to only two-thirds of the story, may well demoralise readers into feeling that they are doomed, as Sagar says, to misinterpret it. Sagar himself has usefully, and with Hughes's blessing, put together a synoptic version of the story, mostly in Hughes's own words, derived from readings (at which he used invariably to frame the poems with some kind of narrative), letters and other sources.[15] It is undoubtedly helpful to have this material in a widely accessible form. However, I believe that the relationship of the narrative to the book *Crow* is more problematic than Sagar suggests, and this belief is strengthened by my examination of the draft material in the Emory archive. Hughes's own views about the essential nature of the project seem to have varied over time. In 1970 he told Ekbert Faas that 'the story is not really relevant to the poems as they stand', and suggested that he might one day finish it and publish it separately,[16] and in a letter to Alvarez, probably in 1969, lamented that he had wasted time on the prose saga when he should have been concentrating on the poems.[17] Yet when he was writing it he consistently described it as a saga or epic and, as we have seen, claimed still to be working on it in 1984.

In this chapter I shall be arguing that the particular impact of *Crow* as a volume, its effect of shock, provocation, occasionally outrage, its arousal of an unanticipated kind of aesthetic pleasure, its combination of desolation and sometimes raucous humour, and of exquisite poetic skill with deliberate crudity, is dependent on its incompleteness, fragmentariness and undecidability. It invokes the worlds of myth and folktale, but has none of the explanatory power of myth. By contrast the narrative frame, in so far as there is one, attempts to corral the unruly meanings of the poems into an overarching and teleological pattern. A particularly crucial point is that Hughes claimed the book as it stands brings Crow to the lowest and darkest point of his adventure.[18] This is the significance of it being 'the first two-thirds': Crow was, according to Sagar, 'just beginning the upward movement of the final third'.[19]

The second part of my argument is that the elements of narrative framework that have been made publicly available, in *The Laughter of Foxes* and Hughes's recording, are themselves fragmentary, often desultory, and bear only the most vestigial relationship to the ambitious narrative scheme, the ruins of which are preserved in the Emory archive. Furthermore, inspection of these ruins suggests that there was never any possibility of Hughes writing the kind of coherent framing narrative that would have marshalled the poems into an interpretive structure. There is, I argue, an inherent incompatibility between the inspiration of the poems and the project of the saga.

First, then, I will say something about the aesthetic effect of the poems as they appear in the volume. Several of the poems conclude with a line about Crow eating, and these lines often exemplify in a particularly strong way Hughes's 'super-ugly language'. These final lines often also exist in a relationship of contrast, tension and even conflict with the rest of the poem. Four good examples of this effect are 'Lineage', 'Crow and the Birds', 'That Moment' and 'A Horrible Religious Error'.

'Lineage' is a parody of the Biblical form, such as the opening of St Matthew's Gospel. The syntax of the lineage form is stripped down to a rapid-fire 'Who begat ... Who begat', and the lineage in question combines Biblical references (Adam, Mary, God) with elemental ones (Blood, Eye, Fear), an incongruous 'Guitar' and an echo of *King Lear* in the line 'Never Never Never'. Something of the solemnity of the Bible is combined with a savage momentum, hint of tragic nihilism and absurdly grotesque juxtaposition. All this is not quite subordinated to a relentless mesmeric chant. The lineage culminates in Crow:

> Screaming for Blood
> Grubs, crusts
> Anything
> Trembling featherless elbows in the nest's filth

This may be 'super-ugly language'; it is also a beautifully concise evocation of an actual nestling; the poem concludes on a note of urgent creatureliness, that contrasts with the solemn tone and personified abstractions of the foregoing poem. The final line is one of the most outstanding examples of the style of *Crow*, with its rhythmically assured shift from the falling, dactyllic opening to the abrupt, spondaic conclusion, and the gathering together of the consonants of the trisyllabic 'featherless' into the monosyllable 'filth'. We may conclude that the end-point of creation is ugly and filthy rapacity; or we may detect, in the creatureliness of the rhythm and image, something more sympathetic and more human than the solemn chant that it concludes.

'Crow and the Birds' also concludes a predominantly parodic series with a rhythmically masterly evocation of Crow's eating: 'Crow spraddled head-down in the beach-garbage, guzzling a dropped ice-cream'. The effect is of an elongated and ramshackle alliterative line, hinging on the alliteration of the two words around the caesura, and a lexical reach from the dialect 'spraddled' to the American-inflected 'garbage'. This line concludes an elaborate series of conventionally poetic evocations of birds – often, it must be insisted, of a beauty that few poets could equal, such as 'When the curlew trawled at seadusk through a chime of wineglasses'. Like 'Lineage' and also 'That Moment', the poem is a single sentence, culminating in the line about Crow. In this poem the effect is enhanced by the previous lines being subordinate clauses dependent on the main clause, which is the final line. At first, as in 'Lineage', the effect is one of shock, as if the reader who has been lured into an appreciation of the foregoing lines is slapped in the face with Crow. But the last line also has a more subtle dialectical relationship with the rest of the poem. We have seen birds rather preciously contained in a lyric frame (as in the line about the curlew) or evading the modern, urban human world ('the heron laboured clear of the Bessemer upglare'). Crow is the only bird that enthusiastically adapts to this world, and does so in a line that typifies the distinctive style associated with him.[20]

'That Moment' is one of the finest poems in *Crow*. This time there is nothing parodic about the lead-up to the final line, which is itself more straightforward and less distinctive than in the previous two poems discussed: 'Crow had to start searching for something to eat.' In this case the poem's stylistic achievement is in the way an intense feeling of desolation is invoked, in twelve lines, by images of personal loss and post-apocalyptic emptiness, and by an unsettling pattern of awkward repetitions and echoes. The reader is drawn to empathise with the strong but strangely unanchored sense of loss and grief in the poem, and for this reason the final line is perhaps the more jarring, since it doesn't entail an obvious revaluation of what has gone before. Again, the whole poem is one sentence in which the main clause is reserved for the last line, so that in retrospect everything is subordinated to this line. Even more than in the other poems, this final line is double-edged. Crow's hunger is a jarring intrusion into the haunting atmosphere of the poem, but this is neither the elemental life-force of 'Lineage' nor the cheerful voracity of 'Crow and the Birds'. The words 'had to' suggest a conflict, as if Crow is not blind or indifferent to the foregoing loss; he may even share in it. 'Had to' suggests reluctance, as if there were something improper about eating in these circumstances, but the biological impera- tive drives him. Yet, a reader might further reflect, this is as it should be: people don't actually stop eating for long even in the most harrowing of circumstances, and Crow represents that which makes life go on despite everything.

The last of the poems that I have grouped together for this discussion, 'A Horrible Religious Error', is perhaps the best of the Garden of Eden poems in *Crow*. In sixteen lines it narrates the appearance of the serpent, God's impotence in the face of it, man and woman's abject worship of it, and Crow's rough and ready response to it: he 'Grabbed this creature by the slackskin nape, // Beat the hell out of it, and ate it.' In these sixteen lines the tone of the poem shifts several times, from the evocation of the snake's enigmatic elegance, 'flexing on that double flameflicker tongue / A syllable like the rustling of the spheres', to the scathing account of man and woman's subjection to it – 'Their tears evacuated visibly' – and the vigorous, condensed narration of Crow's action.

We have seen in the discussion of the other poems that the appearance of the voracious Crow at the end is at least double-edged. His hunger represents an important 'value' in the sequence, but it is a value to which readers might respond in divergent ways. I have tried to emphasise that, in the creatureliness of the actual fledgling, Crow's adaptability to the human world, and the need to go on eating even in the most tragic circumstances, these conclusions represent something at least partly positive, and not a crude let-down or raspberry after the more elevated tone of the earlier lines. A similar response seems at least possible in the case of 'A Horrible Religious Error'. The submission of man and woman to the serpent, and God's impotence in the face of it, are portrayed with obvious satire, and Crow's action is engagingly robust.

Whose is the error in the poem? It may be Crow's, but it may equally be man's and woman's. So, at least, a reader may feel until she or he reads Hughes's context for the poem. He represents it as an episode in Crow's search for his female creator, a search in which he frequently meets her, or her representative, but 'always bungles the encounter. ... It's seemingly monstrous and enigmatic. He misinterprets it. He tries to destroy it.'[21] The function of the 'story', in other words, is to close down interpretation of the poems, to control their enigmatic, provocative quality by hitching them to a moral. It is notable that the commentary on 'Truth Kills Everybody' in Sagar's version of the 'story'[22] is actually quoted from a letter by Hughes to Terry Gifford and myself, responding to what he considered (perhaps rightly) an imperceptive discussion of this poem in *Ted Hughes: A Critical Study*. In other words, it is not part of an *Ur*-narrative out of which the poem emerged, but an intervention in critical debate about it, and has the same status as any poet's comment on his own work. As Hughes himself wrote to Sagar, interpretation is 'everybody's own business, yours as much as mine, finally. ... Finally, poems belong to readers, just as houses belong to those who live in them & not to the builders.'[23]

The open-endedness of individual poems is reflected on a larger scale in the arrangement of the sequence. There is some trace of narrative coherence in the ordering of the first few poems, which concern Crow's birth and early life, but any such coherence soon disappears. The book seems to reflect the spirit of Hughes's introduction to Vasko Popa (published in 1969) in which he writes, 'he will trust no poem with his meaning for more than fifteen or so lines, before he tries again from a totally different direction with another poem' (*WP* 226). This is particularly notable toward the end of the sequence, where 'King of Carrion', which has Crow 'Returning, shrunk, silent // To reign over silence' seems to point to the most pessimistic conclusion, to be shortly followed by 'Littleblood' in which the spirit of life is invited to 'Sit on my finger, sing in my ear'. Hughes probably chose to end with 'Littleblood' because he did not want the conclusion to be too relentlessly pessimistic, and the effect is precisely of such a willed choice, not of a structural necessity following from the shape of the sequence as a whole. In Hughes's recording the poems in the second half of the volume are re-ordered in thematic groups, and several of them are omitted, including 'King of Carrion'.

Despite some difference of detail and of phrasing, the narratives given in Hughes's recording and in *The Laughter of Foxes* are broadly similar, and may be taken together to represent Hughes's conception of the 'epic folk-tale' in his last years. As I have said, this version is only a vestige of Hughes's original conception, as recorded in the Emory archive, and the elements that I have pointed out of interpretive commentary suggest that it is as much a response to (mis)readings as a trace of the original intentions. In this version of the story there are only two developed episodes, at the beginning and the end, and everything in between is unstructured and often desultory.

The story begins with an episode that Hughes titled in drafts 'The Quarrel in Heaven'. After completing his Creation God has a nightmare in the form of a Hand and a Voice. The nightmare mocks His Creation, especially God's masterpiece Man. At the same time, an emissary comes from the world begging God to take life back, because it is unbearable. God's response is to challenge the nightmare to do better, and the consequence is that the nightmare creates Crow, who becomes God's companion, often trying unsuccessfully to improve on His Creation.

I think that this is by far the most effective part of the narrative frame. The idea of God's nightmare – of God having an unconscious – is original and provocative. The relationship between God and the nightmare deconstructs the opposition between God and the Devil: the nightmare is in some sense God's antagonist, but is necessarily a part of God, the suppressed part perhaps. Crow is not part of the 'official' order of God's Creation, but proceeds from precisely that part of Himself that God was trying to exclude from the Creation. It may seem contradictory, after having argued that the poems work best when kept free of the narrative frame, to make an exception of this episode. But I do think it launches the sequence with great imaginative energy and conceptual verve, especially in the elaborated form in which Hughes tells it on the recording. It is important that it opens but doesn't close down the sequence: it gives the figure of Crow a context but does not restrictively explain any of the poems.

The other developed episode, which concludes the story, seems to me a different matter. Crow comes to a river where he meets a monstrous hag. She makes him carry her across the river, and as he does so she asks him questions. These are questions about love, and about his relationship with his female creator. They are dilemma questions. He keeps trying to answer each question, and the more in error his answers are, the heavier she gets, while the more right they are, the lighter she gets. There are seven questions altogether, beginning with the darkest aspects of love and becoming more positive. In the archive there are several sets of questions, which are asked in a variety of narrative situations, including this one, but in the later versions of the story only three questions are ever specified: 'Who paid most, him or her?' 'Was it [presumably their love] an animal, was it a bird?' and 'Who gave most, him or her?' The answers to these questions are, respectively, the poems 'Lovesong', 'The Lovepet' and 'Bride and Groom Lie Hidden For Three Days'. Only the first of these was collected in the English edition of *Crow*; 'The Lovepet' is in the American edition (1971) but curiously not in the augmented sixth printing of the English edition (1972), in which seven other poems are added;[24] 'Bride and Groom' is part of *Cave Birds* and has never been published as a Crow poem, though Hughes has described it as 'a note at the time of Crow',[25] and he reads it on the *Crow* recording. When Crow has finished answering this last question the hag leaps from his back and is transformed into a 'beautiful lithe maiden, who runs towards an oak-wood with Crow in pursuit'.[26] In some versions she also changes shape into various animals.

In contrast to the imaginative power of the nightmare episode, this seems to me little more than a collection of familiar folkloric and mythic motifs: the loathly lady ('The Wife of Bath's Tale'), crossing the river (*The Pilgrim's Progress*), enigmatic questions (*Oedipus Tyrannos*) and shape-changing (the ballad of 'Tam Lin'). In particular it seems weak when offered, as it seems to be, as some kind of counterweight or resolution to the imaginative achievement of the poems in *Crow*, which are predominantly painful and perplexing. While the inclusion of the poem 'Bride and Groom Lie Hidden For Three Days' in *Crow* would undoubtedly have modified readers' impressions of the book's troubling treatment of sexuality (in poems such as 'Crow's First Lesson' and 'Lovesong'), the motif of the transformed hag and the spectacle of Crow in pursuit of 'a beautiful lithe maiden' are likely only to have provided more provocation to Hughes's feminist detractors.

The offered 'upward movement'[27] in the unwritten last third of *Crow* also raises questions about the progression of the project. There is no evidence in the archive that Hughes had written a coherent narrative that had brought Crow to his lowest point just when the deaths of Assia and Shura ended the project. Nor does it seem plausible that between 1965 and 1969 he was deliberately confining himself to writing poems that belonged to this first two-thirds, with a view to writing the poems of the 'upward movement' later. All the evidence suggests that the discovery of the style and persona of Crow liberated Hughes to write the poems that he was capable of writing at the time.

Between the two developed episodes that I have described, there is nothing that could really be called narrative incident. Hughes's links on the recording are mostly little more than very general, and desultory, introductions to individual poems, or groups of poems, such as 'Crow sees wonders, horrors, follies. He learns a thing or two about them' ('A Disaster', 'The Battle of Osfrontalis', 'Crow's Theology') or 'The more he learns about himself the clearer and clearer the real problems come' ('Criminal Ballad', 'Crow on the Beach', 'The Contender', 'Oedipus Crow', 'Crow's Vanity').[28] By finally committing himself in recorded form to this very attenuated version of the narrative (and by authorising Sagar's similar version) Hughes seems to have acknowledged that the original project would never be completed.

There is no doubt, however, that for at least some of the time that Hughes was writing *Crow* he conceived it as an epic folk-tale, and that his plans for the narrative were very ambitious. He wrote a number of outlines, and redrafted some episodes many times. It is difficult to tell whether he ever reached a definitive version of the outline, but one of the more developed ones consists of seven headings: 'Crow's Birth', 'The Desert of Cages', 'The Eskimo Survivor', 'The Palace of Eagleclaw', 'The City', 'Crow in love' and 'Where go'.[29] There are four sub-headings under each heading, though in another note there are twenty-seven sub-headings under 'Childhood of Crow'. The heading 'Where go' is obviously a list of episodes and elements for which Hughes had not determined a place in the scheme, but since he described the narrative as consisting of seven chapters,[30] he is likely to have been thinking of it as a seventh.

Those episodes that Hughes drafted in detail give some indication of the problematic nature of the saga, and the reasons why Hughes eventually published the poems on their own. In one episode Crow finds a television in a desert, showing a stereotypical scene of grotesque people in inert postures, watching televisions showing similar scenes in infinite recession – a curious anticipation of the popular British sitcom *The Royle Family*, but without any of its humanity.[31] In another he comes upon similarly grotesque people in cages, with signs labelling them 'revolutionary', 'millionaire', 'teacher' etc. In the desert Crow is accompanied by a 'Fool' whom he meets sitting by a single tree. In situation and appearance the Fool is very Beckettian: the tree obviously recalls *Waiting for Godot* and he walks with a 'high-stepping staggering walk', reminiscent of Clov in *Endgame*.[32] The various drafts of these episodes do not seem to be moving towards a final version, but suggest indecision about the mode in which Hughes is writing. The television and cage episodes are more suggestive of contemporary satire than of folk-tale. The latter is faintly reminiscent of Swift, yet none of the figures has a Swift-like aptness and incisiveness. Similarly the resemblance to Beckett in the two figures wandering in the desert is superficial – it is just a device to get the cage episode going. Crow's typical mode in the narrative is one of aimless wandering (in this he resembles Wakdjunkaga, the Winnebago Trickster[33]): there is no narrative momentum, and incidents either just happen or are manufactured by some narrative device. Much of the time Crow is described as beating a drum as he wanders about, and in one episode he is dismembered: motifs suggesting that he is conceived as a shaman.

The most elaborately drafted episode is an account of Crow's adventures in a fairground. The fairground is full of doors 'humorously shaped like a vagina', and by going through these doors Crow has various adventures. He joins several Shakespearean heroes in a sheep-eating contest; he visits a brothel where the customers are contestants wired to 'copulometers'; he is crucified by Roman soldiers, thrown into a pit with mastiffs and is challenged by a woman in a graveyard to choose a corpse.[34] The episode works not to contain and structure but to generate and multiply narrative incident. At their best these incidents are suggestive of *Crow* poems. Occasionally Hughes goes into verse and the result is precisely the kind of condensed narrative typical of many *Crow* poems. In the different drafts one can often see Hughes experimenting with more and less detail, as if divided between the conflicting impulses of a spare, folk-tale like outline and a carnivalesque riot of narrative.

At various points the titles of poems are inserted into the narrative, but these are usually as answers to enigmatic questions like those put by the hag. There is no evidence that the majority of the poems were written with the narrative in mind, or that any of them, with the possible exceptions of the answers to the hag, have a fixed place in the narrative or are directly illuminated by it.

I want now to turn to some of the imaginative contexts that shaped *Crow*: Hughes's relationship with the American artist Leonard Baskin, his interest in Trickster mythology, and the influence of East European poetry.

It has often been stated that *Crow* was originally inspired by Leonard Baskin's drawings of crows, and that Baskin suggested that Hughes write poems about them.[35] Elaine Feinstein states that this happened in 1967, but Hughes wrote to Baskin that he was already at work on 'The Book of the Crow' in October 1965.[36] In this letter Hughes refers to an 'opening' published in *Encounter* three months earlier: this is in fact an extract from the play *Eat Crow*, including a passage in verse that was to become the poem 'Crow Wakes', which Hughes considered for the volume *Crow* but eventually rejected.[37] However, it may be that Crow made his first appearance in the film scenario version of *Gaudete*, written in 1964–5, where the image of a crow is central to the title sequence: 'The crow stoops, a switchback lobbed glide – embellished with a malicious flare and underhand twist – to an ugly drop, onto the cropped grass above the water. It is a murderer and a clown, this sanest of birds.'[38] The connection of *Crow* with Baskin was certainly very strongly impressed on readers of early editions of the book, since a very striking image by Baskin, of a crow with closed wings, disproportionately thick, tree-trunk-like legs, and male human genitals, appeared on the cover. However, there is no evidence of close collaboration with Baskin during the composition of *Crow*. Hughes's next letter, in March 1968, acknowledges that he has not written to Baskin for two years, and tells a version of the Crow story, with which Baskin is obviously unfamiliar.[39] This letter does propose a joint book, and later Hughes sent Baskin nearly forty poems, in addition to those in the trade edition, for a limited edition, which never appeared. Baskin contributed twelve illustrations to a Faber limited edition in 1973; but these were evidently done after the poems, and it seems fair to say that he was not significantly involved in the project after first suggesting it.

One of the distinctive features of *Crow*, at its best, is its air of being primitive yet absolutely contemporary: combining the innocence of folk-tale with the sophistication of a late twentieth-century intellectual. This impression is relevant to the two most frequently noted influences on this collection: Trickster mythology and the work of a generation of East European poets, slightly older than Hughes, of whom he particularly singles out Vasko Popa, Miroslav Holub and Zbigniew Herbert for comment. If we look closely at his writings about these apparently divergent influences, however, we see that Hughes does not portray them as the opposite poles of *Crow*'s imaginative universe, but tends on the contrary to conflate them.

In *Winter Pollen* Hughes reprints an essay entitled 'Crow on the Beach'. This had previously appeared as an introduction to the poem of that title in an anthology, but was a revision of a still earlier essay entitled 'A Reply to My Critics'. In other words, it was originally, like his commentary on 'Truth Kills Everybody', another polemical intervention in critical debate about *Crow*, in this case to counter the idea that *Crow* could be understood in terms of Black Comedy. The essay represents Trickster mythology and Black Comedy as 'absolute opposites, as negative and positive are opposites' (*WP* 239). I have commented at length on this essay elsewhere, arguing that Hughes's commentary simplifies and distorts *Crow*, which is best understood as a synthesis of Trickster mythology and Black Comedy.[40] Here I want to draw attention to the way the terms of that contrast replicate those of Hughes's earlier essay on the poetry of Vasko Popa. Whereas Black Comedy is an expression of 'misery and disintegration', Trickster mythology represents 'the renewing, sacred spirit, searching its depths for new resources and directives, exploring towards new emergence and growth' (*WP* 240). It is of key significance that Black Comedy is 'modern' and 'modish', whereas Trickster mythology belongs to 'early and primitive literatures' (*WP* 239). We might recall here Hughes's assertion that *Crow* was in the tradition of 'the primitive literatures', which was his 'own tradition.'[41]

In 'Vasko Popa' Hughes contrasts his chosen East European poets with Samuel Beckett: 'Their poetic themes revolve around the living suffering spirit, capable of happiness, much deluded, too frail, with doubtful and provisional senses, so undefinable as to be almost silly, but palpably existing, and wanting to go on existing – and this is not, as in Beckett's world, absurd. It is the only precious thing, and designed in accord with the whole universe' (*WP* 222). (I quoted in the last chapter Keith Sagar's application of this passage to the poem 'Wodwo', which concludes Hughes's preceding volume. It applies equally to the last poem in *Crow*, 'Littleblood'.) This opposition, which is replicated in that between Trickster mythology and Black Comedy, is echoed again in a further distinction that Hughes draws between Popa's early work, influenced by 'literary surrealism', and his mature work which is aligned with 'the far older and deeper thing, the surrealism of folklore' (*WP* 226). In other words, these poets, in Hughes's presentation of them, are drawn away from versions of literary modernism and towards archaic or universal models.

There is no doubt that Hughes was susceptible to the influence of this poetry to a large extent because of its imaginative engagement with the atrocities of recent history, and in that sense because of its modernity. He is explicit in his essay about the 'attempt these poets have made to record man's awareness of what is being done to him, by his own institutions and by history, and to record along with the suffering their inner creative transcendence of it' (*WP* 220–1). Examples of this can easily be found in all the poets; this one is from Holub's 'Five Minutes After the Air Raid':

[she] settled herself
to wait
for the house to rise again
and for her husband to rise from the ashes
and for her children's hands and feet to be stuck back in place.[42]

Michael Parker has written that these poets, along with Keith Douglas and Sylvia Plath, 'helped Hughes to purge his poetry of rhetorical self-indulgence'.[43] The flatness of the language and enervation of rhythm that belong to the anti-rhetorical effect may be present in the Czech of Holub (and in the Serbo-Croat of Popa and, to a lesser extent, the Polish of Herbert), but they are also an effect of poetry in translation. The influence is particularly notable in a poem such as 'Crow's Account of the Battle', where the enervated rhythm is similarly combined with an ostensibly grotesque and affectless objectivity:

Reality was giving its lesson,
Its mishmash of scripture and physics,
With here, brains in hands, for example,
And there, legs in a treetop.

Of the poets with whom he implicitly aligns himself, it seems to me that Hughes has least in common with Zbigniew Herbert who, as his translators John and Bogdana Carpenter write, 'strived to repossess the culture of the past',[44] in contrast to Hughes's aspiration to 'produce something with the minimum cultural accretions of the museum sort – something autochthonous and complete in itself, as it might be invented after the holocaust and demolition of all libraries.'[45] If we draw Hughes's earlier quoted statements into the magnetic field of this utterance, the implication seems to be that 'primitive literature', Trickster mythology and 'folktale surrealism' are autochthonous, in contrast to Black Comedy, the writings of Beckett, and 'literary surrealism'. It is no accident that it is Vasko Popa on whom Hughes focussed in his essay, since of all these poets it is Popa who draws most obviously on folkloristic sources. Popa is also the poet from whom Hughes most directly borrowed, especially the 'Once upon a time' formula that he found in 'The Yawn of Yawns'.[46]

Another important element in this series of contrasts is that the art at the primitive or autochthonous pole 'supports a society or individual', shares 'the standpoint ... of participants' and is 'urgently connected with the business of trying to manage practical difficulties', while that at the modernist pole 'draws its effects from suicidal nihilism', is 'more detached, more analytical,' has 'abandoned the struggle with circumstances' (*WP* 239, 221, 226). However sceptical a reader might be about attributing 'autochthonous' value to certain kinds of cultural production, it is important to recognise that such a belief is largely responsible for the remarkable poems that Hughes published in *Crow*, and moreover that it is a fundamentally ethical attitude, that helps to explain why *Crow* is not a work inspired, as some of its hostile critics have thought, by nihilism.

# 7
# The 'Plath Wars'

In Chapter 5 I discussed the effect of Sylvia Plath's death, combined with her poetic breakthrough in *Ariel*, on the style and themes of Hughes's poetry from 1963 onwards. In this chapter I will be focussing on the effect on Hughes of public discourse about Plath and his relationship (both personal and literary) with her, from the early 1970s through the 1990s. The situation in which Hughes found himself in the last thirty years of his life was surely unique for a writer. His wife had committed suicide after a marital breakdown provoked by his infidelity. Such an experience would profoundly affect a writer's work. It is a truism to say that in creative writing private experience is transformed in ways that may or may not show visible traces of it. At least until after the writer's death the experience remains private unless, for literary or other reasons, she or he chooses to expose it (as, for instance, Robert Lowell did in *Life Studies*). Hughes's own inclination, until the last years of his life, was decidedly *not* for exposure, and he complained about critics treating the living as if they were dead.[1] He wrote in a late letter that when poets such as Lowell, W.D. Snodgrass and Anne Sexton 'deal[t] with the episode directly, as material for an artistic work' he had 'despised it'. He believed that 'it would have to emerge obliquely, through a symbol, inadvertently', and gave *Venus and Adonis* and the long poems of Coleridge and Keats as examples. He thought that for him this process had begun to happen in *Crow*. However, by 1998 he had come to believe that his 'high-minded principal [*sic*] was simply wrong – for my own psychological & physical health.' He came to wonder whether an autobiographical account of his relationship with Plath, at a much earlier stage, might have freed him to 'deal with it on deeper, more creative levels'. The public outcry about Sylvia Plath that began in the early 1970s prevented him from letting his experience 'sink away to the levels on which I might deal with it naturally and creatively'.[2]

These considerations are obviously relevant to *Birthday Letters*, but Hughes's words imply that his creative life somehow took a wrong direction because of what he called 'public interference'. It is true that he never again expressed the feeling of creative exhilaration that he had when working on *Crow*, but during the 1970s he published *Season Songs, Gaudete, Cave Birds, Remains of Elmet* and *Moortown*, to be followed shortly by *Under the North Star* and *River*. This was not only the most prolific period of his career, but the one in which his work was most varied and experimental. Yet, at the end of his life, Hughes referred to the achievement of this decade as 'little things I'm glad to have got down' into which he had been 'deflected'.[3] He wrote at the same time that the aftermath of his relationship with Plath had blocked him ever since her death.[4]

Sylvia Plath was, of course, not just Hughes's wife but a great poet much of whose best work was a product of the same personal crisis that eventually claimed her life. Plath was not, really, a 'confessional' poet in the manner of Lowell, but she had been liberated by the example of *Life Studies* to write in a way that allowed her private feelings – most relevantly her anger against Hughes – to energise her work. Although Plath became a cult figure even before the publication of *Ariel* in 1965, her early reputation, mediated by Lowell himself and A. Alvarez among others, was of a writer who had faced the most destructive and dangerous aspects of her own psychological experience, paying the ultimate price for her creative triumph. Her later transformation into a poet whose work was centrally concerned with masculine oppression, epitomised by her personal and literary relationship to Hughes, was probably inevitable, and the result of a particular combination of circumstances. The first of these, obviously, was the rise of the women's movement in the early 1970s. This gave rise both to crude personal attacks on Hughes, and, at a more sophisticated level, to feminist analyses of her work that began to implicate him as husband, fellow-writer and mediator of her writing. The other circumstance was the sequence of publications of work by Plath beginning with the reissue of *The Bell Jar* under her own name in America, and culminating in the heavily cut edition of her *Journals* published only in America in 1982. The increased circulation of *The Bell Jar* extended Plath's reputation to a readership that might not otherwise have engaged with her often difficult poetry, and the history of the publication of Plath's work, under Hughes's control, itself became a matter of intense controversy.

Hughes undoubtedly had a strong personal predilection for privacy. He was ambivalent about the literary world and hostile to academia and journalism. He disliked having his photograph published,[5] and protested against the person projected in his poetry being identified with himself.[6] These are not incidental personal characteristics, but intimately linked to the nature of his writing and his attitude to language. We have seen in Chapter 2 that, at least in his more extreme moments, Hughes believed that 'all discoursive [sic] prose vocabulary' is 'essentially false'.[7] In Chapter 4 I have argued that the intense focus on English scenes, and unresponsiveness to his actual American environment, in *Lupercal*, testifies to the profound inwardness of his poetic imagination. The usurpation of his private life by the public sphere was to him, even in its most responsible manifestations (as, for example, Alvarez's *The Savage God*) an attack on this inwardness by forces that he believed to be inimical to it. Increasingly he felt the need to engage with those forces on their own ground – that is, discursive prose – and to adopt a position outside his own experience in order to validate what was essentially inward. The effect on him of the publicising of his relationship with Plath is perhaps best suggested by the *Gaudete* Epilogue poem, 'Waving goodbye, from your banked hospital bed'. Hughes denied that this poem had anything to do with Plath;[8] nevertheless its final lines epitomise the harsh intrusion of crass publicity on the private self:

> In the morgue I kissed
> Your temple's refrigerated glazed
> As rained-on graveyard marble, my
> Lips queasy, heart non-existent
>
> And straightened
> Into sun-darkness
>
> Like a pillar over Athens
>
> Defunct
>
> In the blinding metropolis of cameras.

In this chapter I will discuss several key episodes in the public discussion of Plath's life and work, that were particularly troubling to Hughes. I will particularly focus on A. Alvarez's *The Savage God*, criticisms of Hughes's editing of Plath's work, newspaper correspondence about Plath's grave, and the publication of biographies of Plath.

Plath biography is peculiarly agonistic. Biographers do not merely take sides or have strong opinions about particular events or people in their subject's life. The more of them one reads, the stronger sense one gets not only of, in some cases, overt malevolence, but of an underlying struggle of narratives against each other, and of dirty tricks often being played. During Hughes's lifetime five biographies were published. The first of these, Edward Butscher's *Sylvia Plath: Method and Madness* (1976), is crass[9] and full of inaccuracies, but is at least in intention fair-minded towards Hughes and not actively malevolent. Linda Wagner-Martin's feminist *Sylvia Plath: A Biography* (1987) is even-handed if rather bland, perhaps, by the author's own account, because Ted and Olwyn Hughes insisted on the deletion of 15,000 words. Anne Stevenson's *Bitter Fame: A Life of Sylvia Plath*, the most notorious of the biographies, was written with the close co-operation of Olwyn Hughes, and is the most sympathetic to Ted. However, it became a matter of all too public knowledge that the relationship between Stevenson and Olwyn had seriously deteriorated when, late in the project, Stevenson read archive material that disposed her to a more favourable view of Plath. The text bears an 'Author's Note' expressing gratitude to Olwyn and describing it as 'almost a work of dual authorship' – a classic example of what Mikhail Bakhtin called 'a word with a sideward glance',[10] actually insinuating that the named author does not accept full responsibility for the book. Despite its obviously problematic nature this is probably the fullest and most factually reliable of the biographies. Finally, in 1991, two books were published, Ronald Hayman's *The Death and Life of Sylvia Plath* and Paul Alexander's *Rough Magic: A Biography of Sylvia Plath*, in which for the first time an active malevolence against Hughes is clearly a motive. Alexander's book, in particular, is fairly described by Janet Malcolm as an attempt 'to see how outrageously it can slander Hughes and still somehow stay within the limits of libel law.'[11] To these I should add Janet Malcolm's *The Silent Woman* (1993), a kind of metabiography, or study of the biographising of Plath, which is by far the best written and most intelligent book written on the subject during Hughes's lifetime. Malcolm is particularly informative and illuminating about the composition of *Bitter Fame*.

I will illustrate what I have called the agonistic nature of Plath biography by referring to the treatment in various books of two incidents. The first of these is a quarrel that supposedly occurred between Plath and Olwyn Hughes during a Christmas visit in 1960. Butscher narrates this episode from Plath's point of view, based on a second-hand report by her friend Elizabeth Compton (later Sigmund), who was hostile to the Hugheses. This was the only account available to Butscher, and he is at pains to stress that it 'may tell only one side of a complicated story'.[12] However, such use of second-hand testimony by possibly biased witnesses is endemic to Plath biography, and is one of the reasons for Hughes's rage at, as he felt it, losing ownership of his own life and being 'reinvented'.[13] Anne Stevenson gives the same incident entirely from Olwyn's point of view, obviously drawing on information that Olwyn had given to her for the purpose. She does not refer to the Compton account, but says that in a letter to her mother Plath 'complained in characteristically extreme language about the scene'.[14] The passage referred to is cut from the version of the letter published in *Letters Home*,[15] so that Stevenson's reader is given Olwyn's version and a prejudicial comment on Plath's, with no opportunity to read what Plath actually wrote. According to Janet Malcolm, Stevenson had wanted to quote Plath's letter, but Olwyn had 'insisted that the passages be removed'.[16] Ronald Hayman gives Plath's version of the quarrel, this time paraphrasing the unpublished part of the letter to her mother, and makes no reference to Olwyn's version, even though this was now available in *Bitter Fame*. Stevenson's and Hayman's versions are clearly in breach of good biographical practice, each suppressing evidence – in Stevenson's case, motivated by Olwyn's feelings, in Hayman's by a *parti-pris* against the Hugheses.

My second example concerns a holiday that Hughes and Plath spent with W.S. and Dido Merwin at the latters' property in France. A vivid and highly prejudicial account of this holiday (and of Plath's personality in general) is given by Dido Merwin in her memoir, 'Vessel of Wrath', published as an appendix to *Bitter Fame*. While no reader is likely to accept Merwin's memoir as an objective account, it is obvious that the holiday was not a happy experience. Linda Wagner-Martin's biography, published before *Bitter Fame*, gives no account of the French trip, which it is natural to attribute to the author having no information about it. However, Janet Malcolm reports that Dido Merwin had withdrawn permission for Wagner-Martin to use the letters she had written to her.[17] In the light of this, the absence of the French trip from Wagner-Martin's book is a significant, even subtly polemical silence. More certainly (though implicitly) polemical, is Paul Alexander's brief account of the holiday: 'they ate generous portions of the Merwins' home-grown produce, continued to relax, and generally enjoyed life on a working farm.' He gives no indication of any tension. To the reader of Merwin's memoir, Alexander's mention of eating 'generous portions' is clearly a 'word with a sideward glance' at her barbed comments on Plath's gluttony.[18] The tendentiousness of Alexander's book can be judged from the fact that he repeats an allegation, second-hand and from an unnamed source, that Hughes attempted to murder Plath on their honeymoon,[19] but suppresses Merwin's account of Plath's behaviour in France which, however prejudiced, is published and attributable.

Hughes's exposed position as the still living participant in the contending narratives of Plath's life increasingly made him vulnerable not only to crudely libellous attacks such as the American poet Robin Morgan's allegation that he murdered Plath,[20] but to more subtle polemics. A peculiar tone, or range of tones, is detectable in many writings on the subject. Consider, for example, this passage from Ronald Hayman's book, narrating events immediately after Plath's death:

> Meeting Jill Becker [the friend with whom Plath spent the weekend before her suicide], Hughes asked whether Sylvia had left a coat at their house, and, when it was found on the coat-rack, his first question was: 'Are her keys in the pocket?' They were – both car keys and house keys. But Gerry [Jill Becker's husband] remembered her take a set of keys out of her handbag to let herself into the house. 'Were they found later?' Ted Hughes asked. Why did she have two sets, and why were the keys uppermost in his mind?[21]

This is the tone of a forensic investigation, or even of a murder-mystery. Not only does it – characteristically of Plath biography – unquestioningly accept people's memories nearly thirty years after the event as absolutely authoritative – but it gratuitously implies that Hughes had something to hide concerning events that immediately led up to Plath's suicide.

The effects of Hughes's peculiar exposure can be seen even in the commentaries of the most distinguished scholars. Marjorie Perloff's 'The Two *Ariels*: The (Re)Making of the Sylvia Plath Canon', compares the published *Ariel* (arranged by Hughes) with the contents-list of the collection that Plath had planned before her death (made public, incidentally, by Hughes himself in Plath's *Collected Poems*). Perloff argues that Hughes's editing changes the 'narrative structure' and therefore the meaning of the book:

> [Plath's sequence] begins with the birth of Frieda ... and moves through the despair Plath evidently experienced when she learned, in April 1962, that Hughes was having an affair with another woman, to the period of rage and mysogyny [*sic*] that followed upon his actual desertion in mid-September ... and then to a ritual death and a move towards rebirth, as chronicled in ... the Bee sequence.
>
> [In the published collection however] the poems that make it only too clear that Hughes's desertion was the immediate cause of Plath's

depression are expunged; instead, the volume now culminates in ten death poems, poems written, as it were, from beyond rage, by someone who no longer blames anyone for her condition and reconciles herself to death.[22]

Perloff's account of the different effects of the two sequences is broadly accurate, except for the assertion that all the last ten poems are 'death-poems'.[23] Hughes is being criticised, in his role as an editor, for distorting the meaning of the book. Strictly on these terms, arguments could be made in Hughes's defence. Some of the poems Plath wrote in January-February 1963 are among her most highly regarded, and Hughes would have been vulnerable to criticism from later scholars if he had left them out. The priority for those overseeing the publication of *Ariel* was to establish Plath's status as a major poet by disseminating her best poems, rather than to preserve what Perloff calls her 'narrative structure'. Angry and vengeful poems such as 'The Jailer' and 'A Secret' (both omitted by Hughes) are highly regarded now, but might have figured very differently to Plath's 1965 readership. Critics who condemn Hughes for his editing of *Ariel* never acknowledge that their own response to the poems he omitted has been conditioned by a valuation of Plath's genius based on the poems he did publish.

However, Hughes has himself said that he cut out 'one or two of the more openly vicious' poems, out of 'concern for certain people' (*WP* 166–7), which naturally included himself. Hence Perloff combines criticism of Hughes's editorial practice with references to his 'actual desertion': the scholar who deftly exposes the difference between the two *Ariels* passes judgement with equal confidence on Hughes's private conduct. Indeed, this slippage between scholarly and personal judgement is precisely what gives the impression that Hughes is being hounded even by respectable critics such as Perloff. And even respectable critics such as Perloff are drawn into strange but symptomatic errors. Plath did not learn of Hughes's affair with Assia Wevill in April. There could have been no possible grounds even for suspicion before the Wevills visited Hughes and Plath on 18–19 May; the affair did not begin until late June; and Plath did not find out about it until 9 July.[24] Why April? As Perloff writes, 'with the exception of seven poems, all the *Ariel [1]* poems [Plath's selection] were written between 19 April and 14 November 1962.'[25] The poem written on 19 April was 'Elm', one of the most celebrated in the book. 'The Rabbit Catcher', 'Berck-Plage' and 'The Other' were also written between this date and 9 July. In other words, Perloff has been drawn into distorting the biographical record by the needs of her argument about the text and Hughes's role as the villain of the narrative.

Ironically, Hughes's public trials began with a dispute with a friend and one of his and Plath's most influential promoters, A. Alvarez. Plath had visited Alvarez in London several times late in 1962, when she was writing the *Ariel* poems, and he was the first audience of some of them, when she read them aloud to him. Hughes stayed with Alvarez for a time after his separation from Plath, and Alvarez accompanied Hughes to the undertaker's to see Plath's body. In November 1971 Alvarez published the first part of a two-part memoir of Plath in *The Observer*. After the first part Hughes sent Alvarez a telegram asking him to withdraw further instalments and two long, impassioned letters protesting against Alvarez's having published details of Plath's suicide. He pressed Alvarez to consider the effect on Plath's children (then aged eleven and nine), but it is clear that even without this consideration he felt the memoir to be an abomination. It is above all the publishing of concrete details of her death that he objects to, 'to have her last days exhumed ... for classroom discussion', and 'to make a public spectacle of ... her infinitely humiliating private killing of herself'.

Alvarez wrote in defence of himself that the memoir was 'written with great care and as a tribute to Sylvia', but Hughes retorted that this is beside the point, what does the damage is the 'close up details as public monument'.[26] He uses both these phrases more than once in this correspondence, and it seems to me that they represent the nerve of Hughes's distress. The passage that he most specifically has in mind is likely to be the following:

> Around 6 a.m. she went up to the children's room and left a plate of bread and butter and two mugs of milk, in case they should wake hungry before the *au pair* girl arrived. Then she went back down to the kitchen, sealed the door and window as best she could with towels, opened the oven, laid her head in it and turned on the gas.[27]

This scene, and these details, are imprinted in the consciousness of every admirer of Sylvia Plath's poetry, so much so that it is almost a shock to realise that they have a determinate source. Alvarez is clearly justified in protesting that he has taken great care to avoid sensationalism: the tone is one of quiet, restrained sadness, the feeling conveyed entirely through the details and not at all indulged or appropriated by the writer. Yet Alvarez was surprisingly insensitive when he told Janet Malcolm that the letters gave him the impression that Hughes had been driven 'kind of barmy' by 'the realization that, however tactfully handled, this was public-domain stuff'.[28] The very familiarity and, as it were, inevitability, almost impersonality, of these details, as if they were the final scene of a literary tragedy, make it hard for the latter-day reader to understand how Hughes was affected by them; yet that very familiarity is what proves him right about 'close up details as public monument'. That is precisely what this scene has become. Considered as literary criticism, Hughes's attack on Alvarez is clearly unreasonable. But it is surely not at all unreasonable, and certainly not 'barmy', to be angry when a friend publishes private details. For Alvarez, Plath's death simply *is* in the public domain, whereas for Hughes, such things get into the public domain by determinate breaches of privacy. Alvarez agreed to withdraw the second instalment in the *Observer*, but published the whole memoir in *The Savage God*. The fact that his memoir is, in its own terms, such a sensitive and responsible piece of work makes it all the more telling as an example of the intractable difficulty Hughes faced.

The year in which *The Savage God* appeared, 1971, also saw the first American publication of *The Bell Jar*. Plath's autobiographical novel had originally been published in Britain, days before her death, under a pseudonym, Victoria Lucas. It was republished in Britain under her own name in 1966, but had not been published in America out of deference to the feelings of numerous people who were the originals of characters in the book, most significantly Sylvia's mother Aurelia, who is portrayed as the heroine's martyred and emotionally oppressive mother, Mrs Greenwood. However, Hughes's American publisher discovered that works published by American citizens abroad but not in America go out of copyright seven years after the author's death. Therefore *The Bell Jar* would be published anyway, and the family would get no royalties. In the light of this, Hughes persuaded Aurelia to agree to American publication.[29]

The American publication of *The Bell Jar* greatly increased Plath's visibility and public curiosity about her. It also had another consequence. Aurelia was understandably distressed by the public dissemination of the image of her as Mrs Greenwood – she had a heart attack[30] – and wanted to correct this by publishing a selection of Sylvia's letters to herself. The result was the now notorious *Letters Home*, published in 1975. This publication rebounded on Aurelia, since the relentless presentation of a successful and happy facade, and the often palpably inauthentic style of the letters – their jarring dissonance with the manner of Plath's published poetry and prose – intensified the public impression that the relationship between mother and daughter was dysfunctional. It also had a consequence for Hughes. For the first time he had authorised the publication of personal writing by Plath; although Aurelia was the editor, he, as he told his brother, had the editorial last word.[31]

Hughes's feelings about the effect of this publication were confused and contradictory, but it is clear that he regarded it as a crucial event in the exposure of his life with Plath. In a letter to Daniel Weissbort, anticipating what he was to write over twenty years later to Keith Sagar a propos of *Birthday Letters*, he said, 'I now have to seal myself off from that huge exposure. I might have solved it all for myself in writing, but now a straight public amputation is compulsory.' He nevertheless thinks this could be a liberation for him, since the situation has become more definite.[32] That period of his life had come into, as Alvarez put it, the 'public domain', but Hughes thought that this was preferable to the uncontrolled circulation of gossip. He contemplated publishing all of Plath's writing and then, rather unrealistically, disappearing from public view.[33]

The American publication of *The Bell Jar* had another consequence for Hughes. It made a large amount of money for the Plath estate, which left him with a large tax bill. This induced him both to sell Plath's archive to Smith College, her *alma mater*, and to publish a selection of her *Journals*.[34] Aurelia having also sold her papers to the Lilly Library at Indiana University, a situation now existed in which scholars could see for themselves exactly how Hughes had edited Plath's texts. At the same time, Hughes made his most damaging confession regarding his dealing with Plath's writing. He referred to two notebooks which 'survived for a while after her death'. One of these, the last, he 'destroyed, because he did not want his children to have to read it'. The other, he ambiguously wrote, 'disappeared more recently (and may, presumably, still turn up)' (*WP* 177).[35] The destruction of the journal is the locus of the most starkly opposed views of Hughes's behaviour, and therefore of the conflict between the private and the public. For Hughes's critics, the destruction of any piece of Plath's writing, and above all a piece that was certain to contain damaging allegations against him, by the estranged husband who is nevertheless left in legal possession and control of her work, is an almost unsurpassable paradigm of patriarchal oppression. For Hughes, on the other hand, 'he did not want his children to have to read it'.

The destruction of the journal was a private act on which I do not think a critic is qualified to comment. I do however want to note a significant feature of the public reaction. Plath's own wishes regarding the preservation and publication of her personal writings are unknowable: it is unlikely that she ever thought about it. In the absence of Plath's own voice in the matter, Hughes's critics stand in for her. *Their* desire to read the journals, and the public's, becomes a matter of justice to *her*. The editing of the journals on the contrary was a public act albeit, problematically, in defence of privacy. Now that Plath's unedited journals have been published, it is clear that the text is far less damaging to Hughes than the edited one was. The very fact of editing had become the issue, and the omitted passages, read by scholars in manuscript, inevitably appeared in a different light than if they had been published. The classic example of this is Plath's account of her first meeting with Hughes.

> We shouted as if in a high wind, about the review, and he saying Dan knew I was beautiful, he wouldn't have written it about a cripple, and my yelling protest in which the words 'sleep with the editor' occurred with startling frequency. And then it came to the fact that I was all there, wasn't I, and I stamped and screamed yes, and he had obligations in the next room, and he was working in London, earning ten pounds a week so he could later earn twelve pounds a week, and I was stamping and he was stamping on the floor, and then he kissed me bang smash on the mouth *and ripped my hairband off, my lovely red hairband scarf which has weathered the sun and much love, and whose like I shall never again find, and my favourite silver earrings: hah, I shall keep, he barked.* And when he kissed my neck I bit him long and hard on the cheek, and when we came out of the room, blood was running down his face.[36]

In the 1982 text the italicised passage is omitted.[37] In commenting on the unwisdom of this I first want to note the highly literary nature of the writing. It combines various kinds of humour: self-mockery, conscious exaggeration, comic stereotyping of 'primitive' masculine aggression, juxtaposition of the mundane and the extraordinary, and parodic romanticism. In this context Hughes's actions are examples of playful sexual aggression, possibly exaggerated for literary purposes, and the startling act of violence (though still in the context of sexual challenge) is Plath's bite. The omission of the theft of the hairband and earrings not only risks making them seem more aggressive than they are, but becomes itself an act of textual 'violence' against Plath.[38]

Hughes was not alone in his battle with the 'public domain'. His sister Olwyn acted as his literary agent and as the agent for the Plath estate, and it was she with whom writers such as Linda Wagner-Martin, Anne

Stevenson and Jacqueline Rose mostly dealt. Olwyn was formidable in her defence of what she saw as her brother's interests, but her role became part of the problem. As we have seen in the case of *Bitter Fame* and the Christmas quarrel with Plath, she was herself a protagonist in the narrative, and her control of Plath's writing inevitably raised a conflict of interest. Olwyn did not like Plath and, despite (or perhaps because of) being a strong, independent woman herself, was anti-feminist. In the ideological context of Plath studies from the early seventies on, this was inevitably a provocation.[39]

Olwyn Hughes's discourse is, to borrow another term from Bakhtin, highly monologic. It opposes 'fact', which tends to be in the possession of the Hughes family, to 'speculation', which is any version of events that challenges the family's account. This language, however, is also used by Hughes himself, and signifies not merely an arrogant dismissal of alternative viewpoints, but a rejection of equivalence between himself as the person who lived the events and scholars or journalists who analyse the textual evidence. As he put it in a retort to one such writer, Ronald Hayman, 'I hope each of us owns the facts of her or his own life.'[40] Jacqueline Rose has analysed this statement and its context in *The Haunting of Sylvia Plath*. She points out that 'a fact never comes independently of its context and enunciation (who is offering the facts and why)', that the 'potential for misreading which lies between speech and its reception also resides internally to subjectivity itself', and draws attention to the ambiguity at the heart of Hughes's would-be constative utterance: 'own as possession, own as to acknowledge, to admit to, or confess'.[41] The ambiguity may be said to exemplify Hughes's unstable and untenable yet unavoidable position in relation to Plath's life and writings.

To an extent, Hughes's brusque use of the word 'fact' is a justifiable response to demonstrable falsehood. In the letter in question he was clearly exasperated by Hayman's pose as the dedicated seeker after truth ('The need for biographical information is urgent') but casual perpetration of blatant errors: his article begins with a reference to Plath's 'house in Cornwall'.[42] This is a trivial falsehood, but Plath biography is beset by more serious narratives against which the word 'fact' can justifiably be invoked, from Butscher's misdating of the quarrel with Olwyn, making Plath eight months pregnant when she rushed out into the winter night, to Alexander's retelling of an anecdote that in September 1956, three months after her marriage, Plath sailed from England to America on the *Queen Elizabeth II* (a ship that was not built until ten years later) for an abortion, despite the dating of letters written from Yorkshire that make such a journey clearly impossible.[43]

A more serious narrative that exercised Hughes in this correspondence was the status of his marriage at the time of Plath's death. Hayman's article concerned the fact that, in early 1989, Plath's grave was unmarked, and earlier in the same month a letter appeared in the *Guardian* from two students accusing Hughes of a 'failure to honour her memory'.[44] As is well-known, the reason why the grave was unmarked is that the tombstone, which bore the name 'Sylvia Plath Hughes', had several times been vandalised by people who objected to the name 'Hughes'. The authors of the *Guardian* letter insinuate that the vandalism was Hughes's fault, for putting his name on the grave despite the fact that 'they had signed divorce papers'. This is echoed in Hayman's statement, 'divorce proceedings were under way'. Hughes vehemently rejected both these statements, both in his *Independent* letter and in one that he wrote at the same time to the *Guardian*. It is possible that he was motivated to write this letter not so much by the original one from the students, as by a letter that appeared a few days later in support of it, written by Hayman, in his characteristic forensic tone, but co-signed by a number of distinguished figures including Alvarez (with whom Hughes was by now reconciled), Peter Porter and the Nobel Prize winning poet Joseph Brodsky.[45]

Linda Wagner-Martin's biography, published in England the year before this correspondence and presumably the source of the students' statement, reports a conversation between Plath and her neighbour Trevor Thomas shortly before her death, in which she is said to have 'told him she had reluctantly signed the divorce papers the previous week'.[46] In his *Guardian* letter Hughes writes, 'Sylvia Plath and I were not divorced.' This is undoubtedly a statement of fact. It is however a response to a number of more approximate assertions: Plath had (or said she had, or was said to have said she had) 'signed divorce papers'; Plath and Hughes had both 'signed divorce papers'; 'divorce proceedings were under way'. The purpose of these statements is to suggest something about the moral status of Hughes's relationship with Plath at the time of her death, and therefore his moral right to put his name on her grave (a metonymy for the more substantive matter of his right to control her literary estate). This is equally clearly not a matter of fact. However, Hughes would naturally consider himself to have more authority than anyone else to speak on the matter, and his memories would naturally for him have the status of facts. Unfortunately for him, they did not, and could not, have this status for others. Again he is impaled on his double relationship to the events of his own life: inside and private, outside and public.

In a letter to Anne Stevenson, Hughes wrote, 'My simple wish [is] to recapture for myself, if I can, the privacy of my own feelings and conclusions about Sylvia, and to remove them from contamination by anybody else's ...'[47] As a matter of private life, this is a wish that anyone can understand. As a statement by someone who is unavoidably in the public sphere, it is a refusal of dialogue that was bound to antagonise those for whom he and Plath existed only in that sphere. Hughes's way of dealing with the situation was to write *Birthday Letters*, a public text in the form of a private address to Plath. Whether Hughes was correct in his apparent belief that the consequences of Plath's death blighted his creative development, it certainly is within the critic's competence to judge, and I will be addressing this question in the chapters that follow.

# 8
## The Shaman-Poet and Masculine Guilt: *Gaudete* and *Cave Birds*

In the early 1970s, as after the death of Plath, Hughes wrote little poetry. Assia Wevill committed suicide in March 1969, taking their daughter Shura with her. In May of that year his mother died of a heart attack. As Diane Middlebrook writes, 'Hughes believed that the shock [of Assia's suicide] had killed [his mother], adding yet another woman's death to a lengthening list of fatalities caused by his blunders.'[1] It is not surprising that his most important works of the following decade, *Gaudete* and *Cave Birds*, centre on female victims and a guilty male protagonist. In *Cave Birds* this victim identifies herself as his daughter, wife and mother: 'Just as you are my father / I am your bride' and 'I shall deliver you // My firstborn' ('A Riddle').

As always, Hughes was not literally writing nothing in the period following these tragedies. In 1968 he had collaborated with Peter Brook on a highly successful translation of Seneca's *Oedipus* (see Chapter 14), and subsequently Brook invited him to collaborate again in a remarkable theatrical experiment. The resulting performance at the Shiraz Festival in Iran used the ancient Persian language Avesta and the Greek of Aeschylus, but most importantly an invented 'language' called Orghast, which was also the title of the work. This 'language', which Hughes developed, first working alone and then experimenting with Brook's company, is not like Esperanto, an attempt to overcome the obstacles to signification inherent in the diversity of languages. It is rather an attempt to break through the very notion of 'signification' in the highly charged sense that the word has accrued in post-structuralist theory, with connotations of absence, substitution and deferral. Although it is unlikely that Hughes ever read the work of Derrida, his account of normal language in the Epilogue of *Gaudete*, which illuminates the spirit of *Orghast*, strikingly evokes one of the French philosopher's most famous terms: 'speech // Is a fistula // Eking and deferring' ('I hear your congregations at their rapture'). As the title of this poem, referring to animal sounds, suggests, Hughes's model for really meaningful utterance is what he calls 'animal music', the utterances of birds and animals that, as he put it in an interview about *Orghast*, 'make the spirits listen'.[2] The poem makes it clear that he thinks this is a faculty that through history or even evolution humanity has lost:

> And I hear speech, the bossed Neanderthal brow-ridge
> Gone into beetling talk
> The Java man's bone grinders sublimed into chat.

It is significantly in the context of *Orghast* that Hughes made the statement, quoted in Chapter 5, about the potential for transgressing the barrier between the Symbolic and the Real: 'the deeper into language one goes, the more dominated it becomes by purely musical modes, and the more dramatic it becomes – the more unified with total states of being and with the expressiveness of physical action.'[3] The work with actors was an essential part of this.

The linguistic experiment of *Orghast* tells us a great deal about Hughes's attitude to language. The drama itself is equally important, as a product of a period in which Hughes's work was both structurally and thematically most strongly influenced by mythology, and as perhaps his most purely 'mythological' work. Although Hughes at one time contemplated writing an English text of Orghast,[4] this came to nothing and we are mainly reliant on the outline given by A.C.H. Smith in *Orghast at Persepolis*.[5] This is itself very long and complex, and I will highlight those elements that I think most illuminate Hughes's work in the 1970s. In the world of *Orghast* the ultimate reality is divine light which takes two forms, Moa, 'the palpable matter of creation, chaos of all, womb of all' and 'Sun', 'spirit fire ... the sire of organic life, which Sun proceeds to get on Moa'. The offspring of these is Krogon, who 'aspires to stop time: to amass power and riches, to hold off his death and replacement'. Krogon enslaves and rapes Moa, who becomes 'a revengeful demon', but her offspring only replicate Krogon. The protagonist of the drama is Pramanath (Prometheus), 'the divine self of creation in human form', who is 'himself Light, creative fire, the original single substance ... the Sun and Moa' but is fractured, a victim of Krogon, his mortal and immortal natures at war with each other. Eventually, in the form of Sogis, he destroys Krogon and restores the original harmony.

In one aspect this is an obviously syncretic myth, influenced by Manichaeism, Zoroastrianism, Greek mythology and Blake among others. But it does manifest important aspects of Hughes's world-view, including the ecological. One of these is the belief in an original harmony that humanity potentially embodies but actually destroys. Hughes represents the cosmos of *Orghast* in a drawing of a human body:[6] the body *is* the world, Pramanath *is* 'the original single substance'.

Of more specific relevance to the works that followed is the way gender is imagined in this myth. The female is part of the 'original single substance', therefore part of the protagonist, but also his victim. This calls to mind works of Blake such as *Visions of the Daughters of Albion*, as well as Jung's concept of the Anima. Gender is more explicitly central to *Gaudete* and *Cave Birds* than to any other work of Hughes. The 'crime' or 'error' that is mythologically represented in *Orghast* is the subject of many of Hughes's prose works, above all *Shakespeare and the Goddess of Complete Being*. He associates it historically with Socratic rationalism, monotheism, the Reformation and the scientific revolution, and has even been tempted to trace it to the very evolution of *homo sapiens*.[7] The perpetrator of this crime is however always imagined as male and the victim as female. In a Notebook in the Emory archive there is a poem in which he portrays himself as a spider of love in whose web women are caught and die.[8] There is therefore a parallel (to use no stronger word) between the mythology that expresses Hughes's deepest beliefs about the world, and his feelings about the tragedies in his personal life, especially in the early 1970s. This parallel certainly imaginatively strengthens the works in which it is most clearly expressed. Whether it conceptually strengthens them is a more problematic question.

Hughes did produce one important poetic text in the early 1970s, directly inspired by his work on *Orghast*. This was *Prometheus on his Crag*, an austere and static sequence of twenty-one poems centred on Prometheus's ordeal by vulture. Hughes described this work to Keith Sagar as a 'little myth of sinister import and total inner stasis', the only thing he wrote in the period after Assia and his mother's deaths, while he 'escaped' into work with Brook.[9] This sequence was not widely available until it was published in *Moortown* in 1979. It was however published in limited edition in 1973 by Olwyn Hughes's Rainbow Press. In doing this Hughes inaugurated a pattern for the publication of his work throughout this decade. He had previously published *Recklings*, *Eat Crow* and other works he regarded as secondary in this way, and small pamphlets of poems in his major collections, but in the 1970s *Season Songs*,[10] *Cave Birds*, *Remains of Elmet*, *Moortown Diary*[11] and *Adam and the Sacred Nine* – all his major work except for *Gaudete* – was first published in limited editions by Rainbow or, in the case of *Cave Birds*, Scolar Press.

It is in the period 1973–6 that Hughes's work in this decade is truly remarkable. In this period – equivalent to that covered by each of his first two collections – he wrote *Gaudete*,[12] *Cave Birds*, *Season Songs*, *Moortown Diary*, *Adam and the Sacred Nine*, *Orts* and 'Caprichos'.[13] This body of work is remarkable for its volume, quality and variety, but perhaps most of all for the fact that Hughes, at least in retrospect, seems to have valued it much less than many of his readers and critics: 'little things I'm glad to have got down' into which he had been 'deflected' by his inability to creatively address his relationship with Plath.[14] In 1982 he wrote that he 'lost concentration ten years ago [which I take to mean after *Crow*] and never regained it', and that what he knew he 'ought to be writing' was unwritten.[15] (At the time Hughes did, it must be acknowledged, show more enthusiasm for *Gaudete*, at least, than these later comments suggest.) By contrast, to take three examples from critics writing shortly after this period, Keith Sagar judged *Gaudete* to be 'the most important poetic work in English in our time',[16] while both Gifford and Roberts and Graham Bradshaw thought *Cave Birds* Hughes's best book to date (the early 1980s).[17] Yet for different reasons these, of all Hughes's works, are in danger of becoming invisible texts: *Gaudete* because, apart from the Epilogue lyrics, it is the only major work Hughes published that is left out of *Collected Poems*, and *Cave Birds* because Hughes himself disliked it, and it has never been reprinted with the Leonard Baskin drawings that are an integral part of the work and without which some of the poems are incomprehensible.

I mentioned the variety of the work of this period, and the most important work falls into two main groups, with which I shall deal in separate chapters. There are the texts with strong narrative and mythological characteristics: *Gaudete* and *Cave Birds*, which I discuss here, but also shorter poetic sequences such as 'Adam and the Sacred Nine' and 'Seven Dungeon Songs', which are discussed in some detail in *Ted Hughes: a Critical Study*. In marked contrast to these are *Season Songs* and *Moortown Diary*. These sequences are, at least on the face of it, much less ambitious: *Season Songs* manifests a traditional lyricism that had only occasionally been evident in Hughes's work before this, and *Moortown Diary* is strongly empirical. Something of this ostensible lack of ambition can be seen in the way Hughes presented these texts to the public: the former was marketed as a book primarily for young readers, while the latter, at least in the 1989 reprint, he almost denied to be poems at all: 'the method excludes the poetic process' (*MD* xi).

*Gaudete* was of all the works of this period the one about which Hughes himself was most enthusiastic and which he most vigorously defended. Immediately before publication he predicted that it 'will lose me all my following though I like it',[18] and at about the same time he said that he would like to develop the style of writing and of composition in the narrative – something that he never did.[19] In fact, some of the reviews, at least in Britain, were highly favourable: Hermann Peschmann in the *Times Educational Supplement* wrote, '*Gaudete* confirms Ted Hughes as the most powerful and original voice in English poetry today', and Oliver Lyne in the *Times Literary Supplement* declared that 'the central action is splendid, available, and generally fine writing' (a marked contrast to the *TLS*'s reception of *Wodwo* and *Crow*). In contrast Philip Toynbee was 'left with the impression of monstrous waste' and Martin Dodsworth thought *Gaudete* was 'a fantasy that has enslaved its creator'.[20] Significantly, however, both these more hostile reviewers cited Shakespeare as the standard by which to judge Hughes – a notable sign of the esteem in which he was held even by sceptical critics. The book was less well received in America, where Robert Pinsky complained that it 'makes violence and eroticism both seem merely literary and boring'.[21]

*Gaudete* is Hughes's one extended attempt at continuous original verse narrative. At the same time it is a highly experimental work that brings narrative itself into question. Before continuing with my discussion of it I will offer a brief outline. The first section is a Prologue in which Rev Nicholas Lumb finds himself in a Northern town that is filled with corpses, as if in the aftermath of an atrocity. The scene shifts without explanation to a cave, a wood and something resembling an abattoir as he is shown a woman with a 'half-animal' face, tended by an 'aged aboriginal' (*G* 14) who seems to be both dead and alive. He is required to save her but protests that he can only pray. He is then tied to a tree and flogged. When 'he' awakes, his memory and personality have been taken over by an 'elemental spirit' (*G* 9) made out of the tree, who in turn undergoes an initiation by being immersed in the blood of sacrificed bulls.

This 'changeling' is the protagonist of the main narrative, which is quite different in setting and tone. It takes place during a single day in a stereotyped but curiously charged southern English rural scene. During its first half Lumb has sex with an improbably large number of his female parishioners. Much of this is focalised through the men of the village; the visually technical narratological metaphor is unusually appropriate, since these men look through binoculars, telescope and camera viewfinder: they are literally voyeurs of their own lives. The manner of this narrative is like a sombre farce or Ealing comedy. Lumb's exploits are inherently comic but the sex is mostly joyless and the effect on the women as well as the men is oppressive. The progression of the narrative hinges on a conflict within Lumb. The double motif signifies of course a division within a single person. Lumb's compulsive sexual activities represent an imperative of the natural world, disconnected from feeling or relationship. In an account of *Crow* Hughes said the Trickster represents 'the immortal enterprise of the sperm' (*WP* 240). Lumb answers much more than Crow to this description. It is appropriate because his compulsion is not only to have sex with all the women but to make them pregnant: whether sincerely or cynically, he tells them that one of these births will be of a Saviour, hence the title, which is a quotation from a sixteenth-century Christmas hymn.[22] There seem to be no children in the community: one sign of its sterility which is also conveyed in descriptions of 'barren' domestic interiors (*G* 32). But Lumb also desires an 'ordinary' human destiny, and has selected a partner, a still adolescent-seeming eighteen-year-old girl, Felicity, with whom to escape. Felicity's youthfulness and naivety should alert the reader that this relationship is not a responsible alternative to his mass seductions but another symptom of his incompleteness. In the second half of the narrative two forces combine to drive Lumb to his destruction. Felicity's former boyfriend photographs Lumb *in flagrante* with one of the wives and distributes the picture among the men of the village. And Lumb's housekeeper, Maud, a mysterious sepulchral figure who does not seem to have sex with Lumb herself but to be nevertheless dedicated to his 'mission', exposes his escape plan to the assembled women. This happens at the 'Women's Institute' meeting which Lumb has turned into a theriomorphic ritual with hallucinogenic drugs: in a powerful and horrific scene Maud stabs Felicity and Lumb tries to escape, pursued across the landscape by the enraged husbands. The final, and most compelling, section of the narrative is an extended account of this chase, culminating in Lumb's death.

The two halves of the narrative – the farcical, repetitive first half and the unfolding of tragic consequences in the second – are divided by two episodes that recall the atmosphere of the Prologue. In one, that seems out of synch both temporally and spatially, Lumb is fishing with Felicity in a mountainside lake, out of which a naked, demonic double emerges, and they fight. In the other, a pair of hairy hands[23] takes control of his car, and he finds himself in a scene of mud where his male parishioners lie dead and the female ones buried up to their necks and screaming. Here he is again called on to heal a female, a woman of 'baboon beauty' (*G* 104) whose face seems to be stitched together from many faces, and whose beauty he restores by, it appears, simultaneously giving birth to her and being born from her.

The narrative ends with Lumb's death. It is powerful, disturbing and bewilderingly negative in its effect, given that the theme of shamanic invocation of natural forces, to cure a spiritually and sensually atrophied human society, is of such central importance to Hughes. The greatest challenge that *Gaudete* poses to a reader is to recognise that the narrative is incomplete. In a letter Hughes referred to the 'unwritten half' of the text: 'what happened to [the original] Lumb in the "other world". The written part – what happened to the wooden Lumb – is a parallel, but with all the episodes inverted and as it were depraved.'[24] *Gaudete* was originally written as a seventy-one page prose film scenario in 1964–5. This version consists entirely of the story of Lumb's exploits in the village, following the same outline as the published story but different in almost every detail, with numerous uncanny hints but no explicitly 'other world' episodes.[25] The most important differences between this and the final version are the addition of the Prologue (initially as a dream inserted into the main narrative[26]), the fight with the double, the encounter with the 'baboon beauty' woman and most importantly the Epilogue. When he returned to the film scenario in the early 1970s Hughes thought the 'underworld plot' was 'the more interesting part of the story' but 'became more interested in doing a headlong narrative'.[27]

In the Epilogue the 'original' Lumb reappears by a lough in the West of Ireland. He demonstrates to three young girls his affinity with nature by calling an otter out of the lough: a feat which Hughes has said is not difficult,[28] and which recalls Plath's account of him in early poems such as 'Faun'.[29] Lumb leaves a notebook full of 'densely corrected' verse which the girls carry to their priest, telling him about the otter. The priest plays down the 'miracle', as Lumb called it, of the otter, but is mysteriously transported by his own vision of the whole of Creation as 'an infinite creature of miracles' (*G* 175). The main substance of the Epilogue is these poems, which are markedly different from the main narrative in style and manner. They are – most often explicitly but always at least implicitly – apostrophic lyrics addressed to 'a nameless female deity' (*G* 9) which, I shall be arguing, *take the place of* the 'underworld plot' and dialogically challenge the main narrative.

Unavoidably, my account of what 'happens' in the main narrative gives the impression that *Gaudete* is centrally about sex. To rest in this idea, however, would be to fall into the same trap that Lumb himself falls into. It is true that in notes during composition of the poem Hughes wrote, 'What the woman needs is Eros – her sickness is deprivation of that', but he immediately writes of 'The initiation into total openness to the eros of the natural world'.[30] The most important quality of the narrative, without which everything else is meaningless, is an exceptionally intimate representation of natural processes that are represented not as background to the human drama but on the same level as human experiences and actions. In the following passage Joe Garten, the young poacher and rejected lover of Felicity, spies on one of the women waiting for Lumb.

Garten rises in his hole, peering. Mrs Westlake, the doctor's wife, winds down her window, throws out a spent match, puffs smoke, relaxes tensely, waits.

The wood creeps rustling back. The million whispering busyness of the fronds, which seemed to have hesitated, start up their stitchwork, with clicking of stems and all the tiny excitement of their materials.

Garten half-lies, watching the white fox-fine profile, under dark hair, in the car window. Her stillness holds him. He eases his elbows and knees, hunching gently to his attentiveness, as to a rifle. His eyes, among bluebells and baby bracken, are circles of animal clarity, not yet come clear of their innocence.

Clouds slide off the sun. The trees stretch, stirring their tops. A thrush hones and brandishes its echoes down the long aisles, in the emerald light, as if it sang in an empty cathedral. Shrews storm through the undergrowth. Hoverflies move to centre, angle their whines, dazzle across the sunshafts. The humus lifts and sweats.

Garten's eyes are quiet, like a hunter's, watching the game feed closer. His heart deepens its beat, expectant. (*G* 29–30)

The human scene is not only set against the vivid portrayal of the manifest natural world – the bluebells, the thrush – but this in turn merges into details of the natural world that are not manifest, or ambiguously so: is Garten, or anyone, aware of the 'busyness of the fronds', the storming shrews or the lifting and sweating of the humus? At the same time, the fronds, the thrush, the shrews and even the humus are active protagonists in the scene, a vital part of its meaning.

The main narrative is set on a warm, sunny day in late May in southern England. Apart from the 'otherworld' episodes there is none of the violence or extremity of natural conditions that there is in the *Wodwo* stories, for example. Nevertheless the writing frequently suggests something uncanny and even threatening about the largely domesticated natural scene, an effect that is far more subtle than that of the weather in the stories.

> The vista quivers.
> Decorative and ordered, it tugs at a leash.
> A purplish turbulence
> Boils from the stirred chestnuts, and the spasms of the new grass,
> and the dark nodes of the bulls.
>
> (*G* 26)

> He leans at the door, emptied, merely his shape,
> Like a moth pinned to a board,
> While the nectars of the white lilac
> And the purple of the dark magenta lilac
> Press through the rooms.
>
> (*G* 88)

In the second extract quoted, the phrase 'press through' makes the genteel scent and colour of lilac reminiscent of the terrifying 'Ghost Crabs' in *Wodwo* which 'in a slow mineral fury / Press through our nothingness where we sprawl on beds'. 'These crabs own this world': they are symbolic representations of powers excluded by human consciousness, which in *Gaudete* are sensed everywhere in the most domestic of scenes.

The narrative is a mixture of prose and verse. This gives a ragged, formally careless air to the text, but it is the result of deliberate choices. The original film scenario was in prose; the earliest draft of the poem was entirely in verse; gradually through the redrafting process Hughes reintroduced prose. Hughes has written self-deprecatingly about the style of the *Gaudete* narrative – 'a language of enactment, nowhere fine or studied, nowhere remarkable in detail'[31] – but it *is* a remarkable achievement, and often 'in detail'. The frequent use of the long line might seem to be a lazy compromise between verse and prose, but consider the rhythmic control of these two examples, both representing states of mind. The first is an elderly man's discomfort with the sexuality of his young adult daughters:

> Like leopard cubs suddenly full-grown, coming into their adult power
> and burdened with it. (*G* 41)

Up to the word 'power' this line evokes both semantically and rhythmically the newly discovered adult energy of the daughters; up to this
point it also holds together as a rhythmic unit. The addition of 'and burdened with it' rhythmically 'overburdens' the line and, ending with
three unstressed or lightly stressed syllables, closes it on an enervated
note. The structure of the line subtly suggests the gap between the
daughters' own feeling and the father's. The second example is Lumb, in
the final chase, trying to call on his mental powers to drive on his
exhausted and wounded body:

> He imagines he is effortless Adam, before weariness entered, leaping
> for God. (*G* 163)

This line falls into three clearly defined rhythmic units. In the first the
light, anapaestic rhythm corresponds to the unbounded energy of
the new, paradisal world; in the second this shifts to a falling rhythm,
suggestive both of the labour of the 'fallen' world and of Lumb's actual
condition; while the spring from trochee to iamb in the final phrase
represents Lumb's momentarily renewed power.

In Chapter 5 I discussed Hughes's account of the 'single adventure'
that structures *Wodwo*: the 'invitation or importuning of a subjective
world' by the horse in 'The Rain Horse', the refusal of the invitation and
consequent 'mental collapse into the condition of an animal'. Hughes
explicitly identified the protagonist of this 'adventure' as himself: 'I
refused the invitation, & so I was forcibly abducted.'[32] The story of
*Gaudete* echoes this 'adventure' in a number of ways. In the version of
the 'Argument' printed in the first edition, Hughes writes that Lumb is
'abducted by spirits into the other world'. Animals, especially bulls, are
an uncanny presence throughout the narrative, and at one point
Hughes planned that 'All discoveries of Lumb are triggered by some
creature or intervention of nature'.[33] If Lumb is, by implication, one
who has 'refused the invitation', and has been 'forcibly abducted', one
way of regarding the career of the 'changeling' is 'mental collapse into
the condition of an animal'. In Chapter 5 I agreed with Daniel
Hoffman's interpretation of the 'invitation' as the call to the shamanic
life. In the film scenario Lumb is described drumming on a Siberian

shaman's drum.[34] This version was written shortly after Hughes's discovery of Mircea Eliade's *Shamanism*, and he may later have thought better of such a crudely direct allusion. In a later note he contemplated incorporating Lumb's initiation by a Siberian shaman,[35] but in the final text there are no direct allusions to shamanism. Keith Sagar says bluntly, 'Lumb is no shaman. He cannot hold the two worlds [in John Sharkey's words, "divine and animal aspects of man"] together.'[36] In *Ted Hughes: a Critical Study* Terry Gifford and I follow Joseph Campbell's three stages of shamanism – 'spontaneously precipitated rupture with the world of common day', 'instruction under a master' and 'career of magical practice' – and note that Lumb undergoes the first, the second is absent and the third goes disastrously wrong.[37] It is no accident that Lumb is a priest: what Campbell calls the 'shamanistic crisis' befalls one who already has a religious mission. But there is no social form, no tradition or imaginable 'initiation', to structure the practice of a shaman in Lumb's society. In notes on the poem Hughes insists that Lumb 'has a high-minded self-commitment – he's not just dabbling', but also refers to his 'hocus pocus' and 'amateur magic'.[38]

If *Gaudete* is a more coherent and consciously developed version of *Wodwo's* 'single adventure', it has become a 'double adventure'. Hughes gives us two Lumbs, or two alternative destinies for the same man. In comparing these alternative destinies, and the meaning of the two-part structure of the book, the question of gender is central.

In traditional monotheistic religion, with a male God, He is encountered through the medium of His representative or interpreter, who is also almost invariably male. God is sexless (though not genderless), and the priest is male because he is more perfectly created in God's image. (There are of course exceptions such as St Teresa and the Indian poet Mahadeviyakka.[39])The disadvantaged position of women in such a religion is obvious. However, Hughes's imagined (or reconstructed) Goddess religion is not the mirror image of traditional monotheism. The Goddess is not sexless, and man is, at least symbolically, Her sexual partner. This is Hughes's interpretation of Shakespeare's *Venus and Adonis*, where Hughes locates the starting-point of Shakespeare's myth in Adonis's sexual refusal of the Goddess (*SGCB* 65–7). So it happens that in this religion too, at least in Lumb's version of it, the priest is male. He has the direct encounter with the Goddess. A woman has the alternatives of 'being' the Goddess or of encountering Her through the man. The first of these is a hidden issue in the *Gaudete* Epilogue poems, and the narrative is based on the second. Rand Brandes has pointed out that the central narrative of *Gaudete* 'obliquely parodies the utopian impulses and promises of the numerous "false" Messiahs of the 1960s and 1970s' such as Timothy Leary, Allen Ginsberg, or more sinisterly Charles Manson and Jim Jones, who 'simply reproduced the diseases and psychoses of the patriarchal political body'.[40]

There is some evidence in Hughes's notes that he considered showing the women to be empowered by Lumb's intervention, with healing powers and the ability to be in two places at once.[41] But this is not reflected in the published text. One of the women, Mrs Holroyd, seems to be happy after sex with Lumb, but this is portrayed as ordinary sexual contentment, as she lies listening to 'a sizzle of music/ And transatlantic happy chat' on her transistor radio (*G* 58). Mrs Davies, an older woman, has some traditional witchcraft skills, including singing to an adder and preparing fly agaric; however, this suggestion of an independent feminine 'line' to pagan religion is undeveloped, and Mrs Davies features very little. More typical of the women are Mrs Hagen in whom a 'bunching beast-cry inside her shudders to be let out' and who wants to 'scream straight downward' into the earth (*G* 32), Mrs Westlake who 'waits / Like a beaten dog / At her trembling cigarette' (*G* 40), Janet Estridge who hangs herself, and her sister Jennifer in whose eyes Dr Westlake sees 'the steel-cutting acetylene/ Of religious mania' (*G* 57). In Lumb's 'W.I.' ritual, the women are possessed by music that is 'a tight, shuddering, repetitive machine' of which they are 'mechanical parts'. The music is described as 'a slogging, deadening, repetitive labour' (*G* 139). As Stuart Hirschberg says, 'Lumb is guilty of the very sin of reducing womanhood to the status of living dead which he came into the story to reverse.'[42]

What particularly excited Hughes about Mircea Eliade's book, however, was not the idea of practising as a shaman in the traditional sense, but that the equivalent of the shaman in a modern society is the poet, or a certain kind of poet with whom he identified himself: 'the poetic temperament we call "romantic". In a shamanizing society, *Venus and Adonis*, some of Keats's longer poems, *The Wanderings of Oisin, Ash Wednesday*, would all qualify their authors for the magic drum' (*WP* 58). Graham Bradshaw has struck a note of scepticism about this identification, remarking that the utterances of shamans 'do not depend on considerations of literary quality', and that the shaman's role being 'defined in relation to a body of communal beliefs' makes analogies with 'the poetic temperament we call "romantic" ' problematic.[43] This however is merely restating the problem (as Hughes would see it) that the shamanic function in conditions of modernity is impossible: the problem that is dramatised in the narrative of *Gaudete*. It remains perfectly plausible that the 'temperament' which is subject to 'rupture with the world of common day' of a kind that it feels to be potentially revelatory and not merely disintegrative, might in one kind of society become a shaman and in another a poet. This latter is the course taken by the Lumb of the Epilogue.

The Epilogue poems form the strongest imaginable contrast with the narrative on a number of axes: generically, stylistically and, it has been argued by Rand Brandes, ideologically: 'the "Epilogue" attempts to deconstruct [the patriarchal] ideologies [of the narrative] by offering a subjective, fluid, open, and decentred text informed by matriarchal mythopoetics.'[44] In a review of the poem, Terry Eagleton complained that Hughes's language never 'self-reflectively takes the measure of its own limits and capabilities', that it is 'locked tight in the bursting fullness of its presence' and so 'ironically closer to traditional realism than it would superficially seem.'[45] This is a good description of the language of the narrative, and it corresponds to Hughes's own statement of his intentions: 'I wanted nothing that was not organically part of enactment, and that didn't contribute to a sense of claustrophobic involvement.'[46] But it is *only* a description of the language of the narrative, and the presence of the radically different style of the Epilogue poems necessarily makes the language of the book self-reflective.

The epilogue poems are brief lyrics with mostly short lines, despite which they often have a more complex syntactical structure than the predominantly paratactic style of the narrative. ('I know well' (*G* 190–1), one of the best, is a poem of seventeen lines containing three main clauses, four subordinate clauses and four participle phrases dependent on subordinate clauses.) Whereas the narrative deliberately excludes reflection in favour of 'enactment', the Epilogue is all reflection. While the narrative is ruthlessly extradiegetic the Epilogue is deeply intradiegetic. Stuart Hirschberg has perceptively written that Hughes's poetry moves 'from a shamanistic identification with powerful, violent predators ... in a style at once self-controlled, self-possessed and vehement ... to become the poetry of the suffering victim, the self offered to the self as sacrifice, crucified, motionless, in the grip of anguish and self-purgation.'[47] This move is enacted, stylistically at least, in *Gaudete*. If the narrative is 'self-possessed and vehement', or as Eagleton puts it 'locked tight in the bursting fullness of its presence', the Epilogue is static, preoccupied with absence, and strangely absent itself.

> How will you correct
> The veteran of negatives
> And the survivor of cease?
> (*G* 176)

But all it finds of me, when it picks me up
Is what you have
Already
Emptied and rejected.

(*G* 182)

And for all the rumours of me read obituary.
What there truly remains of me
Is that very thing – my absence.

So how will you gather me?

(*G* 187)

The address to the 'unnamed female deity', the predominance of questions, a curious tonelessness, the consistent surrender of agency to the addressee, all contribute to an effect that is the opposite of 'fullness of presence'. The effect is enhanced by the unavoidable sense one has, in reading them, that they are intensely personal to Hughes, but also the utterances of a fictional character – they slip between subjects.[48] In my experience of attending readings by Hughes in the 1970s, his reading of these poems was uniquely unsuccessful, as if they were incompatible with his literal presence as a speaker. Some of them, such as 'I know well' and 'Your tree – your oak', are among Hughes's best poems, but a critical demonstration of why these individual poems are good somehow does not catch the spirit of the whole, which is largely an accumulation of effects such as in the passages quoted above.

Questions of style cannot be separated from questions of genre. Jonathan Culler has argued that apostrophic lyrics, in contrast to narrative, occupy a 'detemporalised space' in which '[n]othing need happen'. Such poems 'substitute a temporality of discourse for a referential temporality ... something once present has been lost or attenuated ... . Apostrophes replace this irreversible structure by removing the opposition between presence and absence from empirical time and locating it in discursive time.'[49] To the speaker of these poems, the Goddess is both present and absent, or ambivalently present. His own presence/absence is intimately bound up with hers, in the form of a dilemma: as Hirschberg puts it, 'to have her come is intolerable because it brings a dissolution of ego. To have her go out of one's life is more intolerable.'[50] By establishing an apostrophic relationship with the Goddess, Hughes ensures that this relationship exists in Culler's 'temporality of discourse'. The apostrophic address presupposes the presence of the addressee even in the act of lamenting her absence. Hughes does not narrate Lumb's adventures in the spirit world because they are unnarratable, and this realisation implicitly casts a self-reflective light on the narrative that Hughes *did* write.

This self-reflective light is ideological as well as stylistic, as Brandes suggests when he describes the Epilogue poems as attempts to 'deconstruct' the ideology of the narrative. The problem inherent in Goddess religion is still there in the Epilogue: that of women being caught between embodying the Goddess and encountering Her through men, especially if we read the poems in the light of the information that 'Lumb adds up several women in his life, assuming them, as he does so, into that female in the other world' and that some of them are inspired by real people.[51] However, the stylistic and enunciatory characteristics of the poems, described and illustrated above, establish a chastened and self-questioning persona who is the antithesis of the dominating Priapus of the narrative. The Lumb of the Epilogue is a man whose sexuality seems to be in abeyance, or has been completely subsumed into 'the eros of the natural world'. And it is important to remember that they are the same man, and that he is chastened partly by the memory of his narrative life: 'what I did only shifted the dust about' (G 187); 'I forestalled God – // I assailed his daughter' (G 179). Brandes argues that in the Epilogue Hughes is attempting to write about Sylvia Plath, and is sceptical of the poet's denial that one particular poem, 'Waving goodbye from your banked hospital bed' (G 185–6) has anything to do with Plath.[52] It is not necessary to posit any direct autobiographical reference, but the victimisation of women in *Gaudete*, the troubled representation of male sexuality and its inescapable relationship to the Goddess, the divided male protagonist and the figure of the chastened shaman-poet invite us to read *Gaudete* as an attempt to 'deal ... creatively' with his tragic experiences. As we have seen, Hughes did not think so,[53] and he may have had something quite different in mind when he wrote of 'dealing creatively', but as readers we may feel that the exploration of guilty masculinity in *Gaudete* and – very differently – in *Cave Birds* is among his most enduring, and most humanly significant, achievements.

*Cave Birds* is the result of Hughes's most thorough collaboration with Leonard Baskin. Baskin may have inspired *Crow* and illustrated other books such as *Season Songs* and *Under the North Star* but in *Cave Birds* most of the poems were directly inspired by Baskin drawings. Unlike *Gaudete*, the text of *Cave Birds* is printed in full in *Collected Poems*, but this publication loses the vital relationship between the poems and drawings, so I shall cite the first Faber edition (1978) in my discussion. The project began in 1974 when Baskin sent Hughes nine drawings, around which Hughes composed a sequence of poems in which a male protagonist is accused, tried and executed for a crime against a female victim, and finally brought back to life and redeemed, all the parts being played by symbolic birds. Again, this can be seen as a version of the 'single adventure' of *Wodwo*: in an unpublished introduction to the sequence Hughes wrote, 'The protagonist is to be imagined leading his earthly life, until one day he wakes to the fact that Higher Powers have become interested in him ...'[54] Hughes considered this a complete sequence, but Baskin sent him a further ten drawings, requiring Hughes to 'create an underworld episode between execution & resurrection – between raven & falcon'.[55] This may have been the first stress that Hughes felt about the project, but his dislike seems to have been directed as much at the original sequence as at the supplementary one: the poems seemed to him 'too cold and far off', and 'studied'. He thought they had a 'funny atmosphere' that he disliked. For 'relief and contrast' he wrote twelve more poems without bird symbolism, paralleling the drama in more explicitly human terms, and the poems he liked best, especially 'Bride and Groom Lie Hidden for Three Days', were in this group.[56] For this last group Baskin supplied illustrations after composition. The sequence was commissioned to be read at Ilkley Literature Festival in 1975, which may have put a further strain on Hughes: he evidently found the Festival an ordeal,[57] and had to take into account public performance as well as Baskin's drawings when composing the sequence. A very expensive limited edition of the second group of poems was published by Scolar Press at this time, but the full sequence, extensively revised, was not published by Faber till 1978.

*Cave Birds* is Hughes's most difficult book, partly because of the 'studied' language which Hughes came to dislike and which contrasts instructively with the language of *Gaudete*, but also because it is unusually densely allusive. The mythological, occult and other intertextual aspects of *Cave Birds* are well expounded by Graham Bradshaw, Stuart Hirschberg and Craig Robinson, and I do not intend to go into detail about them here. They include the *Egyptian Book of the Dead*, Johann Valentin Andreae's *Chemical Wedding of Christian Rosencreutz*, Plato's *Phaedo*, Jung's writings on alchemy, Farud Ud-din Attar's Persian epic *Conference of the Birds* and Orphic rituals. An awareness of such sources as these is mainly important for understanding how profoundly Hughes's consciousness was attuned to cultures other than, and counter to, the rational humanist Western civilisation into which he was introducing his works. It is however quite possible both to appreciate the quality of the poetry of *Cave Birds*, and to follow its narrative, without a detailed knowledge of Hughes's sources.

If *Gaudete* is Hughes's only original narrative poem, *Cave Birds* is his only fully integrated narrative sequence. It has nothing of the narrative drive of *Gaudete*, but as the sequence progresses it takes the reader through the stages of a story. *Crow* is a loose assemblage in which poems could easily be differently ordered, with a narrative background that could not be construed from the poems. For *Cave Birds* the only equivalent of the lengthy *Crow* 'saga' is a series of brief narrative links that Hughes wrote for the Ilkley reading, which are little more than explicatory notes. In this book the narrative is genuinely embedded in the poems.

Unlike Hughes I think *Cave Birds* is one of his best books, and in the discussion that follows I will explain why I think highly of some of the poems, and give a critical account of the story, or 'drama' as the subtitle calls it, as another version of the guilty male and female victim. Three of the birds in Baskin's drawings are cockerels. One of them has its head bowed between its folded wings submissively; another lies on its back and has its head raised with a look of comical indignation; the third is Chaucer's Chanticleer or the rooster beloved of blues singers, the gorgeous and complacent sexual conqueror (*CB* 15, 25, 47). In the bird drama this represents the original form of the hero, who protests that he is 'imbecile innocent' (*CB* 20). This 'innocence' is, however, his guilt: a complacent insulation from the realities of his own life and existence in general:

> And the inane weights of iron
> That come suddenly crashing into people, out of nowhere,
> Only made me feel more brave and creaturely.
>
> ('The Scream', *CB* 7)

The scream of the first poem's title 'Vomited itself', as it were the visceral protest of his own body against the detached, complacent consciousness.

As 'The Scapegoat' (the third of the cockerels) suggests, the guilt is also that of the sexual male: 'The beautiful thing beckoned, big-haunched he loped, / Swagged with wealth, full-organed he tottered' (*CB* 46). Hughes described it as 'the guilt of the extraverted, beady-eyed, predatory career of the organism making its way, clearing its space and setting up its fort and satisfying its needs.'[58] Among the things the hero 'confesses' in 'The Accused' is 'his hard life-lust – the blind / Swan of insemination' (*CB* 24), a fine example of the Shakespearean density of the poetry of *Cave Birds* at its best.

'The Accused' was, however, at one time titled 'Socrates' Cock',[59] an allusion to Socrates' dying words, in which he jestingly asks Crito to offer a cock to Aesculepius, the god of healing, because death is the cure for life.[60] Another 'palimpsestic' identification of the hero with Socrates is a discarded subtitle: 'The Death of Socrates and his Resurrection in Egypt', signifying that aspect of *Cave Birds* which is 'a critique of sorts of the Socratic abstraction and its consequences … . His resurrection in Egypt … would imply his correction, his re-absorption into the magical-religious archaic source of intellectual life.'[61]

A reader might at this point protest that Hughes is trying to pack too many and contradictory meanings into the sequence: the hero represents *both* 'the predatory career of the organism' *and* 'Socratic abstraction'? This may be so, but if there is a contradiction there is also a crucial common term: masculinity. 'The predatory career of the organism' is not overtly male, but the 'hard life-lust' of 'The Accused' and the 'full-organed' cockerel of 'The Scapegoat certainly are. The masculine character of Socratic rationalism will be obvious to anyone familiar with the tradition of thought with which Hughes aligned himself – most obviously *The White Goddess*, in which Graves mounts an attack on Socrates' 'ideal homosexuality' as 'the male intellect trying to make itself spiritually self-sufficient'.[62] The hero can be seen as repeating the crime of Krogon in *Orghast*, 'to amass power and riches, to hold off his death and replacement': in the Ilkley version of *Cave Birds* one of the accusations is 'You amassed, you wallowed in engrossment'.[63]

The cockerel hero is confronted by a number of bird figures that have legal titles but represent aspects of his own physical existence, which he experiences as other to himself, just as the scream of the first poem seemed autonomous. This begins a process that is equivalent to the 'abduction' of Lumb. The first bird figure is 'The Summoner', with whom the hero disputes in 'After the First Fright':

> When I said: 'Civilisation',
> He began to chop off his fingers and mourn.
> When I said: 'Sanity and again Sanity and above all Sanity',
> He disembowelled himself with a cross-shaped cut.
>
> (*CB* 10)

Graham Bradshaw commented that these lines 'indicate the relativity of different cultural responses to the facts of existence',[64] to which Craig Robinson retorted that 'the poem's primary field of reference is psychological rather than cultural'.[65] However, there is no real contradiction here. The key term for what the hero is experiencing is otherness: this otherness is certainly part of himself (as the changeling is part of Lumb), and a symptom of the hero's psychological crisis, but it is also culturally determined, and is effectively figured in the unnerving kind of experience of cultural difference portrayed here. One might say the difference is between a symbolic culture and a culture of bodily enactment, or between the 'Eking and deferring' speech of the *Gaudete* Epilogue and the 'animal music' to which Hughes aspired in *Orghast*.

The first truly memorable pairing of poem and drawing is 'The Interrogator' (*CB* 12–13). Both are works of superb and sepulchral wit. The drawing is of a vulture, humpbacked, staring past the frame of the picture towards the poem, but with something in its black plumage and frilled collar of a legal dignitary. In the poem this bird is 'the sun's keyhole', both a visual image of the outline of the vulture in the sky, and a more metaphysical joke about the agency through which the sun (the source of life) keeps the cycle of life going. The legal conceit of the sequence and the grotesque physical reality of the bird are combined, in a way that beautifully catches the spirit of the drawing, in the lines, 'Some angered righteous questions / Agitate her craw'.

The most important figure in the bird-drama, apart from the hero himself, is his victim, who appears as 'The Plaintiff'. This bird is one of two owls in the sequence (the other is 'The Owl Flower', one of the best of the Baskins, and an extreme case of the dependence of poem on drawing) whose plumage is suggestive of tongues, leaves and wounds. Drawing on these suggestions, she is 'your moon of pain' but also 'the life-divining bush of your desert' (*CB* 18). The clashing connotations of victimised marginality and intimacy in these images epitomise the paradoxical relationship between the masculine protagonist and the feminine principle that the Plaintiff represents. In a later poem, 'A Riddle', this figure represents herself as the compensatory sufferer for the triumphs and satisfactions of his life: 'As your laughter fitted itself / My dumbness stretched its mouth wider' (*CB* 44).

In the third sequence that Hughes wrote, the male protagonist usually speaks in the first person, and the story is explicitly human, without bird symbolism. In this sequence the relationship between the protagonist and his victim is portrayed in terms of his absent disengagement while she suffers:

As I hung up my coat and went through into the kitchen
And peeled off a flake of the turkey's hulk, and stood vacantly
    munching

Her sister got a call from the hospital
And gasped out the screech.

('Something was Happening', *CB* 30)

There is nothing autobiographical about this, but it is revealing to compare Hughes's account, in *Birthday Letters*, of his vacant unawareness while Plath suffered at his failure to call on her after their first meeting:

When you tried
To will me up the stair, this terror
Arrived instead. While I
Most likely was just sitting,
Maybe with Lucas, no more purpose in me
Than in my own dog
That I did not have.

('The Machine')

The first poem in the limited edition *Howls and Whispers*, comprising poems omitted from *Birthday Letters*, was at one time titled 'The Scream'.[66] In it Hughes portrays himself, two years before meeting Plath, as an innocent young man who 'could never imagine, and can't hear / The scream that approaches him.' Eventually he changed the title to 'Paris 1954', but the image of the scream approaching the unconscious male protagonist, and especially the intention of giving this first poem in *Howls and Whispers* the same title as the first of *Cave Birds*, indicates that at least in retrospect Hughes intended a parallel.

The second outstanding example of synergy between poem and drawing is the poem that narrates the hero's death, 'The Executioner'. The right hand page is half filled with the black outline of a raven looking towards the poem like the vulture of 'The Interrogator'. The poem develops this suggestion of the blackness of death as presence rather than absence:

The tap drips darkness darkness
Sticks to the soles of your feet

He fills up the mirror hc fills up the cup
He fills up your thoughts to the brims of your eyes.

(*CB* 22–3)

With its repetition and lack of punctuation the poem builds up a momentum that is relentless yet alluringly sensuous. At the end of the poem there is a hint that this 'death' is the death of the ego, even a return to the pre-Oedipal state, and that the hero might be given a second chance: 'It feels like the world / Before your eyes ever opened.'

In the first sequence of nine poems, 'The Executioner' was immediately followed by the last substantial poem, 'The Risen', in which the hero is resurrected as a falcon. Despite Hughes's hints of working under duress to extend the narrative when he received the second batch of poems, this second stage enormously enriches the sequence, which in its first form took the hero from death to resurrection abruptly and without explanation. Instead an underworld sequence gives meaning and substance to this development, in some of the finest poems Hughes ever wrote. 'The Knight', inspired by a drawing of a bird's skeleton, introduces the motif of the quest, which Hughes developed further in the third stage poem, 'First, the Doubtful Charts of Skin'. The Knight has 'conquered', but his victory is his submission. The natural process of decay is beautifully integrated into the narrative of voluntary submission:

> His sacrifice is perfect. He reserves nothing.
> Skylines tug him apart, winds drink him,
> Earth itself unravels him from beneath –
> His submission is flawless.
>
> (*CB* 28)

'A Flayed Crow in the Hall of Judgement' takes the hero into the Egyptian underworld, where the ego's passivity in the face of self-renewal is given intimate subjective expression:

> Do purposeful cares incubate me?
> Am I the self of some spore
>
> In this white of death blackness,
> This yoke of afterlife?
> What feathers shall I have? What is my weakness good for?

The third, 'human' sequence takes up the narrative of the hero's renewal in a group of poems about sexual relationship, most notably 'Bride and Groom Lie Hidden for Three Days', which as we have seen (Chapter 5) Hughes also thought of as the culmination of *Crow*, in which Crow breaks through to a vision of mutual relatedness as the lovers literally construct each other's bodies.

The sequence concludes (almost) with the resurrected hero as 'The Risen', a falcon. This poem is one of Hughes's finest expressions of his sense of nature as both immanent and transcendent:

> Where he alights
> A skin sloughs from a leafless apocalypse.
>
> (*CB* 60)

This is, however, entirely a poem about a natural creature, and it ends, 'But when will he land / On a man's wrist'. Keith Sagar complains that this makes 'nonsense of the whole conception'.[67] More positively, one might say it is an acknowledgement of the difficulty at the root of Hughes's mythopoetics: the attempt to conflate the relationship between man and woman, and that between man and nature, the Goddess or his deepest self. The fact that the interpersonal story and the religious allegory come apart at the end is not a weakness of *Cave Birds* but a profound aspect of its meaning: in the words of the brief 'Finale', 'At the end of the ritual // up comes a goblin' (*CB* 62).

# 9
## Farmer Hughes: *Moortown Diary* and *Season Songs*

Some time in the 1970s, out of curiosity, I looked up Hughes's name in the Exeter telephone directory. Not surprisingly I did not find Ted Hughes, Poet, Court Green; but I did find E.J. Hughes, Farmer, Moortown Farm. He bought this farm in North Devon, a few miles from his home in North Tawton, in 1973, and raised beef cattle and sheep there with his wife Carol, whom he had married in 1970, and her father Jack Orchard, a retired farmer. According to Hughes, at this date 'the ancient farming community in North Devon was still pretty intact and undisturbed' (*MD* vii). He portrayed the area as an enclave in which people who were 'almost a separate race' lived in the 'long backward perspective of their ancient landscape and their homes' (*MD* viii). When, in 1976, Jack Orchard died, Hughes wrote that his farming had been 'intimately tied up' with his father-in-law's 'unique archaic personality'.[1] In one aspect the farming venture was an attempt to find a real-life expression of his identification with pre-modern, autochthonous ways of life. There was also another motive, which Hughes did not mention in his public comments: he hoped that his brother Gerald would return from Australia and join him on the farm. The failure of this plan finally and painfully brought home to Hughes that Gerald would never return.[2]

Hughes told Gerald that there was not a lot of work to the farm,[3] but it is nevertheless remarkable that the period when he was working it, 1973–6, was also his most prolific period as a poet. Between 1975 and 1979 he published *Season Songs*, the long narrative poem *Gaudete*, *Cave Birds*, the compendious volume *Moortown*, the substantial limited edition *Orts*, the children's collection *Moon-Whales* and the translation of Janos Pilinszky's *Selected Poems*. The vast majority of this work was done between 1973 and 1976. I have discussed the two most ambitious of these books, *Gaudete* and *Cave Birds*, in my last chapter. In marked contrast to these are *Season Songs* and the title sequence of *Moortown*. These works were better received on publication,[4] have remained more popular and proved – unpredictably at the time – to be more prophetic of the second half of Hughes's career. Both volumes, and especially the *Moortown* sequence, were the direct product of his farming experience.

While he was a farmer Hughes wrote about forty poems that he described as follows:

> I set them down in what appears to be verse for a simple reason. In making a note about anything, if I wish to look closely I find I can move closer, and stay closer, if I phrase my observations about it in rough lines. So these improvised verses are nothing more than this: my own way of getting reasonably close to what is going on, and staying close, and of excluding everything else that might be pressing to interfere with the watching eye. In a sense, the method excludes the poetic process as well. (*MD x*)

He goes on to say that he tried to make these records on the same day as the experience, because if he delayed, 'the processes of "memory", the poetic process, had already started'. When this happened, he had 'missed the moment'. When he subsequently tried to revise the rough drafts in which he felt he had captured the experience, he found that he could not do so without spoiling them. Drafts in the Emory archive confirm that the majority of these poems were written straight out, almost uncorrected.[5] But we must distinguish between these texts and those poems such as 'Hawk Roosting' and the second part of 'An Otter', which Hughes claimed 'arrive[d] instantaneously'.[6] These last represent an ideal of poetic inspiration, in which access to the imaginative source is miraculously facilitated by an almost occult process: he claimed that he literally hallucinated the second part of 'An Otter' as a scroll hanging in the air.[7] In the case of the *Moortown* poems, he seems ambivalent about whether they are genuinely poems at all: they are records of experience rather than imaginative events. But perhaps the most interesting thing about his commentary is the notion that the 'poetic process' can actually be *destructive* of certain kinds of writing.

These poems were first published as the Rainbow Press limited edition *Moortown Elegies* in 1978. The first trade publication was in *Moortown* (1979), where they formed the first of four sections, and they were republished separately as *Moortown Diary* in 1989. Uniquely for Hughes, the texts of these different editions are identical, reinforcing his claim about the impossibility of revising them, but in *Moortown Diary* he added a Preface and notes to some of the poems. This edition also gives dates for most of the poems, which should however be treated with caution – the date given for 'Sheep II' is later than its first publication.

The experience recorded in these poems is most characteristically that of witnessing the suffering of animals. Sometimes this is inflicted by humans, as a necessary consequence of domestication, as in 'Dehorning':

> The needle between the horn and the eye, so deep
> Your gut squirms for the eyeball twisting
> In its pink-white fastenings of tissue.

Note here that although the speaker's 'gut squirms' in recoil from the spectacle, the lines give an unflinching detailed close-up of it. At times this priority of registering the animals' suffering results in a kind of note-form from which the speaker's subjectivity is almost withdrawn:

> Wind out of freezing Europe. A mean snow
> Fiery cold. Ewes caked crusty with snow,
> Their new hot lambs wet trembling
> And crying on trampled patches, under the hedge.
> ('Bringing in New Couples')

We can also see in this example that, as in some of Hughes's earlier poems that I have discussed, the diction is predominantly Anglo-Saxon. In these poems the diction has a distinctive effect. It helps to establish the persona of the speaker as a farmer: a sensitive but practical man who responds emotionally to the suffering of the animals, but asks no metaphysical questions about it.

> A lamb could not get born. Ice wind
> Out of a downpour dishclout sunrise. The mother
> Lay on the mudded slope. Harried, she got up
> And the blackish lump bobbed at her back-end
> Under her tail. After some hard galloping,
> Some manoeuvring, much flapping of the backward
> Lump head of the lamb looking out,
> I caught her with a rope.

There is a notable paucity of metaphor in these poems. Most of the metaphors that do occur are unassuming and domestic, like 'dishclout'.

Phrases like 'blackish lump' and 'back-end' suggest the plain, unpretentious speech of the farmer. These lines are from the best-known of these poems, 'February 17th', in which the speaker cuts off the head of the dead half-born lamb and pushes the decapitated body back into the mother's womb, so that he can reach in to get a hand on its leg and pull it out. The poem has one startling metaphor which stands out against the background of detailed, practical narrative: when the speaker has decapitated the lamb he places the head 'sitting in the mud / With all earth for a body.' The uncertainty whether this is a profound or casual observation, combined with the speaker's archetypal-seeming struggle to push the dead body back into its mother's womb, against her 'birth push', tempts one to think that this is an artful poem, but like most of the others it was written in one barely corrected draft.

'February 17th', illustrates a new relationship between the human and animal worlds, in both *Moortown Diary* and *Season Songs*. The human and the animal are sharers in the destiny of the natural body. The human is no longer eclipsed by the animal, and there is no longer such an emphasis on the predatory, as in the earlier poems, but the shared fate of being in nature. The human has a greater awareness, and may occasionally be able to help, but mostly can only look on in baffled sympathy.

A poem in which, according to Hughes, he 'missed the moment' (*MD* 64) is 'Orf'. This poem was written two weeks after the event, and there are two drafts, one heavily corrected.[8] The title is the name of an ulcerous infection of sheep and lambs, and in this poem the speaker shoots the lamb for which he can do nothing. It has some of the attentive detail that characterises the other poems – 'his breath wheezed through a mask of flies' – but it has a rhetorical structure that contrasts with the narrative 'record' of 'February 17th', 'Dehorning' and 'Bringing in New Couples'. It opens with a sentence of nine lines, running over two four-line stanzas each beginning 'Because' and culminating in 'I shot the lamb'. This is followed by two one-line sentences beginning 'I shot him', and the poem ends with an eight-line sentence in which the speaker imagines 'the lamb-life in my care' asking permission to be banished, after the death of the lamb's body. Both the artful structures of Hughes's more characteristic poems (of which this is one) and the contrasting 'diary' mode of most of the poems in the book are illuminated by this comparison. The somewhat shamanistic persona of 'Orf', speaking of the 'lamb-life' asking permission 'to be extinct', and of 'the radioactive space / From which the meteorite had removed his body', is also markedly different from the sensitive but practically-oriented farmer of the other poems.

A few poems in *Moortown Diary* have nothing to do with farming. These include one of Hughes's most memorable poems, 'Coming down through Somerset'. In this poem the speaker finds a dead badger on the road and takes it home with him. Its summer coat is 'not worth skinning', so the speaker just keeps it, willing it to resist decay. The poem articulates a powerful complex of feelings, from the natural and almost intimate love of the badger's beauty – 'Beautiful/ Beautiful warm secret beast' – to the irrational confession, 'I want him / To stop time'. There are multiple voices, one of which repeats 'Get rid of that badger', and a much stronger metaphorical activity than in most of these poems: 'Flies, drumming, bejewel his transit' (capturing the longing for permanence in the word 'bejewel', applied to the harbingers of decay) and the concluding lines,

> I stand
> Watching his stillness, like an iron nail
> Driven, flush to the head,
> Into a yew post. Something has to stay

which, in Craig Robinson's words, 'stands for the badger's painful reality', but also for the poem's ability to accomplish the stoppage of time that is beyond the badger's powers.[9] Is it the badger or the speaker who is compared to 'an iron nail'? It anticipates some of the best *Birthday Letters* poems by combining a strong sense of the present moment – 'A badger on my moment of life. / Not years ago, like the others, but now' – with the power of art to make it last. It also combines this artfulness with the notation of contingent details suggestive of the 'diary' mode: 'Now he lies on the beam / Torn from a great building. Beam waiting two years / To be built into new building.' The poem is a curious hybrid, with much more overtly poetic language and more imaginatively vulnerable persona than the farming diary poems, but lacking the artful rhetorical structure of a poem such as 'Orf'.

Another non-farming poem, 'Foxhunt', is less intrinsically interesting but worth mentioning because of what Hughes chose to leave out of it. The poem evokes the suffering of the fox – 'Till blood froths his mouth and his lungs tatter, / Till his feet are raw blood-sticks ...' – in a way that is reminiscent of Plath's 'Burning the Letters' and the poems Hughes wrote after Plath's death (see Chapter 5) – and ends, 'As I write this down / He runs still fresh, with all his chances before him.' Although it is not a farming poem, it is written in the same 'diary' mode, with the same qualities of detail and immediacy. It was written in a single draft, unamended except for the deletion of the original last line, 'O fox, jump into me.' This was amended in typescript to 'Only his soul / Can jump into me, and sit safe' and 'Only his spirit / Can slip under my hair, and sit safe', till he abandoned this attempt to incorporate the fox into himself. The interest of this is that we can see Hughes trying to develop the poem beyond the diary mode, to incorporate motifs that would have aligned it with 'The Thought-Fox' and with his central poetic myth, but finally settling for something more limited.[10]

Three of the *Moortown Diary* poems, the two parts of 'Sheep' and 'March morning unlike others', are also included in *Season Songs*, which was first published four years earlier. However, apart from five 'Autumn songs for children's voices' written for a Harvest Festival at Great Missenden in 1968, these poems were composed contemporaneously with *Moortown Diary*. Like that book, *Season Songs* was first published as a Rainbow Press limited edition, with the title, *Spring, Summer, Autumn, Winter*, in 1974. There followed the American edition (Viking) in 1975, with excellent colour illustrations by Leonard Baskin, and the Faber British edition in 1976. Each of these editions has more poems than its predecessor, though the limited and American editions each have one poem not in the Faber edition, which lacks the colour illustrations. The most complete version is the second Faber edition (1985) which has seven new poems, but omits two.

Comparison of the British and American editions also reveals that the former says it is 'intended primarily for young readers' whereas the latter, despite being more like a children's book in format, makes no reference to audience. Speaking of the book on the radio Hughes sustained this ambiguity by saying that in it he wanted to remain 'within the hearing of children'.[11] *Season Songs*, unlike nearly all Hughes's other writing for children, is included in *New Selected Poems* and *Collected Poems*. Referring to the most obvious point of contrast with its immediate predecessors, *Crow* and *Prometheus on his Crag*, Hughes said that he deliberately made *Season Songs* 'upbeat', but the motive of this was 'to buck me up', not to appeal to children.[12] The peculiar sense of audience is evident in the first poem, 'A March Calf', which begins,

Right from the start he is dressed in his best – his blacks and his
   whites.
Little Fauntleroy – quiffed and glossy,
A Sunday suit, a wedding natty get-up,
Standing in dunged straw.

An adult reader might be charmed by this, and might even have welcomed it with relief as a contrast to *Crow*, but the uninhibited anthropomorphism, so unlike Hughes's earlier poems about real animals, suggests a conscious relaxation and indulgence on the part of the author, which might well be accounted for by writing for children. Yet in this same poem Hughes describes the calf as 'shut up in his hopeful religion, / A little syllogism / With a wet blue-reddish muzzle, for God's thumb', which hardly seems to have been written with children in mind, and whose mixture of the language of religion and logic echoes some of Hughes's harshest writing (for example, 'mishmash of scripture and physics' in 'Crow's Account of the Battle'). The anthropomorphism is repeated in other poems, such as the first, third and sixth sections of 'Spring Nature Notes', but the fourth section of this sequence, about the intuitive sense of approaching spring, conveys an 'extra-sensory' awareness of natural processes that is at the heart of Hughes's poetic identity, and central to works such as *Gaudete*. When Hughes says an oak tree in Spring is 'a giant brazier / Of invisible glare' he echoes poems in the *Gaudete* Epilogue, 'Your tree – your oak / A glare // Of black upward lightning' and 'Glare out of just crumpled grass', in which the word 'glare' signifies the presence of the Goddess.

Several poems in *Season Songs*, such as 'April Birthday', 'Deceptions, 'Work and Play' and 'Christmas Card', are as close as Hughes comes to 'light verse', equally pleasing to young and adult readers. But two of the poems, 'Swifts' and 'A Cranefly in September', are among his finest by any standard. Both focus on dying creatures, showing that by 'upbeat' Hughes did not mean the avoidance of painful subjects.

'Swifts' evokes the birds as vividly as any of his earlier poems, combining a breakneck, almost out of control rhythm with an accumulation of precisely observed detail, in this case describing a bird that has fallen to the ground, where swifts are helpless:

He bat-crawled on his tiny useless feet, tangling his flails

Like a broken toy, and shrieking thinly

Till I tossed him up – then suddenly he flowed away under

His bowed shoulders of enormous swimming power.

More literally than in poems such as 'Pike' and 'The Jaguar', because the swifts are not objective correlatives for powers within the human observer, but creatures with whom he shares the world (as in *Moortown Diaries*), the poem exemplifies Hughes's advice in *Poetry in the Making*: 'You keep your eyes, your ears, your nose, your taste, your whole being on the thing you are turning into words' (*WP* 13). The poem combines the 'reporting' quality of *Moortown Diaries* with a more finely wrought rhythm and structure.

'A Cranefly in September' is another superb poem that employs language ranging from fairytale to biochemistry, and multiple perspective – the bafflement of the insect in conditions in which it is not designed to survive, the metaphorical energy of the poet, the awareness of seasonal change, and the man as helpless onlooker – to evoke the beauty, pathos and heroism of the creature cancelled by the terms of its own being:

> Her jointed bamboo fuselage,
> Her lobster shoulders, and her face
> Like a pinhead dragon, with its tender moustache,
> And the simple colourless church windows of her wings
> Will come to an end, in mid-search, quite soon.
> Everything about her, every perfected vestment
> Is already superfluous.

The proliferation of metaphor distinguishes this speaker from the plain-speaking farmer of *Moortown Diaries*. It registers the astonishingly detailed and delicate haecceity of the cranefly, and the pathos that it entails: the beautiful precision that makes the creature just what it is, is also its limitation, its inability to adapt to conditions in which it is not evolved to survive. The poem is one of the finest examples of a new lyricism in Hughes, which is, as Martin Dodsworth observed, 'utterly original in an un-Victorian, un-Edwardian way' and accommodates a 'wholly unsentimental acceptance of pain and stress'.[13]

# 10
## Return to the Calder Valley: *Remains of Elmet, Wolfwatching* and *Elmet*

The collections *Remains of Elmet, Wolfwatching* and *Elmet* were published over a period of fifteen years, between 1979 and 1994. The contents of these three volumes are closely interconnected. In them Hughes makes an explicit imaginative return to the environment of his earliest years: *Remains of Elmet* and *Elmet* contain the poem 'Two', which I discussed in my first chapter as a record of the 'paradise' of those early years and its loss.

In 1976, after the creative surge of the works discussed in the last two chapters, Hughes embarked on a collaborative book with the photographer Fay Godwin. According to Godwin herself, this venture had its origins as early as 1971, when she took portraits of Hughes: 'He liked the portraits, and asked if I ever did landscape photographs ... He told me there was an area in the Calder Valley which he wanted to write about, but felt the need for a visual "trigger".' Godwin began taking photographs, but Hughes did not contact her again until May1976, when 'I already had some pictures and he had some of the poems'. They worked on the book 'through 1977.' There is a nearly final list of poems dated 12 December 1977.[1] Keith Sagar dates Hughes's enthusiasm for the project to 1975, when he saw an exhibition of Godwin's photographs that Sagar had organised at the Ilkley Festival.[2] This is confirmed by the fact that Hughes took away some rough prints from the Festival.[3]

The collaboration was one of Hughes's most successful: Godwin's meditative black and white photographs, deeply aware of weather, landscape, light and the varying fortunes of people's agricultural and industrial enterprises, harmonise exceptionally well with Hughes's poems. In some cases there is a direct correspondence between poem and photograph, but even when there is not, there is a strong sense of convergence between the poet's vision and the photographer's. However, Hughes was dissatisfied with the resulting volume, *Remains of Elmet*, published in 1979. In 1984 he told Baskin that it ought to be seven-eighths different.[4] In one of his last letters, written to Keith Sagar a fortnight before his death, he wrote that he had begun with 'the auto-biographical pieces (Canal poems, Mount Zion etc)', but 'that diabolical fear of subjectivity [which he had discussed in his earlier letter to Sagar about *Birthday Letters*] argued me into writing impersonal mood pieces'.[5] *Remains of Elmet* went out of print because the printers went out of business and the origination material was lost. Faber were reluctant to do a second edition until, according to Fay Godwin, Hughes allowed her agent to offer the book to another publisher.[6]

In 1989 he published *Wolfwatching*, a miscellaneous collection whose most notable feature was that it contained a number of poems about members of Hughes's family. At this time he wrote that these poems were 'written partly as a correction of the over-determined plan' of *Remains of Elmet*, in which, 'knowing how photographs tend to contradict and displace any associated verbal imagery, I decided to stick to something simple and atmospheric' and 'to avoid hijacking Fay's inclusive vision with the exclusive autobiography'. He compares his aim to writing 'film music: non-visual, non-specific, self-effacing'. Later, he felt that the book needed 'a gallery of detailed, quite subjective portraits of some of the people whose lives gave those dramatic backdrops their meaning'.[7] (Writing during the original project, Godwin revealingly told Hughes that she 'didn't have the feeling you have of people everywhere'.[8]) Then the 1993 volume *Three Books* reprinted Hughes's three illustrated volumes – *Cave Birds, Remains of Elmet* and *River* – without the illustrations. Seventeen *Remains of Elmet* poems, including the title poem, were omitted from this version, three poems added (one of them resuscitated from *Recklings*), and several revised. A number of poems are retitled, always to specify their location. Finally, in 1994, came *Elmet*. This was another book of Hughes's poems and Godwin's photographs, based on the text of *Three Books*, with no newly published poems but fourteen additional ones drawn from *The Hawk in the Rain, Lupercal, Wodwo* and most of all *Wolfwatching*. Likewise, some of Godwin's photographs were dropped and others substituted, though she took no new ones specifically for *Elmet*: they had all either been taken for the original volume, or as part of another project.[9]

The term 'mood pieces' is faintly derogatory, and it corresponds to a quality in some of these poems that recalls Hopkins's notion of 'Parnassian' poetry, which is 'spoken *on and from the level* of a poet's mind, not, as in the other case, when the inspiration, which is the gift of genius, raises him above himself ... In a poet's particular kind of Parnassian lies most of his style, of his manner, of his mannerism if you like.'[10]

> The witch-brew boiling in the sky-vat
> Spins electrical terrors
> In the eyes of sheep. ('Moors')

> The upper millstone heaven
> Grinds the heather's face hard and small.
> Heather only toughens. ('Heather')

> From now on
> The moon stares into your skull
> From this perch.
>
>                   ('Bridestones')

These extracts are unmistakably Ted Hughes, but there is an air of self-mimicry, if not of self-parody, about them. No new note is sounded, as it had been sounded in every volume Hughes had published so far. Such a note is sounded in *Remains of Elmet*, in poems that engage in a more complex way with the interrelations of landscape, history and humanity.

Such a poem is 'First, Mills', which memorably evokes the effect of the Great War on the places from which soldiers were recruited: 'the bottomless wound of the railway station / That bled this valley to death.' This is a technique of superimposition: one visualises the flow of young men away from the valley via the station, and at the same time the bleeding that killed them at the other end of their journey: the effect is one of poignant inevitability. As Elaine Feinstein has written, 'Men from every part of the valley had died in those battlefields, and sometimes an entire street of families lost their sons through a mistaken order to advance.'[11] The landscape in this poem becomes a 'trench' and the sky 'an empty helmet / With a hole in it.' The bleak and stifling atmosphere of human life in the valley is thus both projected on to the landscape and referred back to history. Hughes's wish to write an unromanticised social history of the area is evidenced in the several drafts of an unpublished poem aptly titled 'Clogs'.[12]

A more complex effect is achieved in 'Hill-stone was Content'. This poem narrates the willingness of the personified stone to be 'conscripted/ Into mills' and forget its 'wild roots'. This trope conflates the Great War with the industrial revolution that made it possible, not only technologically, but in terms of the disciplining of men. The stone 'stayed in position/ Defending this slavery', metonymically the slavery of the men working in the mills who 'With bodies that came and went' also 'Stayed in position'. The depersonalised and instrumental nature of the work is powerfully suggested, and the phrase 'stayed in position' has significant military connotations. At the end of the poem another image of war springs up, startlingly suggestive of the time in which the poem was written rather than the Great War: both stones and mankind are fighting against 'the guerrilla patience / Of the soft hill-water.' Hughes was writing in the aftermath of the most humiliating failure of a technologically superior army, in Vietnam, against guerrilla fighters, whose native strength and attunement to the land is not merely a metaphor for the strength of the water but a model of human relationship to the land.

Surprisingly, Hughes omitted from later versions of the sequence some of the most successful poems of this kind. One such is 'Walls'. This poem is accompanied by a photograph of a well-maintained drystone wall that snakes up the side of the field to a house that is equally well-maintained, with bright paint on window frames and drainpipes, and smoke coming from the chimney. In the distance are telegraph poles, linking the human management of the scene with connection to a wider world. (In *Elmet* this photograph less appropriately accompanies the poem 'Wind', imported from *The Hawk in the Rain*.) Though inspired, apparently, by Godwin's photo of the wall, the poem is much more about the lives and deaths of the people who have built and maintained such walls. The relationship of culture, in the form of speech, to work and physical environment is beautifully suggested in the poem's opening in which the 'callussed speech' of the wall-builders is imagined rubbing itself 'Soft and hard again and soft / Again' on the stones which themselves are 'syllables' expressing the contours of the landscape. The two-way operation of the linguistic metaphor is beautifully apt. This poem makes exceptionally effective use of the run-on line, giving each sentence its own precise and energetic rhythm:

> Spines that wore into a bowed
> Enslavement, the small freedom of raising
> Endless memorials to the labour
> Buried in them.

This sentence is rhythmically shaped by three successive line-breaks. In the first two cases the syllable after the line-break is the same, but Hughes enhances his contrast by, in the first case, dropping the stress across the line-break and, in the second, raising it. The word 'Buried' is made to dominate the sentence with its voiced plosive consonant and the extra emphasis gained from carrying across the stanza as well as the line-break. If this makes the sentence seem predominantly gloomy, associating the back-breaking labour of walling with death, the 'small freedom of raising' is not entirely overshadowed; and if these people have disappeared as individuals, their collective identity is memorialised by the walls, which the poem's final lines call with double-edged metaphor a 'harvest of long cemeteries'. The poem's small positive note is strongly reinforced by the photograph.

The effective co-operation of poem and photograph in 'Walls' is enhanced by its relationship to two other poems in *Remains of Elmet*, 'Hill Walls' ('Walls at Alcomden' in *Elmet*) and 'Top Withens'. 'Hill Walls' immediately precedes 'Walls', and its accompanying photograph shows a drystone wall that is contrastingly in ruins. This whole poem is structured round the conceit of agriculture as an optimistic sea-voyage ending in shipwreck. A more profound comparison is offered by 'Top Withens' which, like 'Walls', is omitted from *Elmet*, where it is replaced by 'Two Photographs of Top Withens'. The replacement poem, addressed to Sylvia Plath and recalling a specific incident, is in the manner of *Birthday Letters* (where, curiously, the same occasion is memorialised in another poem, 'Wuthering Heights'). This change epitomises Hughes's attempt to make the sequence more personal and autobiographical.

The photograph accompanying 'Top Withens' (and 'Two Photographs of Top Withens' in *Elmet*) is an eloquent contrast to the 'Walls' photo. The building, in the centre of the frame, is a dark square mass with one tiny hole through which light squints: evidently a ruin. A dark mass of cloud seems to pour down, focussed on the building, while the foreground is occupied by coarse, windblown grass that echoes the turbulent sky. The poem maps the failed human enterprise that the ruined building represents on to the conquest of America. The enterprise was inspired by 'Pioneer hope', the hills were full of 'savage promise'; but the 'skylines, howling, closed in', evoking a stereotypical image of American Indians, and the poem imagines 'withered scalps of souls' swinging in the trees. News keeps coming of 'America's slow surrender', but this place is 'the dead end of a wrong direction' – paradoxically, in this corner of England the wilderness has defeated human attempts to tame it, whereas America has surrendered. The poem shifts from apparently sympathising with the 'Pioneer hope' to a gleeful identification with the 'savage' triumph of the elements: 'swift glooms of purple / Are swabbing the human shape from the freed stones.' 'Swabbing' implies that the 'human shape' is an infection, while 'freed stones' echoes the identification of the stones with the human wage-slaves in 'Hill-stone was Content'.

The replacement poem, 'Two Photographs of Top Withens', intriguingly places Godwin's photo, which is there for the reader to see, beside another, taken by Hughes himself, of Sylvia Plath sitting in one of the trees that feature in Godwin's image, and which is not reproduced. The absence of Plath from the Godwin photograph strengthens the sense of her as, in the poem's final words, 'a ghost'. In the unseen photo the house is less ruined ('most of the roofslabs are in place') and the 'Pioneer hope' of the earlier poem is now attributed to Plath, who exclaims, 'We could buy this place and renovate it!' Like most of the poems in *Birthday Letters*, 'Two Photographs of Top Withens' is addressed to Plath, and the attribution to her of a naïve American exuberance is familiar from some *Birthday Letters* poems. Here the naivety is cut across by an awareness of

> the empty horror of the moor –
>
> Mad heather and grass tugged by the mad
> And empty wind
> That has petrified or got rid of
>
> Everything but the stones.

This is, however, disappointingly lame in comparison with the vigorous, empathetic, almost animistic evocation of the elements in the original poem.

The most important of the autobiographical poems in *Remains of Elmet* is 'Two' (discussed in Chapter 1), which encodes rather than reveals the personal significance to Hughes of his early experiences in the Calder Valley, because it does not announce its autobiographical nature. The others are mostly grouped together in the book. None of these has the 'exclusive' effect that Hughes feared: they tend to present an image of the poet as child, such as one might extrapolate from the other poems. Perhaps the most memorable is 'The Long Tunnel Ceiling', artfully set where the canal in which the boy fishes, fed by high moorland streams, is crossed by the main road, an industrial trade route on which lorries carrying cottons from Lancashire and worsteds from Yorkshire 'fought past each other'. The boy, fishing for small fish called loach, is startled by a crash that he thinks is a brick from the tunnel ceiling, dislodged by traffic. He discovers however that the 'brick' is 'An ingot!/ Holy of holies! A treasure! / A trout!' The epiphanic nature of this experience, enhanced by the sudden reversal from the profane traffic-damage, is entirely convincing:

> Brought down on a midnight cloudburst
> In a shake-up of heaven and the hills
> When the streams burst with zig-zags and explosions
>
> A seed
> Of the wild god now flowering for me
> Such a tigerish, dark, breathing lily
> Between the tyres, under the tortured axles.

However, this excellent poem does not tell us more about the young Hughes's spiritual development than the already classic 'Pike', and lacks the element of terror in that poem.

Because of Hughes's suppression of the human dimension in many of the *Remains of Elmet* poems, and his subordination of his poetry to Godwin's predominantly landscape images, it is not surprising that many critics write as if 'nature' were the hero of the book: for example Patricia Boyle Haberstroh, 'human force will be conquered as nature asserts its power',[13] or Ann Skea, 'Light and soul, which are trapped in the valley, are, here, released from human constraints and can work with the other elemental energies to revive the damaged Earth.'[14] In the light of this, it is particularly interesting that Hughes later described the landscape in the poems as a 'dramatic backdrop' that was given meaning by the lives of the people who inhabited it.[15] The autobiographical and family poems in *Wolfwatching*, some of which were later included in *Elmet*, were Hughes's attempt to rectify this imbalance, as he thought it.

According to Diane Middlebrook, Hughes based *Remains of Elmet* on 'the memory of his mother's voice', and in it he 'begins the process of investigating his mother's role in his vocation as a poet'.[16] In a late letter to Keith Sagar, Hughes wrote that he would really have liked to build the whole sequence round both his father and mother.[17] These motives and inspirations are much more evident in the poems written after the publication of *Remains*. Only two poems, which frame the volume, mention his mother, and his father is not mentioned in *Remains* at all. The last poem, 'The Angel', is a rewrite of 'Ballad from a Fairy Tale' in *Wodwo*. In a 1981 letter he dismissed both poems as 'rather poor attempts to make sense of a dream I didn't understand at all – and still don't'.[18] In both poems the speaker sees 'a swan the size of a city' over the valley (only in 'The Angel' is it explicitly a dream). He asks his mother if it will be a blessing and her answer 'Turned that beauty suddenly to terror' ('The Angel'). This is the only direct reference to his mother's voice in *Remains of Elmet*, and the words are withheld. In both poems the 'angel' wears, instead of a halo, a 'strange square of satin'; later the speaker sees this cloth again, when it is evidently the covering of a coffin. In 'Ballad from a Fairy Tale', first published in 1967, when his mother was still alive, the irresistible impression is that the coffin is Sylvia Plath's. In 'The Angel', the last poem in a volume dedicated to his mother's memory, it equally irresistibly seems to be hers. Evidently Hughes disliked both poems. He omitted 'Ballad from a Fairy Tale' from all the volumes of selected poems, and 'The Angel' from *Elmet*.

In *Wolfwatching* (1989) Hughes published two more poems about his mother, with two about his father and half a dozen more inspired by members of his family or his early life in the Calder Valley. All but two of these poems were reprinted in *Elmet* (1994), together with two more family/autobiographical poems. Surprisingly, the ones he omitted from *Elmet* are 'Dust As We Are' and 'Source', two of Hughes's finest poems about his parents.[19] In 'Leaf Mould', the only new poem about his mother in *Elmet* (in which it replaces 'Hardcastle Crags', a 'mood piece' with which it shares an epigraph and a photograph) Hughes is explicit about the relation between his poems and her voice:

> She hung round your neck her whole valley
> Like David's harp.
> Now, whenever you touch it, God listens
> Only for her voice.

The mother's voice is specifically associated with mourning for the war-dead: 'She grieved for her girlhood and the fallen'. The poet, who was dedicated in her womb to 'this temple of her *Missa Solemnis*', is her 'step-up transformer', magnifying her grief to mourning for 'Paradise and its fable.' Here he suggests that the fall myth underlying his poetry, which can be traced biographically to the loss of his early life in the valley with his brother, originates in family memories of a much greater, world-historical catastrophe. 'Leaf Mould' is a fascinating and revealing poem, but the strange bond between the child and the mother, here somewhat mythically rendered, is conveyed with a more moving personal intensity in the final lines of 'Source', a poem about the mystery of his mother's lifelong fits of weeping:

> You would
> Stop the needle and without a word

> Begin to weep quietly. Like a singing.
> With no other care, only to weep
> Wholly, deeply, as if at last
> You had arrived, as if now at last
> You could rest, could relax utterly
> Into a luxury of pure weeping –
> Could dissolve yourself, me, everything
> Into this relief of your strange music.

The repetition combines with the plangent, run-on rhythm to suggest the insistence and the exhaustive, emptying relief of the mother's weeping. The poem's title, picking up the sense of flow in both the imagery and the rhythm, combines the mystery of the cause of her weeping with the idea of the mother as the origin of the poet and her 'strange music' that of his poetry.

The poem in *Elmet* about Hughes's father, 'For the Duration', picks up the title of Saki's story 'For the Duration of the War', but in a grimly extended sense. As 'Source' is about the mystery of his mother's weeping, 'For the Duration' ponders his father's silence, implying that the 'duration' of his trauma is endless. In this poem, more than any of the other autobiographical poems in *Wolfwatching*, one can see a continuity with the inspiration of *Birthday Letters*: a plain, self-questioning, often prose-like utterance, neither figuratively nor rhythmically remarkable, 'without any of the niceties that any poetry workshop student could have helped me to'.[20] It is typified by these lines:

> Maybe you didn't want to frighten me.
> Now it's too late.
> Now I'd ask you shamelessly.
> But then I felt ashamed.
> What was my shame? Why couldn't I have borne
> To hear you telling what you underwent?

As with 'The Source', I find the poem excluded from *Elmet*, 'Dust As We Are', more memorable and moving, at least in its conclusion:

>                   I divined,
> With a comb,
> Under his wavy, golden hair, as I combed it,
> The fragility of skull. And I filled
> With his knowledge.

After mother's milk
This was the soul's food. A soap-smell spectre
Of the massacre of innocents. So the soul grew.
A strange thing, with rickets – a hyena.
No singing – that kind of laughter.

The child combing his father's head and divining the fragility of the skull under the vigorous golden hair is both tender and harrowing. The psychological inheritance from the father complements that from the mother, but in a far from harmonious way: for her 'strange music' a hyena-like laughter. The poem's title alludes ironically to Book I of the 1850 *Prelude*:

Dust as we are, the immortal spirit grows
Like harmony in music; there is a dark
Inscrutable workmanship that reconciles
Discordant elements, makes them cling together
In one society. How strange, that all
The terrors, pains, and early miseries,
Regrets, vexations, lassitudes interfused
Within my mind, should e'er have borne a part,
And that a needful part, in making up
The calm existence that is mine when I
Am worthy of myself! Praise to the end![21]

The allusion declares both Hughes's likeness to Wordsworth, in that both poets identify the source of their creative power in their childhoods, and in particular localities, and his unlikeness, in that for him 'discordant elements' are not reconciled, but the 'strange music' competes with hyena laughter. The difference is fundamentally historical. History, which impinged on the adult Wordsworth with the French Revolution, has already ravaged the valley of Hughes's birth.

The *Remains of Elmet/Wolfwatching/Elmet* project could be seen as Hughes's *Prelude*. Like Wordsworth, he kept revising it. But Hughes was far more radically dissatisfied with his work than Wordsworth, and with good reason. Whether out of acquiescence to Godwin's photographic art, as he said in 1989, or from 'diabolical fear of subjectivity', as he confessed to Sagar nine years later, there was little of the 'growth of a poet's mind' in the 1979 text, apart from isolated 'spots of time' pieces such as 'The Long Tunnel Ceiling'. When, during the next decade, he took an autobiographical turn, 'the genuine inspiration for the whole scheme had gone' and the result was a 'mongrel effect.' In 1984, when he was already contemplating a revised edition, he told Baskin that revision was blocked by the 'brick wall' of the 'family tomb'.[22] Only in 'Leaf Mould' is the representation of his parents integrated with the evocation of the Calder Valley. In the end, when preparing *Elmet*, he simply piled in everything that related to the area and left the ordering to Fay Godwin.[23] This sense of frustratedly washing his hands of the project may account for the surprising omission from *Elmet* of such poems as 'Walls', 'Top Withens', 'Source' and 'Dust As We Are'. Neither *Remains of Elmet*, with its predominance of 'mood pieces', nor *Elmet* with its unintegrated autobiography and opportunistic recycling of poems from as far back as *The Hawk in the Rain*, is an entirely satisfactory collection. But the sequence of publications examined in this chapter gives us some insight into the struggle of a mature poet to renew himself and change direction.

# 11
## Fisherman Hughes: *River*

Despite Hughes's frustrations with *Remains of Elmet*, there was undoubtedly a strong artistic congeniality between him and Godwin, and the collaboration was in many ways a success. This may have encouraged Hughes to embark on another venture with a photographer. In *River* (1983) each poem is accompanied by a photograph by the Devon fisherman and photographer Peter Keen. This collaboration is much less successful. Godwin's black and white photos are meditative and often sombre compositions that reward repeated viewing. It is obvious that many of Hughes's poems are inspired by the photographs, and the two bodies of work complement each other. Keen's colour photos, though skilful and often beautiful, connect with the poems only on the most superficial level. Indeed, there is never a direct connection between an individual poem and its accompanying photograph. It is evident that none of the poems was inspired by the photos, and their presence on the opposite page is, more often than not, a distraction. Above all, the photographs do not correspond at all to the preoccupation with subjectivity that is central to the most memorable of Hughes's poems in this volume. This was commonly noted in reviews. Peter Redgrove for example was enthusiastic about the poems but wrote that the photographs 'are not of the same interest, and present an embalmed or chocolate-box appearance; they are not awake'.[1]

Hughes himself regretted the collaboration on more practical grounds. The book cost twice as much as it would have without the photographs. Hughes thought no-one would buy it and regretted that his poems were tied up in an expensive book for which he would only get half the royalties.[2] In 1993 he published a much revised version of the sequence in the volume, *Three Books*, without photographs.

As in *Moortown Diary*, the poet-persona of *River* is that of a countryman, in this case a fisherman. Many of the poems focus on fishing, and the persona is a man with a formidable knowledge of fishing technique, the ways of fish and above all the life-cycle of the salmon. The *River* poems, especially in the revised version, are, more than any of Hughes's earlier poetic work, overtly engaged with ecological crisis. '1984 on "The Tarka Trail" ' (*TB*) is a direct polemic against the pollution of rivers, and especially modern farming methods. It is however slackly written and journalistic. Much more resonant are the poems that draw on Hughes's profound knowledge of the behaviour of fish, to represent imaginatively

> how salmon come to be such sensitive glands in the vast, dishevelled body of nature. Their moody behaviour, so unpredictable and myste- rious, is attuned, with the urgency of survival, to every slightest hint of the weather – marvellous instruments, recording every moment-by- moment microchange as the moving air and shifting light manipulate the electronics of the water molecules. (*RCD* 52)

Fishing also has a profound subjective importance for Hughes, as we have seen in much earlier writing such as 'Pike', and his use of fishing as a metaphor for imaginative writing in *Poetry in the Making*. In *River* one does not feel, as in *Moortown Diary*, that an important part of the poet's subjectivity, the part that drew him to shamanism, is withheld. It is in the act of fishing, in the concentration, anticipation and the physical connection of the potentially fatal catch that the human persona shares something of the fish's 'attunement':

> Eerie how you know when it's coming!
> So I felt it now, my blood
> Prickling and thickening, altering
> With an ushering-in of chills, a weird onset
> As if mountains were pushing mountains higher
> Behind me, to crowd over my shoulder.
> ('Milesian Encounter on the Sligachan')

But the fisherman is of course a killer of animals. At least from the 1970s on, Hughes's writings suggest a conflicted and contradictory attitude to all forms of hunting animals, including fishing. In a posthumously pub- lished interview with an American angling magazine he said, 'I would never stop fishing, because I do not want to lose what goes with fish- ing … this last connection. To this whole – to everything. The stuff of the Earth. The whole of life.'[3] Yet in the poem 'Foxhunt', published in *Moortown Diary*, he shows no sympathy with the hunters and in a 1997 letter he wrote, 'I've known for some years what a hunted deer goes through physically. And a hunted fox. And a fish being caught, for that matter', and floated the idea that animals should be given the status of 'fellow citizens'.[4] This conflict recalls the essay on 'Poetry and Violence' (*WP* 251–67) in which Hughes wrote of the hawk and pike that 'their killing is a sacrament' and quoted scathingly the phrase, 'our customary social and humanitarian values'. By using the language of citizenship with reference to animals, he seems to be appealing to precisely those values, and raises the thought that in that essay he may have been externalising conflicting principles within himself.

The word 'sacrament' is in line with the extensive use of religious, and specifically Christian, vocabulary in *River*: 'anoints' ('Flesh of Light'), 'resurrection' ('Under the Hill of Centurions'), 'holy' ('Strangers'), 'Eden' and 'sacrament' itself ('The Gulkana'), 'chapel' and 'altar' ('September Salmon'), 'pilgrim' and 'nun' ('An Eel'), 'liturgy' and 'Sanctus' ('Salmon Eggs'). 'God' and 'spirit' occur frequently. Hughes's use of this language was self-conscious: Joanny Moulin has pointed out that in the *Three Books* version he substituted 'covenant' for 'promise' in 'The Gulkana' and (in *New Selected Poems*) 'advent' for 'tidings' in 'Salmon Eggs'. Conversely, perhaps thinking he had taken his use of this language too far, he cut the words 'Sanctus Sanctus' from the revised version of 'Salmon Eggs'. Presenting Hughes as an anti-Christian poet, Moulin interprets this language as 'a strategy of brinkmanship and subliminal influence'.[5] It is also a strategy of recuperation, an attempt like Crow's in 'Crow Blacker than Ever' at 'Nailing Heaven and earth together' by appropriating, or re-appropriating, the language of the 'sacred' in a wished-for return to the 'religious outlook of the primitive' to which, as interpreted by Mircea Eliade, '[t]he hardness, ruggedness and permanence of matter was in itself a hierophany [sacred mystery]'.[6]

Crow's attempt to nail Heaven and earth together had disastrous consequences. I am not suggesting that Hughes's attempt is equally ill-advised, but in reading these poems we should consider Moulin's notion of 'brinkmanship', the self-conscious and provocative quality of this language in Hughes. This is what is lost when the language is replicated by commentators. Terry Gifford has remarked sardonically that *River* had been elevated to 'the status of a holy book' by certain Hughes scholars.[7] Notable examples can be found in the commentaries of Leonard Scigaj, Ann Skea and Bo Gustavsson,[8] but I will give an example from Keith Sagar, as he is such an important figure in Hughes studies:

The spent salmon is the defeated, torn and sacrificed hero whose acquiescence is a form of worship. The salmon poems are all hymns to the goddess, tributes to the mythic heroism of the salmon, dying in the cause of the goddess. Their sacrifice is also a sacrament, the consummation of being reborn from their own eggs and sperm.[9]

The notion of sacrifice requires that the object sacrificed has the potential of continued existence, a value of which the community or individual is depriving itself and giving to the deity (in the case of self-sacrifice, one's own continued enjoyment of life). As Hughes's own account (*TB* 184–5) of the life-cycle of the salmon makes clear, the fish has no such potential: it has simply reached the end of its life. The idea that the salmon's death is 'a form of worship' is similarly distorted. Worship presupposes a distinction and separation between the worshipper and the deity. In Hughes's world-view, this is the case only with humanity: all other animals are at one with the Goddess, 'at rest in the law'. The particular poem that Sagar is alluding to here, 'October Salmon', is almost devoid of religious language, and one example, 'the machinery of heaven', seems problematically religious. When Hughes does use the trope of sacrifice with reference to salmon, he does so with a provocative and disturbing edge, a conscious extravagance, that is lost in reverential commentary: 'They looked like what they were, somnambulists, / Drugged, ritual victims, melting away / Towards a sacrament' ('The Gulkana'). These lines are aware of what human sacrifice is actually like.

Hughes's enterprise in *River* is much more strained than Sagar's commentary suggests. The strain gives rise to both strengths and weaknesses. The most distinctive weakness is that the persistent feminisation of the natural world results in a vein of arch sexual symbolism. I give just one example, from 'Dee':

> the lit queenliness of snow hills,
> The high, frozen bosom, wears this river
> Like a peculiarly fine jewel.

It would be difficult to find another such frigid and inert simile elsewhere in Hughes's poetry.

However, I want to concentrate on what seems to me the most interesting feature of *River*, and one of its main strengths, which is the representation of a disturbed and displaced subjectivity, through an intriguing shift of subject positions between poems. I will concentrate on five poems, that seem to me the best in the original volume: 'That Morning', 'The Gulkana', 'Milesian Encounter on the Sligachan', 'Go Fishing' and 'October Salmon'.

Before looking closely at these poems I want to comment on the fact that the first two are set in Alaska, and that 'The Bear', perhaps the best new poem[10] added in the *Three Books* version, is set in British Columbia. In my chapter on *Lupercal* I discussed the complete absence of imaginative response to America in that book, the importance of British and specifically Yorkshire scenes for Hughes's imagination, and suggested that despite the apparent dominance of the outwardly directed eye in his work, these scenes actually represent an intensely protected inwardness. The sub-Arctic wilderness is unique among foreign environments in having inspired some of Hughes's greatest poetry. Hughes visited Alaska with his son Nicholas in 1980. He wrote to his brother, 'I never liked any place as much. I just can't tell you what a paradise it is.'[11] Such enthusiasm does not necessarily signify inspiration: Hughes wrote equally enthusiastically about his trip to Australia in 1976, and about a 1983 visit to Nick in Africa (where Nick was working on his PhD), but neither journey produced any poetry.[12]

It may be that we can find the key to the importance of Alaska for Hughes in the word 'paradise', and specifically in what is perhaps the most paradisal poem in his oeuvre, 'That Morning'. In this passage the fisherman is wading in the river:

> Solemn to stand there in the pollen light
> Waist-deep in wild salmon swaying massed
> As from the hand of God. There the body
>
> Separated, golden and imperishable,
> From its doubting thought.

The emotive and religious gestures of this passage are anchored in the artistry of the second line quoted. The pattern of assonance and alliteration combines with a spondaic rhythm that is the opposite of 'bludgeoning'.[13] The predominance of semivowel, sibilant and nasal in the spondaic stresses produces a soft, surging, rather than abrupt, movement, while the interweaving of assonance and alliteration binds the words into a whole suggestive of massive, mobile fluidity. The line approaches in quality the greatest of all poetic evocations of fishy abundance, Yeats's 'The salmon-falls, the mackerel-crowded seas' ('Sailing to Byzantium'), but Hughes goes beyond Yeats by placing the subject *within* this abundance. Yeats's line 'sings', but Hughes's *senses* its object. The conceit of the 'golden' body (with alchemical connotations) separating from the doubting mind is supported by the way language inhabits sensation in this line, and the 'body' of the language asserts itself so powerfully. Note that the subject *is* this body, the passage is written from this perspective of freedom from the 'doubting mind'. The golden body is echoed later in the poem when

> Two gold bears came down and swam like men
>
> Beside us. And dived like children.
> And stood in deep water as on a throne
> Eating pierced salmon off their talons.

Here the language is simple, almost childlike. At first it seems like a fable: the bears swimming 'like men' seem like visitors from another world, spirit guides. In a way they are, but they are also simply bears, and this momentary erasure of the boundary between the spirit world and the objective world, between the aspiration of the golden body and the human subject, permits a lightness rare in Hughes's most deeply engaged poetry.

There is, however, an element in this poem that disrupts the 'paradisal' atmosphere. It opens by describing the salmon as

> so many
> So steady, so spaced, so far-aimed
> On their inner map, England could add
>
> Only the sooty twilight of South Yorkshire
> Hung with the drumming drift of Lancasters
> Till the world had seemed capsizing slowly.

This comparison of salmon to warplanes is later echoed in the word 'formations'. Hughes's note on this poem in *Three Books* is almost entirely about this passage, which he calls 'simply a memory of South Yorkshire from a late phase of the Second World War' (*TB* 186). But how could it be 'simply a memory'? The memory must be motivated. In the note Hughes contrasts the sensation of listening to the Lancasters with that evoked earlier in the war by German Dorniers on their way to bomb Sheffield. The memory of British bombers may well have benign connotations, but it still seems incongruous. One possible explanation for this incongruous memory illuminates the poem's importance in Hughes's *oeuvre*.

Although the poem does not identify its protagonists, 'That Morning' is so compelling partly because it is a reversal of 'Two', a poem that does implicitly identify its protagonists as Hughes and his brother Gerald, and that narrates the end of a life and a relationship that were 'paradise to me'.[14] Hughes told Gerald that Alaska was 'paradise'. The fact that

Hughes visited Alaska with his son bears tangentially on this, since it replicates and reverses Hughes's quasi-filial relationship with Gerald. Hughes enjoyed that earlier paradise in West, not South Yorkshire, but it was to South Yorkshire that he was exiled when he was separated from Gerald, and Gerald joined the RAF. In 'Two', 'the war opened', ending the relationship between the boy and his 'guide'. That relationship, and its ending, I have suggested, are what sealed the inwardness of Hughes's relationship with the natural world, and gave it its persistent note of loss, longing and nostalgia. The reference to wartime South Yorkshire is not 'simply a memory' but a reminder, perhaps subliminal, of the loss of the world in which 'the stream poured oracles of abundance / And the sun poured out at their feet' ('Two'), and that has been regained in remote Alaska.

Several poems in *River* (especially in the *Three Books* version) are in the form of a loose autobiographical narrative in which the narrator enters the river or its environment and encounters there, in the river itself and its fish, something that calls to the hidden self who belongs to the natural world, and who is usurped in social existence. But the position of the speaker, the subject, of these poems, in relation to this hidden self, is unstable. We have seen that 'That Morning' is spoken by or from the 'golden body' that has separated from 'doubting thought'. This is what makes the poem 'paradisal'. In other poems the subject position is more conflicted.

The most substantial of these poems is 'The Gulkana' ('Gulkana' in *River*), which was extensively revised between *River* and *Three Books*, and again for *New Selected Poems*. Except where otherwise stated I quote from the final version. The speaker walks along the 'tightrope shore' of the river and starts to feel afraid, as if he is being 'hunted'. He explains this to himself as

> my fear of one inside me,
> A bodiless twin, some doppelgänger
> Disinherited other, unliving,
> Ever-living, a larva from prehistory,
> Whose journey this was, who now exulted
> Recognising his home,
> And whose gaze I could feel as he watched me
> Fiddling with my gear – the interloper,
> The fool he had always hated.

This is reminiscent of the two Lumbs in *Gaudete*, especially the scene in which the naked Dionysiac double rises from the lake and fights with the vicar. It is this double, not the speaker, to whom the wilderness is 'home' and who, implicitly, identifies himself with the salmon. From this point of view the speaker is an inauthentic 'interloper'. But this speaker is fully the subject of the poem: he is not distanced like the inauthentic protagonists of early poems such as 'Egg-Head' and 'Meeting'.

The central trope of the poem is the 'voice' of the river, which is associated with its alien-sounding name, 'a deranging cry / From the wilderness'. At the beginning of the poem the speaker reflects on the river's name and asks, 'What does it mean? / A pre-Columbian glyph.' There is a small but significant revision of tense from the *River* text, 'What did it mean?' Pre-Columbian means Native American and the language that gave the Gulkana its name might still be spoken. The poem's representation of Native Americans, and their relation to the values suggested by the words 'pre-Columbian', 'prehistory' and 'aboriginal', seems to be contradictory. The Indian village is 'comatose – on the stagnation toxins / Of a cultural vasectomy.' But the poem ends with the voice of the river telling of its denizens, the last of which is the old Indian Headman, who 'smiled / Adjusting to our incomprehension – his face / A whole bat, that glistened and stirred.' This appears to be an entirely subjective representation, but the image of the bat effectively suggests a consciousness that is 'attuned' to the 'body of nature'.

It is, however, the salmon that are described as 'Aboriginal Americans' in the poem's central passage:

> They were possessed
> By that voice in the river
> And its accompaniment –
> The flutes, the drumming. And they rose and sank
> Like voices, themselves like singers
> In its volume. We watched them, deepening away ...
> Aboriginal Americans
> High among rains, in an opening of the hills,
> They will begin to circle,
> Shedding their ornaments,
> In shufflings and shudderings, male and female,
> Begin to dance their deaths –
> The current hosing over their brows and shoulders,
> Bellies riven open and shaken empty
> Into a gutter of pebbles
> In the orgy of eggs and sperm,
> The dance orgy of being reborn ...

This passage is considerably extended and strengthened from the *River* version. Its rhythm and lexis remind me of Eliot's evocation of a very different scene in the first section of 'East Coker':

> In that open field
> If you do not come too close, if you do not come too close,
> On a summer midnight, you can hear the music
> Of the weak pipe and the little drum
> And see them dancing around the bonfire
> The association of man and woman ...
> ... Round and round the fire
> Leaping through the flames, or joined in circles ...
> ... Feet rising and falling.
> Eating and drinking. Dung and death.[15]

Eliot's use of alliterative metre is much more consistent than Hughes's, but such a metre forms the base of Hughes's rhythm. In both cases the metre is lightened by a long, loose, meditative sentence-structure. Lexically, the pipe and drum, dancing (both shamanistic motifs in Hughes's imaginative world), circling, the centrality of sexual union and death are intriguing echoes. (I have omitted the quotations from Ecclesiastes and Sir Thomas Elyot in 'East Coker' that have no equivalent in the Hughes.) Both passages narrate visionary experiences induced by a form of hypnosis – Eliot is '[h]ypnotised' by the 'electric heat', Hughes encounters '[h]ypnagogic rocks'. Both end with the speaker placing himself in relation to the scene narrated: 'I am here / Or there, or elsewhere' ('East Coker'), 'I came back to myself' ('The Gulkana'). Both poems are concerned with origins, and with cyclic return ('In my beginning is my end', 'East Coker'), though the settings of their explorations are so different.

Hughes's revisions to 'The Gulkana' emphasise the shamanistic elements in the poem, and in 1988, in the middle of the period during which he made these revisions, he wrote 'The Poetic Self', the essay in which he identified Eliot as, with only Shakespeare as his peer, the epitome of the shaman-poet. In this essay Hughes interprets Eliot's early poem 'The Death of St Narcissus' as the representation of the 'other more or less articulate personality hidden inside' the ego, a '*doppelgänger*' whom he identifies as the 'poetic self' (*WP* 274–5). The Laforguean[16] companion poem 'Humouresque' is 'Eliot's parody of the ego who longs to be that other' but is really 'no more than a shadow' (*WP* 281–2). The feared 'doppelgänger' in 'The Gulkana' is clearly

Hughes's representation, or intuition, of this 'poetic self', and the ego who returns home in a Boeing 747 is a 'spectre of fragments', though Hughes lacks an equivalent of Eliot's Laforguean idiom to give it such memorable expression.

Eliot's 'poetic self' and 'shadow' ego (in Hughes's reading) are confined in separate poems. In 'The Gulkana', however, the 'doppelgänger' and the 'spectre' are brought together. It could be argued that, in the central passage that narrates the speaker's vision of the death-dance of the salmon, he has been taken over by the 'doppelgänger'. 'I came back to myself' signals a reversion to 'A spectre of fragments'. But this 'spectre' is not sealed off from the experience of the 'doppelgänger'. Even in the plane,

> Word by word
> The voice of the river moved in me.
> It was like lovesickness.
> A numbness, a secret bleeding.
> Waking in my body.

'Milesian Encounter on the Sligachan' (set on Skye) is a similarly structured narrative, but shorter and less solemn in tone. It includes the account of 'attunement' quoted at the beginning of this chapter, but this is prefaced by a comic account, in long prose-like lines, of the speaker 'lurching' along a bogland river to find salmon-pools. This passage is framed by two very short lines that announce the 'shock' of finding the pools and encountering the 'superabundance of spirit' that they contain. In the context of 'The Gulkana' the most interesting line is, 'And now where were they, my fellow aliens from prehistory?' In 'The Gulkana' it is the 'doppelgänger' who is a 'larva from prehistory'. We might deduce that this poem is spoken *by* the 'doppelgänger', though there is a note of comic exaggeration in the line that should warn us against taking this difference too seriously. The line is double-voiced, incorporating the anticipated mockery of a reader unsympathetic to Hughes's exploit, but not conceding to it. There is a more obvious effect of the same kind later in the poem, when in a series of exclamations Hughes identifies the little salmon he finds with a Gruagach, a Boggart and a Glaistig.

'Milesian Encounter' concludes by usurping the speaker's point of view with that of the salmon, who watches him 'As I faded from the light of reality.' The loss of ego hinted at here is more fully explored in the completely serious-toned poem 'Go Fishing'. This poem is written entirely in the imperative mood, so that grammatically at least the subject is divided, and there are no personal pronouns. Here the 'speaker' is not a dramatised protagonist as in 'The Gulkana' and 'Milesian Encounter' but a disembodied and depersonalised voice which, nevertheless, participates in the experience it commands, through the materiality of its language. If it is a voice beyond the ego, just as the 'doppelgänger' is beyond the ego, the closeness of speaker and addressee in this poem warns us of the ultimate artificiality of separating these personae.

> Join water, wade in underbeing
> Let brain mist into moist earth
> Ghost loosen away downstream
> Gulp river and gravity

As in 'That Morning', a predominantly spondaic metre combines with assonance and alliteration, though to different effect. The effect here is not of movement but of dissolution. Consider the way words melt into each other, via a chain of echoes, in the sequences water / wade / being / brain; mist / moist / ghost / loosen; ghost / gulp / river / gravity. The effect is enhanced by the absence of punctuation. As the poem proceeds, passive forms of the verb predominate – 'Be supplanted', 'Be cleft', 'Displaced', 'Dissolved', ' Mangled'.

The last poem that I want to discuss, 'October Salmon', differs from the others in that it is not explicitly concerned with the speaker's subjectivity, nor is it about fishing. It is a complementary companion-poem to 'The Knight' in *Cave Birds*. In that poem the foreground is occupied by the image of a knight dedicating his victory in some unspecific religious ceremony, but through the chivalric language appears (with the help of Baskin's drawing) the image of a dead bird. 'October Salmon' is much more naturalistic. The dying fish is in the foreground, and the speaker is distinguished less by his divided subjectivity than by his informed ability to interpret the spectacle that unfolds. This speaker is able to read the whole life-history of the fish into its present 'death-patched' appearance in 'poor water', and to contrast the present scene with 'the sea-going Aurora Borealis / Of his April power – / The primrose and violet of that first upfling in the estuary'. This speaker knows both that 'He was probably hatched in this very pool' and that 'If boys see him they will try to kill him': he is intimate both with the fish's world and with the human world in which the fish is stranded. There are traces of chivalric language that echo 'The Knight' – 'hero', 'vigil', 'epic poise' – but these are combined with images more suggestive of modern warfare and the impact of Hughes's father's ordeal on his imagination: 'veteran', 'regimentals', 'decorations'. Unlike the Knight who has 'conquered', the salmon 'suffers the subjection, and the dumbness, / And the humiliation of the role'. The poem has a grim, facing-the-facts quality, but it is at root celebratory, as the following passage makes clear:

> And that is how it is,
> That is what is going on there, under the scrubby oak tree, hour
>    after hour,
> That is what the splendour of the sea has come down to,
> And the eye of ravenous joy – the king of infinite liberty
> In the flashing expanse, the bloom of sea-life,
>
> On the surge-ride of energy, weightless,
> Body simply the armature of energy
> In that earliest sea-freedom, the savage amazement of life,
> The salt mouthful of actual existence
> With strength like light

The 'savage amazement of life' is grammatically subordinated to 'what is going on there', but it surges from the lines as the object of the speaker's desire, evident in the unmistakably human aspect of the fish's imagined existence. In this way the speaker's subjectivity, and the exultation of the 'doppelgänger', leaks even into this ostensibly outwardly focussed poem.

# 12
## The Poet Laureate

The office of Poet Laureate has been considered a poisoned chalice. No national institution has been so consistently an object of derision; no public office has been so guaranteed to make its holder a laughing-stock. Since the Restoration the Laureateship has been held by four poets of the first rank: John Dryden, William Wordsworth, Alfred Tennyson and Ted Hughes. Compare with this short list the following rather longer one: Thomas Shadwell, Nahum Tate, Nicholas Rowe, Lawrence Eusden, Colley Cibber, William Whitehead, Thomas Warton, Henry Pye, Alfred Austin. The first seven men on that list held the Laureateship continuously from 1688 to 1813. They include some talented playwrights and distinguished scholars, but none of them was outstandingly gifted as a poet. For a century the Poet Laureate was required to compose Odes in honour of the King or Queen on their birthday and at New Year, a task which was considered beneath the best poets of the age. Here are the words in which Thomas Gray declined the office in 1757:

> If any great man would say to me, 'I will make you rat-catcher to his Majesty, with a salary of £300 a year and two butts of the best Malaga' ... I cannot say I should jump at it .... I would rather be sergeant-trumpeter or pin-maker to the palace. [1]

In 1790 William Cowper said, 'It would be a leaden extinguisher, clapped on all the fire of my genius, and I should never more produce a line worth reading.'[2] In 1813 Sir Walter Scott considered accepting, but was advised against by his patron, the Duke of Buccleuch: 'I shall frankly say that I should be mortified to see you hold a situation, which by the general concurrence of the world, is stamped ridiculous.'[3]

Most of the early Laureates were more famous for the mockery they attracted than for their poetry. Two of them, Thomas Shadwell and Colley Cibber, had the misfortune to be immortalised in two of the greatest English satirical poems, Dryden's *Mac Flecknoe* and Pope's *Dunciad*, as was a rather better poet, Robert Southey, in Byron's *Vision of Judgment*. The tradition of mocking the Laureate has survived to the present, and even the most gifted of poets is not immune to it. When Hughes wrote a poem celebrating the wedding of the Duke and Duchess of York he was derided for the lines, 'A helicopter snatched you up. / The pilot, it was me', even though they are obviously meant to be funny. When he published his third birthday poem for the Queen Mother, in 1995, *The Guardian* invited fellow-poets to respond in verse, and Hughes was perhaps lucky that we do not have a satirist of the calibre of Dryden, Pope or Byron. The best response, from Peter Redgrove, a friend and admirer of Hughes, was more gently mocking:

> One can always tell the Queen Mother,
> An old woman whose cheeks are cool
> And fragrant to kiss and whose robes
> Smell faintly of lily of the valley;
> One can tell the Queen Mother anything.[4]

Although in 1984 Hughes was, with Philip Larkin, one of the two most widely admired British poets, there seemed to be something incongruous about his appointment as Poet Laureate. As Seamus Heaney noted at the time, Hughes lacked the 'civic' and 'institutional' aura that clung to predecessors such as Tennyson, Robert Bridges, John Masefield and John Betjeman, and his mind-set was profoundly at odds with 'the mainstream, secular, positivist British way of responding to experience.' Heaney believed that precisely because of this, Hughes's appointment was historically significant: the country (or the Establishment) had chosen a poet with 'an essentially religious vision', whose poetry strove to put its readers 'in vital, imaginative contact with the geological, botanical, historical and legendary reality of England itself'.[5] However, the monarchy is a Christian and since the sixteenth century specifically a Protestant institution, and Hughes's 'religious vision' is pagan in the strongest sense of the word and particularly hostile to post-Reformation Christianity. In a letter to Lord Gowrie shortly after his appointment he described his notion of the meaning of the Laureateship as 'primitive'.[6]

By the time of Hughes's appointment, the Laureate was no longer expected to celebrate Royal birthdays (John Masefield, for example, did not do so), but the monarchical tradition of the post was clearly one of the things that attracted him to it, and he chose to exercise precisely the function that had earlier made the Laureateship a joke. Among the Gerald Hughes papers at Emory there are documents showing both that Hughes's attachment to the idea of monarchy was long-standing, and that he was drawn at an early age to the kind of formal, occasional verse that he produced as Laureate. In a letter to Gerald's wife Joan, undated but probably written at the time of the Coronation in 1953, Hughes enclosed a dialogue between Elizabeth I and Elizabeth II, apparently written at Joan's request. In it Elizabeth I mocks her successor for the diminished role she is assuming, and launches into an argument that helps to illuminate the connection between Hughes's monarchism and his imaginative affinity with predatory violence. The elder queen asserts that a king is a 'symbol of control' which makes every individual 'a more disciplined cohesive unit in the national purpose'. Without this discipline, 'men become animals' and live in a state in which it is the moral right 'of every individual to kill whoever stands in his way.' (This argument illuminates the early poem 'Law in the Country of the Cats'.) The human group 'degenerates ... until they get one popular leader' who becomes 'the image by which each man organises himself ... instinctively'[7] More than thirty years later, in notes for the 'Birthday Masque' for Elizabeth II's sixtieth birthday, Hughes echoed these thoughts when he wrote of the symbolic birds in his poem finding 'their true selves (their spiritual selves) by finding the spiritual unity of the Islands, which is "the ring of the people", which is also the Crown ... which is the Queen' (*RCD* 55). There was however a more irreverent side to Hughes's attitude to the monarchy, expressed in his letter to his daughter Frieda on receiving the Queen's Medal for Poetry, nine years before he became Laureate. He says he felt inclined to be a 'cheeky upstart', could not 'treat royalty with the right tone of reverence', and was afraid of being thrown out for saying something 'utterly impossible'.[8]

Most of the extant unpublished juvenile poetry is elaborately formal and occasional, almost certainly because what has survived is what Hughes wrote for other people and was kept by them. The freshest and liveliest is a marriage poem for his childhood friend Edna Wholey, in a formal, ode-like style, whose last section, 'The Ring', begins each part with the line that ended the previous one, as in Donne's 'Corona'.[9] There are also four poems written for Gerald, in an elevated, sometimes bombastic style, including a long 'Birthday Ode'. This consists of 'Invocation to the nearest Muse' (later collected, as 'Song'), 'Lustral rites for the mortal imagination', and an 'Overture', three movements and an

'Epithalamium', amounting to some 750 lines of blank verse, the last part dated 20 October 1950.[10] In style and manner these poems anticipate such Laureate poems as 'A Birthday Masque' and 'A Masque for Three Voices' far more than any of Hughes's other published verse. One of the birthday odes for Gerald opens with these lines, which appear to lament Gerald's departure for Australia:

> The year's sweet cry climbs no more through the woods;
> Clouds, wind, leaves starve, forsaken of that voice.[11]

Hughes's first Laureate poem, published immediately upon the announcement of his appointment, turned out to be uncharacteristic of the work he would produce in this role. Its full original title was 'Rain-Charm for the Duchy, A Blessed, Devout Drench for the Christening of His Royal Highness Prince Harry'. Even in this title there is a tension between its inspiration and the occasion that it serves: the pagan rain-charm and the Christian baptism. The poem evokes a tremendous thunderstorm and the exultation of the personified rivers of Dartmoor:

> Thunder gripped and picked up the city.
> Rain didn't so much fall as collapse.
> The pavements danced, like cinders in a riddle ....
>
> What a weight of warm Atlantic water!
>
> The car-top hammered. The Cathedral jumped in and out
> Of a heaven that had obviously caught fire
> And couldn't be contained ....
>
>       I was thinking
> Of joyful sobbings –
> The throb
>
> In the rock-face mosses of the Chains,
> And of the exultant larvae in the Barle's shrunk trench, their
>     filaments ablur like propellors, under the churned ceiling of
>     light ... .

Hughes originally wrote this poem without any thought of the Prince's christening,[12] but the decision to use it for this occasion was an inspired one. It acquires a new dimension: throughout it runs a sense of the contrast between this 'drench' and the sprinkling that the Prince will receive in Church, the feebleness of the echo of pagan fertility symbolism that survives in Christian ritual. There is nothing confrontational about this: the implied comparison is warm, humorous and mannerly. At the time, in an essay welcoming Hughes's appointment, I wrote, 'if he is able to sustain the poise and integrity of this first poem he might turn the Laureateship into an organ for creatively exploring the role of religion, ritual and mythology in our society.'[13] He probably believed that, in such poems as the Masques for the Queen and the Queen Mother, this was what he was doing. However, I am sure that the vast majority of readers will find this first poem, which wears its Laureate role so loosely, far more successful than the very deliberate pieces that followed it. The facts that Hughes made it the title poem of his Laureate collection, and that it is the only poem from that collection in *New Selected Poems*, suggest that he may have thought so too.

There was an anticipation of the Laureateship in 1977, when Faber marked the Silver Jubilee by commissioning Hughes and Larkin to write quatrains to be incised in stone in Queen Square, outside their offices. An amusing aspect of this episode is that Charles Monteith, the Chairman of Faber, thought the verse Hughes submitted was too sophisticated and asked for something simpler, sending Larkin's poem as an example. Hughes compliantly sent another version that Monteith liked better.[14] Larkin's *Selected Letters* display an unqualified hostility to Hughes, epitomised by the assertion, 'No, of course Ted's no good at all. Not at all. Not a single solitary bit of good.'[15] Hughes by contrast had a very generous attitude to his rival. In *Poetry in the Making* one of his examples of 'Writing about People' is Larkin's 'Mr Bleaney', about which Hughes writes, 'Looking through the lens of this poem, it seems we could see every detail of any situation this man could ever get into' (*PM* 48). Hughes read 'Aubade' on the radio and said it was Larkin's best poem,[16] and read 'Let us now praise famous men' (*Ecclesiastes* 44) at the memorial service for Larkin at Westminster Abbey.[17] Shortly before Larkin's death Hughes wrote to him recommending a healer, and was mortified when he discovered how close to death Larkin had been, and hoped that he had not read the letter.[18] This episode is particularly revealing because Hughes knew that Larkin would be sceptical, even feared giving offence, but felt morally impelled to write.

Not surprisingly, Hughes also had less favourable things to say about Larkin, though not about his poetry. He was exasperated by the 'prostrated' critical response to Larkin's book of occasional prose, *Required Writing*, and resented Larkin's narrowness of taste and hostility to poetry in translation. He thought him, 'a sour old cuss'.[19] Intriguingly, Hughes thought that Larkin was 'too obviously right-wing' to be Laureate, and his own candidate, when asked, was Charles Causley, 'a man of the people, with a great gift for turning likeable verses on sacred, ceremonious themes'.[20] Hughes was certainly wounded when Larkin's malicious remarks about him were published in his *Selected Letters* (1992).[21] In the original title of 'Rain-Charm for the Duchy', the phrase 'Devout Drench' was quoted from Larkin's poem 'Water', a gracious homage to the poet whose refusal of the Laureateship allowed it to be offered to Hughes. In *New Selected Poems* (1994) the allusion to Larkin is omitted.

Neither of the Queen Square quatrains is a very memorable piece of verse, but they give a fascinating insight into what kind of Laureate each poet might turn out to be.

In times when nothing stood
but worsened, or grew strange,
there was one constant good:
she did not change[22]
(Larkin)


A Nation's a Soul.
A Soul is a Wheel
With a Crown at the hub
To keep it whole
(Hughes)

Obviously they are both conservative poems, but that was to be expected: a poem celebrating a royal Jubilee is bound to be conservative. What is interesting is the difference between them: the different kinds of conservatism they represent. Behind Larkin's poem is the tradition of lament for the mutability of earthly life, and the yearning for constancy, traditionally attributed to the stars. The Queen is merely a symbol of this constancy. As a historical comment on Elizabeth II this is of course untrue. The monarchy changed enormously during her first twenty-five years, mainly through her decision to open up her family life to the media. But this is irrelevant to Larkin's poem. It is the idea of constancy that matters. The poem belongs ideologically with an advertisement for the *Daily Telegraph* that combined a Constable-like rural scene with the slogan 'Times change, Values don't.' If we want to know what more precisely lies behind the poem, we don't have to look far. It will be forever shadowed by another quatrain that Larkin wrote in the same year and circulated privately, entitled 'from an unwritten Jubilee poem to HM':

> After Healey's trading figures,
> After Wilson's squalid crew,
> And the rising tide of niggers –
> What a treat to look at you.[23]

So we know what it was that 'worsened, or grew strange'. In 1984 Larkin was offered the Laureateship but turned it down. He died in 1985 and these verses were published in 1992. Larkin's reputation as a poet has survived the scandal of his racism, but it would be interesting to speculate on what would have happened if that scandal had engulfed the Laureateship, the monarchy, and the whole network of conservative institutions of which the Laureateship is a very small part.

Whereas Larkin adapts a traditional figure of mutability and constancy for the purposes of the petty right-wing politics of the time, Hughes's poem is more plausibly universal. His association of the metaphor of the wheel with the Soul and the idea of Wholeness shows the influence of Jungian psychology. For Jung the wheel was an example of the mandala, a symbol of spiritual wholeness or, as he called it, individuation.[24] It was for him and no doubt for Hughes as well an archetype, transcending history. That Hughes shares this perspective is evident in his notes to his most ambitious Laureate poem, the Masque for the Queen's sixtieth birthday, where he writes that

> The Crown ... does not belong to historical time and the tabloid scrimmage of ideologies, but to natural time, where the flower of five million years ago is still absolutely up to date ... . The Crown ... is the reminder and the presence of this mystery in life – that historical time comes second. (*CP* 1217)

Later we shall be seeing that Hughes does not consistently hold to this extreme anti-historicism. At present I just want to consider that however archetypal, his image of the Nation is vacuous unless it informs history, including those historical changes that Larkin so unarchetypally referred to in his unofficial Jubilee poem. The mandala image of the wheel is very much elaborated in the Birthday Masque, where as we shall see Hughes explicitly, if glancingly, alludes to Black and Asian immigration. But an even more pressing historical problem is raised by the fact that Hughes's image of the nation as a spinning wheel kept whole by the hub of a Crown very obviously echoes some of the most famous lines of twentieth-century poetry, the opening of Yeats's 'Second Coming':

> Turning and turning in the widening gyre
> The falcon cannot hear the falconer.
> Things fall apart: the centre cannot hold.[25]

Yeats's poem was written in the context of the Irish Civil War, which reminds us that, for Hughes's compatriots, the idea of the nation is not a simple one, and is certainly not transcendent. This echo raises the question, what nation is the Laureate the national poet of? The idea of British nationhood has been complicated and even threatened, throughout the period of Hughes's Laureateship and since, by three historical factors. First, there is devolution, which threatens to undermine the very integrity of the state known officially as the United Kingdom of Great Britain and Northern Ireland. At the same time it exposes the constructed nature of that state, which before 1921 was called the United Kingdom of Great Britain and Ireland, before 1801 Great Britain, and the largest portion of it at earlier periods Britain and England. Most of these names are still used, often interchangeably. The second factor is European union, which has proved traumatic for the United Kingdom from its outset. British identity has to an important degree always been defined *against* the Continent, and the political momentum of union, with the powerful material symbol of the Channel Tunnel, is a real threat. Thirdly, the ethnic character of British, and especially English, identity has changed dramatically as a result of Commonwealth immigration.

The institution of the Laureateship has seen the two Acts of Union, between England and Scotland in 1707, and between Britain and Ireland in 1801. Hughes's earlier poetry does not often refer explicitly to nationality, but when it does so most resonantly the nation in question is England. In the Laureate poems however he consistently calls it Britain. One of the most ambitious of them, 'A Masque for Three Voices' written for the Queen Mother's ninetieth birthday, maps the history of the twentieth century on to the Queen Mother's life. One of the voices explicitly ponders the question of 'British' national identity at various points in the century. At first this voice is deliberately naïve and confused:

> Being British is the mystery. Can you see
> That it is you or you or you or me?
> I do not understand how this can be.

What enables this voice to answer its question about national identity is the Second World War:

> Being British was no mystery when man's future
> Depended on one nation's soul – a creature
> No zoologist ever glimpsed in nature.

However, in the notes to his published collection of Laureate poems Hughes reveals that being British remains, as E.M. Forster might have said, if not a mystery then certainly a muddle. There he speaks of 'the Celtic common quarrel with the Norman-Anglo-Saxon dominance, which eventually pulled Southern Ireland out of the marriage-truce, still keeps Ulster uncontrollable, and yet has produced the energy of some of Britain's greatest personalities, as well as the steady flow of her cultural wealth' (62). So here what binds the 'soul' of the nation is a 'truce', implying that the normal relationship between its members is one of war. Yet in the same note Ireland is erroneously described as part of 'Great Britain'. It seems then that Hughes was a rather confused Unionist, and in this respect he was probably representative of his fellow-countrymen.

Hughes is in good company. Shakespeare was never Poet Laureate, but John of Gaunt's famous speech in *Richard II* would probably answer most people's idea of what a Laureate poem should be:

> This royal throne of kings, this sceptr'd isle
> This earth of majesty, this seat of Mars,
> This other Eden, demi-paradise;
> This fortress built by Nature for herself
> Against infection and the hand of war;
> This happy breed of men, this little world;
> This precious stone set in a silver sea,
> Which serves it in the office of a wall,
> Or as a moat defensive to a house,
> Against the envy of less happier lands;
> This blessed plot, this earth, this realm, this England.
> (II, i, 40–50)

When *Richard II* was written Scotland was a separate kingdom with its own monarch and a long history of conflict with England, but Shakespeare clearly imagines *England* as an island, as did Tennyson in his first and greatest Laureate poem, the 'Ode on the Death of the Duke of Wellington'.[26]

Hughes's Laureate poems have been dismissed by most commentators as ludicrous. Peter Reading, for example, suggested that 'the poet laureate has been superseded by the court jester'.[27] In my opinion these poems, at least the two long 'Masques' written for the sixtieth birthday of the Queen and the ninetieth birthday of the Queen Mother, represent a project as serious and ambitious as his great mythological works of the 1970s such as *Crow* and *Cave Birds*. In the Emory archive there are 112 pages of heavily corrected manuscript drafts of the 'Masque for Three Voices', suggesting the seriousness with which he approached the task.[28] If Hughes's Laureateship was a failure it was an heroic and, let us hope, a meaningful one.

In 'A Birthday Masque for Her Majesty Queen Elizabeth's Sixtieth Birthday', Hughes develops three images which enormously elaborate on the crown mandala of the Jubilee quatrain. The first of these is a crown of flowers, giving rise to the comment I have already quoted about natural time taking precedence over historical time. The third is an image of a birthday cake with sixty candles, representing thirty pairs of birds, which correspond to the protagonists of the Persian epic *Conference of the Birds*, in which the birds' quest for the Divinity ends with their finding it in themselves: so, according to Hughes, 'the birds of the British Isles ... find their true selves (their spiritual selves) by finding the spiritual unity of the Islands' (55). As one might expect, the evocation of the living world in these poems gives us many examples of Hughes at his best, such as the Gull who

> Flips over, a scream and a scarf in the sea-cliff's
> Wheel of wind. Or down there under the wind
> Wing-waltzes her shadow
> Over the green hollows.

The idea of 'the spiritual unity of the Islands' however brings us back to the confused Unionism that I have already discussed. But Hughes was not a narrow and petty nationalist. The middle section of the Masque is based on the image of the 'ring of the people', borrowed from the celebrated Sioux shaman Black Elk, for whom this image, according to Hughes, 'embraced, finally, all the different peoples of the earth, not only his own tribesmen' (*CP* 1217). Hughes's version of this ring is, inevitably, a Crown, but one that is forged 'out of laminated metals' representing 'the past and present invading groups that make up modern Britain'. The thought of the more recently arrived groups as 'invading' may be an uncomfortable one, but Hughes is merely putting them on a par with the Celts, Saxons, Danes and Normans. They are represented in the poem itself by these lines:

> And here in the boil the peacock oils
> From Siva's thumb.
> The Hoopoe's cry
> From the tower. The seed-flame
> From the eye-pupil's
> African violet.

This may not be the most resounding poetic affirmation of multiculturalism, but it confirms that Hughes's trope of the wheel is more accommodating than Larkin's one of constancy and mutability.

Hughes's second Laureate poem of major ambition, 'A Masque for Three Voices for the Ninetieth Birthday of Her Majesty Queen Elizabeth the Queen Mother', attempts to use the Queen Mother's life-span as a frame for narrating the history of the twentieth century and, within that, a developing consciousness of 'British' identity. I have already commented on the fact that, in his earlier poetry, Hughes used 'England' rather than 'Britain'. One of these earlier poems, 'Out', first collected in *Wodwo*, is particularly relevant to his Laureateship. It is one of his most revealing poems, though it is one of his less known. Its first section, 'The Dream Time', begins by evoking the continuing trauma suffered by his father years after the First World War and goes on to portray the effect of this on himself as a young child: 'I, small and four, / Lay on the carpet as his luckless double'.

The third section, 'Remembrance Day', takes as its central image the poppy. The wearing of the poppy on Remembrance Day is one of the signs of a patriotic British citizen. Hughes writes, 'It is years since I wore one', and the poem concludes:

> So goodbye to that bloody-minded flower.
>
> You dead bury your dead.
> Goodbye to the cenotaphs on my mother's breasts.
>
> Goodbye to all the remaindered charms of my father's survival.
>
> Let England close. Let the green sea-anemone close.

Remembrance Day is of course a *British* institution, but the nation on which Hughes turns with such passionate intensity at the end is 'England'. We should not be misled by the fact that the passion is one of renunciation and repudiation. Such outbursts are characteristic of many twentieth-century writers deeply involved with their sense of Englishness, from D.H. Lawrence to John Osborne. The word 'England' has a resonance in Hughes's writing that 'Britain' never has: compare the pond 'as deep as England' in 'Pike'. Above all that final line, beautiful, powerful and mysterious, has a memorableness that obliterates the laboured symbolism of the Laureate poems. The figuring of the nation as a 'green sea-anemone' conflates the sea-imagery of John of Gaunt's speech with the 'green and pleasant land' of Blake's 'Jerusalem'. At the same time there is something disturbing about this animal with a plant's name, a crossing of natural boundaries which is emphasised by the word 'green'. Sea-anemones are a pretty colour but they are amorphous and primitive and when they 'close' they devour their prey. This line brings to a pitch of metaphorical intensity a feeling of national identity that is burdensome and historically determined. And that national identity of course is 'English'. Hughes may later have adopted a more inclusive sense of nationality, but I am sceptical about the way, in the 'Masque for Three Voices', he retrospectively claims that it was a 'British' identity that was confirmed for him in the Second World War.

The first of the 'Three Voices' in Hughes's Masque takes us on a breakneck tour of the twentieth century in a jaunty ballad metre that is intended to be humorous but risks the very banality that it seems to be satirising. The second voice meditates quietly on the Scottish moorland landscape of the Queen Mother's birthplace, while the third, which is perhaps the most autobiographical, traces the development I have already described from puzzlement to affirmation of British national identity. It is in this section that Hughes invites comparison with one of the few great Laureate poems, Tennyson's 'Ode on the Death of the Duke of Wellington'. I will quote again, at greater length, the passage in which, for Hughes, the Second World War solves the mystery of being British.

> Deafened ears and seared eyes found how war
> Sanctifies King and Queen until they are
> One sacred certainty that all can share.
>
> Eyes in the round glow of the burning earth
> Saw what mattered, and how much it was worth,
> That King and Queen must bear, like a new birth.
>
> Being British was no mystery when man's future
> Depended on one nation's soul – a creature
> No zoologist ever glimpsed in nature.

And here are some lines from Tennyson's poem.

A people's voice! We are a people yet.
Though all men else their nobler dreams forget,
Confused by brainless mobs and lawless Powers;
Thank Him who isled us here, and roughly set
His Briton in blown seas and storming showers,
We have a voice, with which to pay the debt
Of boundless love and reverence and regret
To those great men who fought, and kept it ours.
And keep it ours, O God, from brute control;
O Statesmen, guard us, guard the eye, the soul
Of Europe, keep our noble England whole,
And save the one true seed of freedom sown
Betwixt a people and their ancient throne,
That sober freedom out of which there springs
Our loyal passion for our temperate kings.[29]

Of all the Laureate poems ever written, this is the only one that Hughes can have seriously considered as a model for poems such as the Masque for the Queen Mother. In the passages I have quoted there are obvious echoes: the preoccupation with the nation's wholeness, the collective image of the soul and the idea of Britain's responsibility to Europe or the world. Tennyson's poem commemorates the hero of the Battle of Waterloo, which took place when the poet was six years old. It was written thirty seven years after the battle, in 1852, when the Napoleonic dynasty had recently been restored in France, to considerable agitation in Britain. Hughes's poem celebrates a more symbolic heroine of the early years of World War Two, which began when the poet was nine years old. It was written fifty years later, when Britain did not face the kind of threat that Tennyson feared, but when many historical developments, most obviously devolution, European union and multiculturalism, threatened the concept of nationhood as a spiritual unity, which is the theme of Hughes's Laureateship. One can easily imagine Europhobes being roused by Tennysonian phrases such as 'lawless Powers' and 'brute control'.

But a comparison of these passages shows that Tennyson is much more in command of his idiom than Hughes. Despite the solemn rhetoric that dominates the poem his language is nuanced and appropriate to the constitutional reality of Victorian Britain. His greatest praise for the monarchy is that it is 'temperate'. It is Hughes who seems the more anachronistic, reaching with his words 'sanctified' and 'sacred' for a concept of monarchy that was killed off with Charles I in the seventeenth century. As *Shakespeare and the Goddess of Complete Being* makes clear, he thought this was a historical disaster. This also explains his liking for the 'Masque' form, which all but died with the divine king that it celebrated.

Tennyson's phrase 'a people's voice'[30] refers back in the poem to a collective voice honouring Wellington through the ages, but when it is repeated it clearly also refers to the poem itself. Valerie Pitt has commented that when he became Laureate he had the advantage of 'a body of common sentiment' but there was 'no available poetic convention in which to express it'. and that his 'Laureate verse is not ... the verse of a complacent poet working in an outworn convention, but the vigorous creation of new forms for a new national consciousness,'[31] and Matthew Campbell has described Tennyson's new form as a mixture of 'the elegiac, heroic and civic modes of Victorian culture'.[32] Such a mixture is well exemplified by my extract from the Wellington Ode.

By contrast Hughes's idiom seems personal and even eccentric. However, he has helped us to understand the perspective from which the poem – and indeed his whole Laureate project – was conceived in a 'note' that amounts to one of his most important and illuminating essays. It is certainly more illuminating than the poem, and was originally published, like the poem, in the *Weekend Telegraph*, as a response to a reader who found the poem 'incomprehensible'. The poem is written, he says

from the point of view of the son of an infantryman of the First World War. This qualification defines the outlook of an offspring of that war, one for whom it was virtually the Creation Story, and such a shattering, all-inclusive, grievous catastrophe that it was felt as a national *defeat*, though victory had somehow been pinned on to it as a consolation medal ... . Possibly, among the survivors and the children of the survivors of the industrial horde, that sense of paralysing defeat, the shock of massacre, was sealed by the years of the Great Depression. Yet that numbed mourning for the First World War was ominously enlivened, at a deep level, by a prophetic expectation of the Second ... . One who was born of the First World War, who spent his first nine years dreaming of the Second, having lived through the Second went on well into his thirties expecting the nuclear Third and the chaos after. Since these wars were felt to be defensive – against the threats of tyrants and their ideological police-state tyrannies, in which, perhaps, one might not last long – all social theories and even half-political ideas were instinctively screened ... . This would help to explain how the evangelism of ideological dialectics, of alternative, ideal points of view, which were so attractive to a generation born just before the First World War, and became so attractive again, in more sophisticated forms, to a generation born after 1940, sounded to those born between less like the freed intelligence than like the tyrant's whisper ... . In a way, it foreclosed our minds against the great European intellectual debate of the next forty years ... . The British outlook that I describe here, I realize, is now almost entirely limited to those born after the First World War but before the late thirties ... .

Hughes goes on to say that in a time of crisis every nation needs a resource such as 'a constitution, or a Holy Book, or a tradition of heroic leaders', which has to 'be there at the spiritual level as a sacred myth' which in the particular crisis in question 'turned out to be the Crown.' Hughes is writing a distinctive kind of history here, both analytic and interior, both material and mythologising. It helps us to see that his Laureate project is conceived from the point of view of the son of the First World War infantryman who wrote the poem 'Out' about his father being masticated by mud and cenotaphs on his mother's breasts, and who called on the 'green sea-anemone' to close. It also, incidentally, shows us an aspect of Hughes that is surprisingly akin to the 'Movement' writers with whom he is routinely contrasted, and who shared a similar aversion to 'ideological dialectics'. But by historicising his project, Hughes also subverts it: this discourse contradicts that of the note I quoted earlier, in which he claimed that the Crown 'does not belong to historical time'. We can also see that, unlike Tennyson, Hughes is not creating 'new forms for a new national consciousness' but constructing a personal myth, which may be shared by some, though I suspect not all, of his generation.

# 13
# Writing for Children

Hughes wrote more books for children than collections of original poetry for adults. He wrote for children throughout his career, beginning at least as early as the summer of 1956 when, on honeymoon with Plath in Spain, he wrote the first versions of *How the Whale Became and Other Stories*.[1] The role of this writing in his literary life, and its relationship to his writing for adults, is complex and various. There was certainly a financial incentive. He wrote to his brother in 1957 that 'we should all earn our fortunes on it',[2] and at least in the 1960s he not only published more books for children than for adults, but the children's books had longer print runs. But it was by no means a cynical venture. Writing for children, and the related activity of encouraging writing by children, were central to what might be called his ideological project. He wrote in his 1976 essay 'Myth and Education', 'Every new child is nature's chance to correct culture's error' (*WP* 149). Both the seriousness and the delight of writing for children are beautifully manifest in his many letters to his daughter Frieda, that range from practical advice on writing to hilarious narratives of his early meetings with the Queen.[3] Although a great deal of his writing for children is obviously much simpler than the work aimed at an adult audience, and much of the poetry is written in obvious and even McGonagall-esque rhythms, the boundary between the two bodies of work is far from clear. As we have already seen, *Season Songs* is a book written ambiguously 'within the hearing' of children, but included in *New Selected Poems* and *Collected Poems*. It is unquestionably an important stage in the development of Hughes's adult poetry. *Under the North Star* (1981) has a very similar stylistic profile but is, rather inconsistently, excluded from *Collected Poems*. *Moon-Bells* (1978) and *What is the Truth?* (1983) contain several poems published elsewhere for an adult audience; the last poem in *Moon-Bells*, 'Earth-Moon', which is also the title poem of a limited edition of children's poems, was originally the first-written of the 'Bedtime Story' narratives in *Crow*.[4] At a reading in Australia in 1976, perhaps provocatively, Hughes described *Crow* itself as a children's story.[5] In 1995 Faber published four volumes of *Collected Animal Poems*. These were marketed as children's books, but included all the animal poems that Hughes had published in his adult as well as children's volumes. As Lissa Paul has commented, this makes it 'possible to argue that a large proportion of the poems in the *New Selected* are children's poems.'[6] Hughes himself has said that when writing for children he was aware that children respond strongly to some poems that he has written 'at full stretch' for an adult audience.[7]

As well as numerous volumes of poetry for children, Hughes published prose fiction, plays, the poetry primer *Poetry in the Making* and, with Seamus Heaney, edited two major anthologies, *The Rattle Bag* and *The School Bag*. For many years, also, he acted as a judge for competitions, including the *Daily Mirror* Children's Literary Competition (see 'Concealed Energies', *WP* 27–32). Evidence of the work he put into this is preserved at the Emory archive in the many competition entries he had read, on the verso of which Hughes wrote drafts of *Crow*, *Gaudete* and other works.

Hughes's earliest published writing for children is very different in style from his adult work. His first book, *Meet My Folks!*, is written in rollicking, heavily accented verse interestingly reminiscent of Hughes's juvenilia derived from Kipling and Robert Service. He may have recalled that it was these rhythms that first drew him to poetry (*WP* 4–5). He has said that his imagined audience for these poems was aged about seven.[8] Predictably, many members of the imaginary family are closely associated with animals: the sister is a crow, one grandmother is an octopus; the grandfather traps owls, an uncle paints animals and the other grandmother knits clothes for them. More interesting, perhaps, is the uncle who invents useless things such as a toothless saw and a roll-uppable rubber ladder, and the father who is an Inspector of Holes. There is something double-edged about both these poems: they could be taken as humorous representations of masculine abstraction; or, conversely, as figures of imagination inhabiting worlds beyond the functional. The father's occupation, certainly, is more imaginatively appealing than the hole-counting in the Beatles' 'A Day in the Life': you never know 'what fearful thing is creeping from below' through a hole; a crack in the road might mean 'the world is a great egg, and we live on the shell.' For the American edition (1973) Hughes added a poem that, though written in the same reassuring metre as the rest of the volume, is imaginatively on a different level. 'My Own True Family' is a shamanic narrative in which the speaker creeps into an oak-wood and meets an old woman who reveals the trees as his true family. He is made to swear that every time he sees an oak tree felled he will plant two. The experience is a 'dream that altered me', and when he left the wood, 'My walk was the walk of a human child, but my heart was a tree.' As the title indicates, this poem, though literally fictional, is imaginatively true: it is a version of the narrative of visitation, usurpation or abduction that underlies Hughes's imaginative world and emerges in, for example, 'The Thought-Fox', the 'single adventure' of *Wodwo*, *Gaudete* and *Cave Birds*. It also exemplifies the more didactic element that enters into some of Hughes's later writing for children.

In the other collections of children's poetry that he published in the early 1960s, *The Earth-Owl and Other Moon-People* and *Nessie the Mannerless Monster*, Hughes mostly abandons the Kipling/Service metre for a form that is, as Keith Cushman has pointed out, reminiscent of William McGonagall. Cushman suggests that Hughes thought McGonagall's doggerel, 'which sounds inept to an adult, would be delightful to a young listener.'[9] *The Earth-Owl* is the more significant of these volumes. It was aimed at a much older readership than *Meet My Folks!*[10] and inaugurates a preoccupation with the moon as a site of imaginative transformation that was to recur in three more (admittedly overlapping) collections for children: *Earth-Moon* (1976), *Moon-Whales and Other Moon Poems* (1976) and *Moon-Bells and Other Poems* (1978). Some of the most effective poems directly invite the reader to re-imagine familiar objects. 'Moon-Tulips' are 'a kind of military band' presenting a 'deafening bouquet': the adult reader can't help being reminded here of Plath's 'Tulips' which filled the air 'like a loud noise'. In 'Moon-Nasturtiums' Hughes makes inspired use of silly rhyme to contrast the caterpillars that infest the flowers on earth with the 'noisy gorillas' that swarm on the giant nasturtiums of the moon. Hughes's 'Moon-Dog-Daisies' 'run in packs'. Perhaps the poem that puts his young readers most directly in touch with the preoccupations of his adult poetry is 'Moon-Horrors'. The horrors in question are numbers. Here is what the poem says about 'the fearful horde of number sevens' for example:

Whatever they touch, whether owl or elephant, poet or scientist,
The wretched victim wilts instantly to a puff of purple mist
And before he can utter a cry or say goodbye to kith and kin
Those thin-gut number sevens have sucked him ravenously in.

Hughes is obviously adapting for children the thought he was later to express for adults in 'Crow's Account of St George' in which a man who 'sees everything in the Universe / Is a track of numbers racing towards and answer' ends up killing his wife and children. In 'Moon-Horrors' the destructive numbers are compared to the tiger, shark and mosquito: whereas the tiger 'leaves certain signs ... nothing betrays the moon's hideous number nines.' This anticipates 'Tiger-Psalm' in which the tiger who 'Kills frugally, after close inspection of the map' is contrasted with machine-guns that 'go on chattering statistics': one of Hughes's more blatant metaphors of sacred nature against destructive civilisation. For many readers, the comparative lightness of touch of 'Moon-Horrors' might make it a more successful treatment of the theme than either of the adult poems.

*Nessie the Mannerless Monster* is a McGonagall-esque narrative about the refusal of people at large to believe that the Loch Ness Monster exists. Nessie is obviously a figure for the dimensions of reality ignored by modern culture and especially science. A 'world-famous scientist' responds to her by saying, 'You are impossible! ... all Plesiosaurs, say our books, have been dead a million year.' Here the motive to keep open children's imaginative receptiveness to the unknown verges on a philistine caricature of the scientist as a man who can't see what is in front of him.

Throughout his career Hughes was drawn to the creation tale. It is central to *Crow*, and he published three volumes of such tales for children between 1963 and 1995. He thought his first attempt in Spain was too abstract because he had no idea what age he was writing for; he worked on them again the following year in America, with children aged about six in mind.[11] The stories published in *How the Whale Became* (1963) have obvious precursors in Kipling's *Just So Stories*, but the differences are instructive. Kipling's tales, like Hughes's, are set in an early world when animals had not yet taken the form that they have now. But Kipling's world also has a precise geography in Africa, South America, the Far East, Australia and so on. Kipling's reader is told for example that the Elephant's Child 'went from Graham's Town to Kimberley, and from Kimberley to Khama's Country, and from Khama's country he went east by north ... till at last he came to the banks of the great grey-green, greasy Limpopo River.'[12] 'Khama's Country' is Botswana, or Bechuanaland as it was then known, Khama or Kgama III being a Tswana chief who had led a delegation to London in 1885, asking for Crown protection to be given to Bechuanaland. Kipling's reader is being educated in the geography and politics of Empire, as well as imaginatively entertained. The location of Hughes's tales is much less determinate.

Perhaps the most interesting difference, however, is that God plays no explicit part in Kipling's creation, but is a central figure in Hughes's. As in Kipling, Hughes's creatures get their final form as a result of some trick or accident, but they were initially made by God. The God of *How the Whale Became* is not the impotent 'cruel bastard' of *Crow*, but he is written about in a similarly light, irreverent tone. In 'How the Tortoise Became', for example, 'the weather was so hot God had to wear a sun hat and was calling endlessly for iced drinks' (*D* 36). God is a more endearing figure than he is in *Crow* and (unlike in 'A Childish Prank') has the power to breathe life into his creatures. But he is portrayed as a craftsman rather than an all-powerful Creator, who makes mistakes and often has to leave the final form of his creation to chance. Perhaps the strongest anticipation of *Crow* is in 'How the Bee Became', which is also one of the most haunting of the tales. The Bee is made by a demon out of ground gems moistened by the demon's own tears. God 'had no idea that such a creature [as the demon] existed' (*D* 48). This scenario is obviously reminiscent of God's nightmare in *Crow*: there is a force in the world outside of God's creation, of which God is ignorant. The demon cannot breathe life into the Bee but flatters God into doing so. Thus, while God is the most powerful figure in the world of these tales, he has weaknesses and can be tricked. The Trickster tale is an obvious model for a number of these stories, particularly 'Why the Owl Behaves as it Does' and 'How the Fox Came to be Where It Is'. Owl tricks the birds into believing that they will die if they open their eyes in the daytime, and Slylooking the fox tricks Foursquare the dog into taking the blame for his raids on the henhouse. As in many traditional Trickster tales, the tables are turned on the Trickster but he escapes in the end. An important and subtle part of the educative function of these stories, then, is introducing their readers to narrative modes, and associated ways of thinking about the world, from a different cultural context.

Hughes's writing for children was closely bound up with his work for the BBC. Of the fifty-two broadcasts made by him or featuring his work between 1960 and 1965, sixteen were for schools. The most important of these were the programmes for the 'Listening and Writing' series that eventually came to be collected as *Poetry in the Making* (1967).[13] His audience for these broadcasts was aged between ten and fourteen.

Two of the programmes have been frequently cited by Hughes's critics for the insight they provide into his own work. These are 'Capturing Animals', in which he describes writing poetry as a continuation of his early hunting expeditions with Gerald, and 'Learning to Think', in which he compares the creative process to fishing with a float: 'the whole purpose of this concentrated excitement, in this arena of apprehension and unforeseeable events, is to bring up some lovely solid thing like living metal from a world where nothing exists but those inevitable facts which raise life out of nothing and return it to nothing' (*PM* 61). As these examples suggest, Hughes is concerned with the development of the imagination, not with techniques of writing. He repeatedly emphasises that children should be encouraged to write rapidly, against the clock, in order to concentrate their attention on their subject, and that they should not think about the words: if you really imagine your subject, 'the words look after themselves, like magic' (*PM* 18). This is consistent with his frequent assertion that his best poems, such as 'Hawk Roosting' and the second part of 'An Otter', came to him fully formed; in 'Capturing Animals' he says that 'The Thought-Fox' was composed 'in a few minutes' (*PM* 19). Something of the importance that children's writing had for Hughes is suggested by his stated assumption that 'the latent talent for self-expression in any child is immeasurable' (*PM* 12). He acknowledges that this may be a false assumption, but insists that it is a fruitful one. His objective is not to turn children into professional writers: it can accurately be described as religious in character. It was appropriately in a programme in a series about religion that Hughes said, 'to live removed from this inner universe of experience is also to live removed from ourself, banished from ourself and our real life' (*PM* 123–4). The notion of a Fall that structures Hughes's view of history (Greek rationalism, monotheism, the Reformation, the scientific revolution) equally applies to growing up: as Hughes has said in an article about the quality of work in children's writing competitions, 'almost without exception these abilities ... are somehow extinguished in the late teens' (*WP* 31).

'Listening and Writing' also commissioned all but one of the plays that Hughes wrote for children. Most of these were broadcast between 1964 and 1968, but the most interesting, 'Orpheus', was the last, broadcast in 1971. Hughes wrote that after Sylvia Plath's death he had rejected the subject of Orpheus as 'too obvious an attempt to exploit my situation.'[14] This play is the exception, which may explain why it was not widely available in England until the posthumous publication of *Collected Plays for Children* (2001). At the beginning of the play Orpheus's music 'makes the trees dance'. It is represented as 'pop' music on a guitar. When Eurydice dies his music becomes discordant. When he visits the Underworld he sees that Pluto's wife, Persephone, has the face of a closed flower. Pluto never sees her open face because he only has her in the winter. When Orpheus asks Pluto to return Eurydice the god replies that this is impossible, and that her death was the price of his music. However, when Orpheus offers to open Persephone's flower-face, with music that is now 'solemn Handel, Bach, Vivaldi or earlier', Pluto promises 'Whatever you wish' – a promise, however, that he is unable to honour. Orpheus can only have Eurydice's soul. When, returning, he looks back, he does not see her but hears her voice, which stays with him and inspires his new music, which is

> not the music of dancing
> But of growing and withering,
> Of the root in the earth and the leaf in the light,
> The music of birth and of death.
> And the stones did not dance. But the stones listened.
> (*CPC* 105)

The most pivotal event of the myth, Orpheus's tragic backward look, is in effect removed. In Hughes's version, when Orpheus looks back he only confirms what was already the case, that Eurydice is not really there. He does not have to endure the repeated loss. The lost wife's survival in the form of a voice foreshadows the powerful presence of Plath's voice in *Birthday Letters*, especially in 'Visit', where

> I look up – as if to meet your voice
> With all its urgent future
> That has burst in on me.

The relevance of the changes in Orpheus's music to Hughes's own writing career, or at least his perception of it, is obvious: especially the change from the 'undisturbed relationship with the outside natural world'[15] in his early poetry to the more tragic and often nightmarish vision of his work after Plath's death.

Hughes's most celebrated and highly praised book for children is probably *The Iron Man* (1968, *The Iron Giant* in America). This is also the book in which Hughes's serious purpose in writing for children first becomes overt. It is the story of the mysterious arrival of an iron giant in a rural community. The giant eats metal, and the initial response of the community is to destroy him. They catch him in an enormous elephant trap and bury him. He re-emerges, however, and the hero of the story, a boy called Hogarth, befriends him, and arranges for him to be fed in a scrapyard. In the second half of the story the theme of the first half is repeated on a global scale. The earth is threatened by a 'space-bat-angel-dragon'.

Again humanity attempts to destroy the threat, and again it fails. Hogarth asks the Iron Man to help, which he does by challenging the dragon to a trial by extreme heat. The Iron Man wins, and the dragon returns to outer space where it makes the music of the spheres. Hughes discusses the story at length in the first version of his essay 'Myth and Education', which is very different from the version published in *Winter Pollen*. He describes it as a conscious attempt to counter the psychological influence of stories such as St George and the Dragon, in which the monster is destroyed or suppressed. He also emphasises the story's contemporary relevance to, as he puts it, 'the collision with the American technological world and, beyond that, the opening up, by physics and so on, of a universe which was completely uninhabited except by atoms and the energy of atoms.'[16] In what might be called a *faux*-hypothetical manner he says,

> Now if I were some poet of the Heroic Age I could claim for my story that it would, first of all, connect you back to your struggle with ordinary existence and society and outer life, and that beyond that, it would connect you with the deepest and most alien seeming powers in your own mind, which are the correspondents of the outermost demon powers of space ... . I could then claim that my story would cure schizophrenia ... .One doesn't make these claims, of course.[17]

Hughes could rightly claim, however, that he had created an original myth that is also distinctively contemporary. As he put it in a discussion after a reading of 'Myth and Education', 'you only invent the myths you need.'[18]

*The Iron Man* concludes the first phase of Hughes's children's writing, in which the work marketed for children is clearly distinct in style and audience from his books for adults. It was, he has said, the last of the stories he invented for his own children.[19] Between the mid-1970s and mid-1980s he published a series of books in which the distinction is much less clear. The first of these, *Season Songs*, I have already discussed in Chapter 9: my separate treatment of this volume, alongside the adult book *Moortown*, on the grounds that it is included in *Collected Poems*, is a sign of the ambiguity. As I argued in Chapter 9, while the uninhibited anthropomorphism and light-verse technique of some of the poems implies a young audience, there are some pieces, notably 'Swifts' and 'A Cranefly in September', that are among Hughes's finest by any standard.

*Under the North Star* (1981) is a very similar book to *Season Songs*. In this case the British edition is illustrated by Leonard Baskin and has, like the American edition of *Season Songs*, the appearance of a children's book. The jacket describes it as having 'originated as an entertainment for a lively and precocious little girl', but the same jacket advertises *Cave Birds* and *Remains of Elmet*, and none of Hughes's books for children. There are no poems as outstanding as 'Swifts' and 'A Cranefly in September', but most of them read as fully adult nature poems, and the harsh context of the book (the Arctic) makes if anything fewer concessions than the self-confessedly 'upbeat'[20] *Season Songs*: 'Only the Iron Wolf shall know // The iron of his fate' ('Wolf').

*What is the Truth?* (1984) has the subtitle 'A farmyard fable for the young'; so it is, ostensibly, a straightforward children's book. When writing it Hughes had in mind a definite audience: the nine to ten year old children from inner cities who came to the Farm for City Children run by his friends Clare and Michael Morpurgo.[21] It has a narrative frame in which God's son wants to visit mankind on earth, and God tells him that the visit will show that mankind knows everything but the truth. The spirits of various village folk meet with God and his son while their bodies are asleep. The main substance of the book is a series of poems about animals, spoken by these characters. The poems are untitled, and the overall result is a loose, relaxed effect. The boundaries of individual poems are blurred, and several characters voice poems about the same creature. The variety of voices reinforces the variety of style which is a feature of all the 'children's' books of this period. Although relaxed and, mostly, less demanding than much of Hughes's verse, it appeals as much to an adult as to a young reader. One of the poems, a long narrative about the shooting of a fox, has been published separately with the title 'A Solstice', and is a completely adult account of Hughes's ambivalent feelings about hunting.[22] The narrative frame closes with God's announcement that all the animals are collectively himself and the Truth, and his son's decision to stay on earth: this gives the volume a didactic quality, despite the relaxed and varied character of the body of the poems.

In the third and final stage of Hughes's career as a writer for children, his children's books are once again clearly distinct from those for adults, and repeat, with variations, the themes and styles of the first period. There are two more volumes of creation tales, *Tales of the Early World* (1988) and *The Dreamfighter and Other Creation Tales* (1995). These volumes are collected together with *How the Whale Became and Other Stories* in a posthumous volume, also titled *The Dreamfighter and Other Creation Tales*. In this volume the three collections are said to be suitable for children of progressively higher ages, from five upwards to ten upwards. The later volumes resemble *Crow* more strongly than *How the Whale Became* does – for example, God's mother features in a number of them, and in the story 'The Dreamfighter' God has nightmares – and are often more complex. There is a more overt element of religious satire, for example:

> 'It's no good shouting at me,' said Leftovers mildly. You made me. I am what I am. And that's all there is to it.'
> 'I am what I am!' screeched God. He sounded like an almighty Elephant. ('Leftovers', *D* 172)

('I am that I am' is God's reply to Moses when asked his name, Exodus 3.14.) Man and Woman feature more strongly than in the early stories, and the treatment of their relationship accounts for some of the relative maturity and complexity: for example, 'The Making of Parrot', in which Man neglects Woman because he is entranced by the song of the parrot.

If *Tales of the Early World* and *The Dreamfighter* revisit and extend the mode of *How the Whale Became*, Hughes's poems for children in the last fifteen years of his life are also unambiguously addressed to a young audience. He published two little volumes, *The Cat and the Cuckoo* (1987) and *The Mermaid's Purse* (1993), with the small Devon Sunstone Press, illustrated by his friend R.J. (Reg) Lloyd, who had also illustrated *What is the Truth?* These books were later reprinted by Faber with different illustrations. These are simple lyrical nature poems, without the grotesqueness and imaginative extravagance of Hughes's early poetry for children, but with regular rhyme and obvious metre, and a consistently cheerful, humorous tone. With the single exception of 'Gulls', rescued from the early limited edition *Recklings*, there is no ambiguity about the audience of these poems. Like *What is the Truth?*, these books were written for the inner city children who visited the Morpurgos' farm, in this case aged four and five. Hughes has said that he learned a lot about verse from writing them – an exemplary comment from an internationally renowned poet in his sixties.[23]

*Ffangs the Vampire Bat and the Kiss of Truth* (1986) is perhaps the strangest of Hughes's books for children. It begins in rough verse and drifts into prose. The role of main protagonist changes from a cockerel to the vampire to a vampire-hunter. Although unambiguously addressed to children, it is a chaotic riot of narrative incident more reminiscent of the unpublished *Crow* saga than of anything else Hughes wrote. It is as if Hughes were literally following his advice about writing a novel in

*Poetry in the Making*: 'let it grow, like a freakish giant marrow that will not stop' (*PM* 90). It ends with Ffangs in pursuit of his vanished sister, and a promise that his adventures 'will be continued in the next book' (*FVB* 96), which never appeared. Hughes has said that he writes more unguardedly for children than for adults, and that a friend had asked how he could expose himself as he had in *Ffangs*.[24] Perhaps, as Andy Armitage has suggested,[25] the friend had in mind Ffangs's plaintive, 'I don't want to be a vampire. / I want to get back to the world and become human' (*FVB* 30), as if in riposte to Hughes's fate of being cast as the vampire who 'drunk my blood for a year./ Seven years, if you want to know' in Plath's 'Daddy'.

The most important and interesting of Hughes's later writings for children is undoubtedly *The Iron Woman*, a sequel to *The Iron Man*. While the earlier story was a psychological fable about acceptance of and negotiation with technology and modern physics, the sequel is a much more urgent, and didactic, ecological intervention. Despite being made of iron, the Woman is perhaps Hughes's most direct representation of the Goddess. Like the baboon-beauty woman in *Gaudete* she emerges from mud. Hughes has said that the story began with his thinking, 'how does nature feel about being destroyed? Presumably it's enraged, and the obvious response is an aggressive one, to remove the destroyer.'[26] The most memorable thing about her, more even than her size, is a scream, or 'horrible mass of screams, yells, wails, groans' expressing the suffering of the river-creatures from pollution. The scream is contagious, and whenever someone who has heard it touches another person, that person hears the scream. As a lifelong fisherman, for Hughes the most immediately pressing instance of environmental damage was the pollution of rivers. Of all political issues, this is the one to which he devoted most practical energy. It incidentally gives his story the advantage that it can be dramatised as a local issue: the Iron Woman is determined to destroy the local waste-disposal factory in which the heroine, Lucy's father works. Another motivation for Hughes to write the story was the letters sent to him by girls who had read *The Iron Man* and wanted a female equivalent. His response was to 'put together a little girl, and all the elemental power of a woman – her authentic, creative power.'[27] In this can be seen a subtle and important difference from *The Iron Man*. The Man is memorable as an image, especially in the unforgettable first chapter in which, having fallen from a cliff and smashed to pieces, he reassembles himself bit by bit. But the Woman is a conscious force. The Man presents a problem to the human community by existing; the Woman is the answer to the problem created by the human community. It is a destructive answer, that needs to be controlled by human intelligence; but her intervention saves the world from human greed and folly. In no other work that he wrote for children is his conception of this audience as 'nature's chance to correct culture's error' so literally pertinent.

# 14
## Hughes as Translator

Translation occupied Hughes at periods throughout his professional writing life, and became an exceptionally important activity in his last four years, when he wrote, published and had performed six translated works. He 'translated' from Latin, Greek, French, Spanish, German, Hungarian, Hebrew, Russian and Italian. I put the word in quotation marks here to indicate that Hughes's relationship to the original texts that he rendered varied considerably. He was not a polyglot. He was fluent enough in French to converse and correspond in this language, and so I assume that in translating Racine's *Phèdre* he worked directly from the original. In working with Latin texts (two of his most important translations, *Seneca's Oedipus* and *Tales from Ovid*) he used the Loeb editions with the original and a literal translation on facing pages. Here he evidently read the original but worked primarily with the literal version. In the case of János Pilinszy's Hungarian he worked with literal translations by another Hungarian poet, and adopted a similar method with Yehuda Amichai's Hebrew, collaborating with the poet himself and Assia Wevill.

Hughes's translations also vary in their degrees of faithfulness to the original text. With contemporary texts, or at least contemporary poetry, he adhered to a principle of literalness. An important context of his early involvement in translation was the magazine *Modern Poetry in Translation*, which he founded with his Cambridge friend Daniel Weissbort in 1966. Hughes later reflected on the background of the *Zeitgest* of the 1960s, a decade in which he said the modern age 'came to consciousness of itself', especially of what Hitler and Stalin had 'made' or 'revealed' of humanity.[1] Poets whose work bore witness to the Holocaust and/or Stalinist terror were especially important to him – hence the influence of Eastern European poets on *Crow*, discussed in

Chapter 6. To have adapted or taken liberties with the work of poets who had this kind of importance to Hughes would have violated the spirit of his interest in them, and he 'settled for literalness as a first principle' (*WP* 235). Where Hughes is working from a literal translation of a poem in a language he does not know, this principle seems paradoxical – what can Hughes contribute? I shall be discussing this question in the case of the translations of Pilinszky. When translating classical texts, however, Hughes wrote 'versions' that can be counted as important parts of his original *oeuvre*. He freely adapted Seneca's *Oedipus*, Ovid's *Metamorphoses* and Euripides's *Alcestis*; with the *Oresteia* he was more conservative, perhaps because of this text's exceptional canonical status.

Hughes's first professional translation was a version of an extract from the *Odyssey*, broadcast on the Third Programme in November 1960. Later in the 1960s he engaged in projects that launched the two major strands of his career in translation: modern poetry and classical drama. He worked with Assia Wevill on Yehuda Amichai's *Selected Poems*,[2] published in 1968, and was commissioned by the National Theatre to write a version of Seneca's *Oedipus* for Peter Brook, produced in the same year. In 1976 Hughes and János Csokits published the *Selected Poems* of Pilinszky, the outcome of nearly ten years of collaboration, and in 1977 Amichai's *Amen* was a collaboration with Amichai himself. It was, however, in his last years that Hughes was most prolific as a translator, especially for the theatre: Wedekind's *Spring Awakening* (1995), Lorca's *Blood Wedding* (1996), *Tales from Ovid* (1997), Racine's *Phèdre* (1998), Aeschylus's *Oresteia* (1999) and Euripides's *Alcestis* (published 1999, performed 2000). He wistfully wondered what effect this was having on 'my own wings',[3] but at least *Tales from Ovid* and *Alcestis* contributed with *Birthday Letters* to a remarkable late resurgence in Hughes's achievement and reputation. Possibly the last poem he wrote was a version of Pushkin's 'The Prophet', a collaboration with Daniel Weissbort and Valentina Polukhina. In this chapter I shall concentrate primarily on translations which I can compare with texts that Hughes is known to have worked from – Seneca, Pilinszky, Racine and Ovid – but I shall also comment on his *Oresteia* and *Alcestis*, because of the importance that has been attributed to these late additions to his *oeuvre*.

In 1967 Hughes was approached by Kenneth Tynan, then literary manager of the National Theatre, to revise a translation of Seneca's *Oedipus* that the National had commissioned from David Anthony Turner, a BBC radio producer. The play was to be directed by Peter Brook. Initially Hughes was reluctant, partly because he had formed an aversion to Brook from a television appearance. He thought Brook epitomised everything he disliked about the metropolitan intellectual. When Brook phoned him, however, Hughes warmed to his 'hesitant, sensitive, tentatively reaching, sincere' manner.[4] At first he tried to work with the Turner version, but he found it too agitated and melodramatic, and eventually it was agreed that he would write a completely fresh version, working from the original in the Loeb edition with a translation by Frank Justus Miller. The published text has introductions in which Hughes acknowledges Turner's inspiration and thanks him for his co-operation with the change of plan, while Turner renounces any credit for the 'magic' of Hughes's text (*SO* 7–9). This impression of friendly co-operation is, however, far from accurate. Hughes wrote an account of his work on this project which is the longest piece of personal writing in the Emory archive, and a uniquely detailed record of his professional life (it includes vivid and fascinating portraits of Brook, Tynan, John Gielgud and Irene Worth). Turner was humiliated by the abandonment of his text and, according to Hughes, he took legal action against the National. Hughes, in turn, got into dispute with the National over the billing of the play. He had gone along with the phrasing, 'adapted by Ted Hughes from a translation by David Turner' to spare Turner's feelings, but became anxious that his rights in his work might be prejudiced.[5]

Hughes greatly admired Peter Brook and went on to work with him on *Orghast* and *The Conference of the Birds* before withdrawing because he felt the collaboration was distracting from the work he wanted to do. Hughes responded well to Brook's criticism of his drafts of the play, and was impressed by his handling of the actors and his approach to the text: 'we must search into every phrase for its ultimate moral and religious meaning.' He liked the way Brook got the actors to 'drop their tricks' by making them speak the lines very fast. Since one of the actors was Sir John Gielgud, the 'tricks' in question were the most polished and celebrated acting technique of the age.

*Oedipus* was a landmark for Hughes, both as his first large scale, professional, commissioned work of translation, and as his first successful work for the theatre. He commented himself on 'the literary writing in a vacuum of all my previous attempts at drama', but working on a translation for the theatre enabled him to concentrate on style alone, and produce a theatrically effective text.[6] The significance of Hughes's achievement was perhaps not appreciated at the time, because *Oedipus* was received primarily as a work by Brook, and in reviews Hughes was not mentioned at all or said merely (fulfilling his fears) to have adapted Turner's translation. An exception was Ronald Bryden in the *Observer*, who praised Hughes for the best Oedipus translation since Yeats.[7]

The choice of Seneca rather than Sophocles' more celebrated play was predetermined by the National, but Hughes embraced it enthusiastically. He wrote that the 'Greek world saturates Sophocles too thoroughly' and that the world of his play is 'fully civilized', whereas Seneca's people are 'Greek only by convention ... more primitive than aboriginals ... spider people, scuttling among hot stones' (*SO* 8). Sophocles's Oedipus is much more statesmanlike and rational than Seneca's. When he learns that Thebes has been struck by plague because Laius' murder remains unpunished, he tells the citizens that if the guilty one confesses he will suffer only banishment; by contrast, Seneca's Oedipus reacts to the news with an elaborate curse, that the murderer should find himself guilty of the crime Oedipus himself is trying to avoid – thus cursing himself. There is much more emphasis in Seneca than in Sophocles on the gruesome aspects of the plague and of prophecy by examining entrails. Sophocles's Jocasta hangs herself whereas Seneca's stabs herself in the womb. In Sophocles there is a tender scene of farewell between Oedipus and his children, absent from Seneca.

Hughes was undoubtedly attracted by the emphasis on physical suffering in the Seneca, which drew commentators to see parallels with contemporary events in Vietnam, as well as with Artaud.[8] He is likely to have been even more enthusiastic about Seneca's much more overtly shamanistic rendering of the prophet Tiresias, whose visit to the world of the dead, to speak with the ghost of Laius, is narrated at great length. In these lines, Hughes is only slightly embroidering the shamanistic atmosphere of the original:

now the priest begins to call up the things of the underworld      he calls
to death itself over and over working himself into an ecstasy      face
contorted foam thickening around his mouth      he argues with the
dead      he cajoles and threatens      screams mutters sings whispers (*SO* 33)

Brook shared Hughes's enthusiasm for shamanism. In developing the experimental vocal techniques that were such a feature of the performance, the company listened to chants by African shamans, Tibetan monks and South American Indians.[9]

Hughes's text follows Seneca's in outline and in much detail, but there are numerous omissions, usually passages of stale reflection and ponderous epic simile, and some additions. The most significant additions are to the part of Jocasta, which is expanded from twenty-two to 146 lines.

This might initially have been motivated by the need to create a role big enough for Irene Worth, but Hughes is likely in any case to have wanted a strong female presence in a play about the consequence of the masculine intelligence destroying the (female) sphinx. These additions emphasise Jocasta's maternal role. In her first important speech (*SO* 16–18) she recalls bearing sons: the mother's awareness of the pain, fear and 'hard, sharp metal' that await her sons, but also a vitalistic celebration of the new-born child as 'the warrant of the gods ... their latest attempt/ to walk on the earth and to live'. In a later added speech Jocasta says that Laius, the father whom Oedipus unknowingly killed, deserved his fate because he took her son away. In Seneca Jocasta shares the guilt of exposing the baby Oedipus: in Hughes's version she is absolved. However, the greater horror that Seneca bestows on Jocasta's suicide, compared to Sophocles, is further intensified by Hughes, in whose version her final words direct the sword 'where everything began the son the husband/ up here' (*SO* 54), acted out in the production by Irene Worth as 'an act of deadly intercourse with the sword.'[10]

Because of the economy of Latin syntax, Seneca's original text is much shorter than Miller's literal translation. Hughes also compresses the text, not by condensing syntax but by doing away with complex sentence structure and writing in a series of ejaculatory phrases, punctuated (in the form of spaces in the text) on the basis of speech rhythm rather than grammar. For example:

Seneca: Nescisse cupies nosse quae nimium expetis.
Miller: Thou wilt long not to have known what thou desirest o'ermuch
    to know.[11]
Hughes: you command me to speak   you will pray you were deaf (*SO* 32)

Whether he did this consciously in imitation of the conciseness of Seneca's Latin we cannot know. There is little specific evidence of his responding directly to the Latin, though one case in which he may have done so is the following:

Seneca: rigat ora foedus imber et lacerum caput
    largum revulsis sanguinem venis *vomit*
Miller: A hideous shower drenches his face and his mangled brow *spouts*
    streams of blood from his bursting veins[12]
Hughes: the blood came *spewing* out over his face and beard
    in a moment he was drenched (*SO* 52)

Hughes wrote *Oedipus* while he was working on *Crow*, and it is recognisably the product of that phase of his career. His comments on it as being 'crude'[13] and (greatly exaggerating) 'with a vocabulary of about 250 words'[14] chime with his notion of the 'super-simple' and 'super-ugly' style of *Crow*. The vigour, simplicity, emotional power and dramatic eloquence shorn of magniloquence, that made this text so successful in the theatre, are qualities that had become habitual to Hughes through the writing of *Crow*. But it was Brook's avant-garde theatricality that reviewers found memorable: the drumming and glaring lights of the opening; the chorus scattered among the audience, and at different levels, so that one speech seemed literally to descend through the theatre; the chanting, screeching and wailing counterpointed with 'dispassionate monotone';[15] Colin Blakely saying Creon's lines while whirling like a dervish; the adoption by the actors of mask-like expressions. In imitation of the Greek satyr play following the tragedy, the performance ended with the cast dancing round an enormous golden phallus. Hughes had written texts for this epilogue, one of which he published as 'Song for a Phallus' in *Crow*[16] These were not used, and instead a Dixieland band played 'Yes, we have no bananas.' The epilogue wasn't well received by critics, and Laurence Olivier hated it so much that an argument about it with Brook ended with Olivier breaking a mirror.[17] In general, reviewers (with the exception of Charles Marowitz, an erstwhile collaborator of Brook's, who described him as 'the purveyor of avant-garde clichés to the mass audience'[18]) judged the production to be a theatrical success, but most thought it failed in an aspiration that was dear to Hughes as well as to Brook. Brook aimed for an effect of 'true contact with a sacred invisibility' through theatre, but even his Associate Director Geoffrey Reeves, who worked on *Oedipus*, thought the project 'only seemed to underline the impossibility of making such contact now'.[19]

The collaboration with Brook led to *Orghast* but, though Hughes told his brother that Brook had invited him to work on a cycle of plays,[20] he surprisingly did not write again for the English stage, or translate for the theatre, until a quarter of a century later. His next translation project was his long collaboration with the Hungarian émigré poet János Csokits on the *Selected Poems* of János Pilinszky. Hughes's role as the adapter of literal versions by Csokits was, as I have said, paradoxical, especially since he was working in the aura of Theodor Adorno's celebrated assertion that 'to write poetry after Auschwitz is barbaric.'[21] In his introduction, Hughes quotes Pilinszky as saying, 'I would like to write as if I had remained silent.' He compares this with the silence of Indian saints, of Socrates and Christ before their accusers, and even of Christ on the cross: 'what speech is adequate for this moment, when the iron nails remain fixed in the wounds, with an eternal iron fixity, and neither hands nor feet can move?' There is an echo here of a recurring figure in Hughes's poetry – in his Prometheus poems, for example, which contemplate their protagonist fixed on his crag, or 'Crow and the Sea', when Crow tries to walk away from the sea '[a]s a crucified man cannot move'. These are figures of confrontation with necessity, and of resolutely refraining from everything that is not necessity. Hughes speaks, echoing Adorno, of the 'silence of artistic integrity "after Auschwitz" ' (*WP* 232). The 'artistic integrity' of the secondary poet, drafted in to give the translations some literary quality, is obviously an issue for Hughes. Daniel Weissbort has written that Hughes would have preferred to leave Csokits's versions as they were, but was under pressure from editors to contribute – nevertheless, Weissbort thinks, Hughes's versions are an improvement on Csokits's.[22]

In fact, Csokits presented his versions to Hughes in an open, dialogic form. They were usually accompanied by extensive commentaries in which Csokits offered several alternatives, or gave the literal translation but offered something else because he thought it sounded better. Although Csokits's English is excellent there are sometimes false notes in his translations which betray the fact that they are not the work of a native speaker. Hughes, in other words, is not breaking open a sealed artefact to 'improve' it but participating in what is conceived from the outset as a dialogic process.

I want to identify three kinds of contribution that Hughes makes. The first, in which his own poetic skill is most obviously a factor, is where he finds a word that more vividly or powerfully conveys the meaning gestured at in Csokits's version. In his version of 'Fish in the Net', for example, Csokits wrote, 'A tremor passes through our hearts' and commented, 'this is a rather literal version, but perhaps our hearts *tremble* – or *shudder* etc would be better. However it is just *one* quiver, not a continuous movement.'[23] Hughes's version, 'Our hearts convulse', keeps the notion of a single movement, but is much stronger than any of the words suggested by Csokits. For his version of 'By the Time You Come', Csokits wrote a long note on a phrase that he translated as 'featureless man of basket'. He said that the Hungarian word can mean 'featureless' or 'inarticulate'. If the latter, the second word has to mean 'basket-seller', but Csokits had never heard it used in this sense.[24] Hughes's solution is brilliant: 'lumpish basketwork dummy' combines connotations of 'featureless' and 'inarticulate', keeps the literal meaning of the second word, and is much more vigorous and idiomatic than Csokits's phrase. In 'Exhortation' Csokits used the word 'confusion' but was dissatisfied with it: 'The Hungarian word emphasises the nervous movements, or/and the chaotic situation which is the result of it.'[25] Hughes provides the solution with the single word, 'hysteria'.

At times Csokits's versions strike the native ear as stalely literary. Hughes invariably comes up with a fresher alternative in these cases: 'to no purpose' for 'in vain' and 'fierier' for 'more ardent' in 'Complaint'; 'wandering' for 'roving' and 'washing' for 'purling' in 'Impromptu'.[26]

However, the most interesting interventions, and the ones that do most to validate Hughes's claim that 'literalness' is 'the first principle', are the cases in which he reinstates a literal translation that Csokits himself has rejected. In 'Complaint' Csokits says the original means 'mud' but he prefers 'ooze'; Hughes's version reinstates 'mud'. In 'By the Time You Come', Pilinszky uses a word that, according to Csokits, literally means 'orphanage':

> In my orphanage, unburied,
> As on a wintry dump
> Picking among the rubbish
> I keep finding scraps of my life.

Csokits prefers 'forlornness' or 'forsakenness' to the literal rendering. Here, in restoring 'orphanage', Hughes simultaneously reasserts the principle of literalness, rejects feebly literary language, and preserves the metaphorical character of the original.

In the poems for which I have been able to see Csokits's versions and notes, there are several other examples of these kinds of intervention by Hughes. They are fascinating documents in a number of ways. Hughes is genuinely subservient to Pilinszky: there are few occasions on which he can be detected imposing a 'Hughesian' note. At the same time, his contributions undoubtedly enhance the texts as English versions and, in those cases where he restores the literal reading, there is a meeting of minds between the two poets who did not speak each other's language (they corresponded in French), facilitated and mediated by Csokits. Even so, there are far more of Csokits's words than of Hughes's in the published text.

The following year, Yehuda Amichai's *Amen* was a collaborative translation by the author and Hughes, and in 1989 Hughes and Csokits brought out *The Desert of Love*, an expanded edition of the Pilinszky *Selected Poems*. However, after 1977 translation receded from the foreground of Hughes's literary life, until the last few years, when he did more work of this kind than in the whole of his previous career.

His return to translation began with an invitation to contribute to a Faber anthology of versions of Ovid, edited by Michael Hofmann and James Lasdun. Hughes greatly enjoyed this venture, and ended up contributing translations of four extracts – 'Creation; Four Ages; Flood; Lycaon', 'Bacchus and Pentheus', 'Salmacis and Hermaphroditus' and 'Venus and Adonis' – to the volume, *After Ovid*, that appeared in 1994. As a result of this publication, Farrar Straus offered Hughes a big advance to do a whole book of Ovid translations. He wrote to Leonard Baskin in terms suggesting that he was primarily motivated by the money and the ease with which he could do it, estimating that he could write two tales a week. Later, when he had committed himself to the project, he told the same correspondent that it was 'amusing' but wondered if it was 'useful – to *me*?'[27] As far as Hughes's reputation was concerned, it was more than useful: even before the final coup of *Birthday Letters*, *Tales from Ovid* restored his reputation, which had declined at least since *River*, to its highest for more than a decade. Possibly not since *Lupercal* had a book of Hughes's received such overwhelmingly favourable reviews, and *Tales from Ovid*, like *Birthday Letters* the year following, was Whitbread Book of the Year.

For his work on *Tales from Ovid* Hughes referred to at least three existing translations: the Penguin Classics version by Mary Innes, the Loeb edition with translation by Frank Justus Miller, and the Elizabethan verse translation by Arthur Golding. The Innes and Miller translations are both fairly literal, and there are echoes of both in Hughes's text. The Loeb (as in the case of Seneca) has the original and translation on facing pages; Hughes certainly looked at the original, though I have found no clear evidence of his responding directly to it. He probably read the Golding less as a guide to the meaning, than because it is in verse: in particular, he may have been drawn to Golding's 'fourteeners' because they approximate in length to Ovid's hexameters. However, Hughes himself makes no attempt to imitate Ovid's verse form: this contrasts with his earliest known translation, 'The Storm' from *The Odyssey*, where there is a clear attempt to echo the cadence of the classical hexameter. Hughes also abandons the structure of the *Metamorphoses*, which is not a collection of discrete poems but a fifteen-book quasi-epic, a continuous narrative with linking passages and multiple narrators. He translates only a small proportion of the stories in the *Metamorphoses*, and changes their order.

Hughes wrote an Introduction to the volume, in which two features stand out. One is his emphasis on passion – 'human passion *in extremis*' which becomes 'an experience of the supernatural' and in which 'the all-too-human victim stumbles out into the mythic arena and is transformed' (*TO* x). This chimes with an important motif in *Birthday Letters*, on which Hughes had almost certainly been working immediately before *Tales from Ovid*. For example, in 'The Shot', Hughes writes about falling in love with Plath, and being drawn into the 'mythic arena' of her obsession with her dead father:

> For a long time
> Vague as mist, I did not even know
> I had been hit,
> Or that you had gone clean through me—
> To bury yourself at last in the heart of the god.

As we shall see, however, it is not only erotic passion that sparks this transformation.

The second important theme in the Introduction is Hughes's comment on parallels between the age of Ovid and his own. Ovid was writing at a 'unique moment in history' when the 'Roman pantheon had fallen in on men's heads' and the 'mythic plane, so to speak, had been defrocked'. The age was striving for a new form of 'spiritual transcendence', which was about to appear as the crucifix. The poems register 'the psychological gulf that opens at the end of an era', something that 'we can certainly recognise' (*TO* x–xi). Hughes's whole *oeuvre* can be seen as a struggle to articulate spiritual experience in a vacuum of religious forms. A key feature of *Tales from Ovid* is that, despite the 'obsolete' and often corrupt nature of the religious 'paraphernalia', Hughes several times enhances the religious sentiment of the text.

Obvious examples of erotic passion dragging the all-too-human person into the mythic arena are the terrible passion of Tereus for Philomela, which transforms him into the hoopoe and her into the nightingale; Myrrha, whose incestuous passion for her father results in her wishing to be removed 'From life and from death / Into some nerveless limbo', and is changed into the myrrh tree and gives birth to Adonis; and Salmacis, whose fulfilled passion for Hermaphroditus turns the lovers into a single intersexual body. In most cases, as in the first two cited here, the passion is a destructive one, but not always: notably, Hughes omits from the story of Salmacis and Hermaphroditus the resulting 'ill-repute' (infamis) of the fountain of Salmacis, in which any man who bathes will 'go forth half-man' (semivir).[28] In Hughes's version there is no implication of weakening or of travesty in the ultimate union of the lovers. 'Salmacis and Hermaphroditus' also contrasts with the sinister tone of the similar story of passion in *Crow*, 'Lovesong'.

Hughes changes the meaning of 'Salmacis and Hermaphroditus' by omission. Of still more interest are his additions to the text. The extract that he expanded most is 'Bacchus and Pentheus'. There are good structural reasons for this, since, in the original, the story of Pentheus's fatal rejection of the god, deeply important to Hughes, is overbalanced by the interpolated narrative of the Bacchic priest Acoetes. However, it is notable that the Ovidian passion which Hughes most elaborated, the one that projected Pentheus 'into the mythic arena', is one of rejection and religious scepticism. The speech of Pentheus on pages 185–8 of *Tales from Ovid*, in which he rails against the 'painted boy' Bacchus and reminds the Thebans of their historic identity as 'Iron warriors, menhirs of ancient manhood', is expanded to 102 lines from thirty-two in the original. It is a passage of sustained, coruscating invective which one feels Hughes must have thoroughly enjoyed writing:

> How can you go capering
> After a monkey stuffed with mushrooms?
> How can you let yourselves be bitten
> By this hopping tarantula
> And by these glass-eyed, slavering hydrophobes? ...
> You have dunked it all [reason], like a doughnut,
> Into a mugful of junk music –
> Which is actually the belly-laugh
> Of this androgynous, half-titted witch.

Pentheus the denier, the sceptic, the would-be imprisoner and torturer of the god, is, for Hughes, Judas, Pilate and the Pharisees combined, whose fate, being torn to pieces by his mother, epitomises that of many of Hughes's anti-heroes. But, as the reader is carried on the swell of Pentheus's vehement rhetoric, with its capacious lexical reach, he accrues sympathy and even heroic stature.

The other most interesting category of additions bears on Hughes's remark about the religious crisis of Ovid's Rome. In the opening section Hughes matches or even outdoes Ovid in sarcastic comments about the Gods:

> I summon the supernatural beings
> Who first contrived
> The transmogrifications

In the stuff of life.
You did it for your own amusement.

There is nothing corresponding to the fifth line in the original, though Hughes may have misread Miller, 'Ye gods, for you yourselves have wrought the changes' as 'you for yourselves ...'.[29] However, despite the gods being 'defrocked', Hughes both intensifies the religious tone of the original, and marks it with his own signature. There are several examples of this, especially in 'Creation; Four Ages; Flood; Lycaon', but the first is perhaps the most striking. In the brazen age, Ovid writes, although human beings had fallen into violence and savagery, they were 'non scelerata tamen': 'but not yet impious' (Miller); 'but still free from any taint of wickedness' (Innes).[30] Here is Hughes's rendering of this phrase:

But still
Mankind listened deeply
To the harmony of the whole creation,
And aligned every action to the greater order
And not to the moment's blind
Apparent opportunity.

The highly general and almost desultory note of the original and the prose translations is turned into something much weightier and more distinctive: an echo of Hughes's much earlier assertion that 'the living, suffering spirit' is 'designed in accord with the whole universe' (*WP* 222), and of the allegiance throughout his work to attentiveness to an inner depth, as opposed to the momentary, secular satisfactions of the ego.

The other major translations of Hughes's last years were for the theatre, most importantly his *Phèdre*, *Oresteia* and *Alcestis*. These texts were late but major contributions to a flowering of verse translation of classical and neo-classical texts by well-known poets in the late twentieth century. This movement was initiated by Tony Harrison who, of all these poets, was the only one qualified to translate direct from the Greek. Harrison's *Oresteia* (1981) was one of the landmark productions of Peter Hall's National Theatre. Harrison also translated Molière's *Le Misanthrope*, Racine's *Phèdre* (as *Phaedra Britannica*) and, more recently, Euripides's *Hecuba*. His *Trackers of Oxyrhynchus* is based on Sophocles's fragmentary satyr play, the *Ichneutae*. Other notable contributions to this movement are Seamus Heaney's *The Cure at Troy (Philoctetes)* and *The Burial at Thebes (Antigone)*, Blake Morrison's (Sophocles) *Oedipus* and *Antigone* and Sean O'Brien's version of Aristophanes's *The Birds*.

*Phèdre* is the one translation on which Hughes may have worked entirely or primarily from the original. He described it to Ben Sonnenberg as 'reasonably literal'. He 'stripped off' the Alexandrines with their 'hauteur', which he obviously wanted rid of, but also their 'resonance', which he regretted.[31] This translation is indeed more literal than, for example, *Tales from Ovid* or *Alcestis*, but there are nevertheless notable moments when Hughes departs from the strictly literal. The high point of his translation is the long speech in which Théramène narrates Hippolytus's death by the sea-monster that his father Theseus has ignorantly invoked to punish Hippolytus for his supposed rape of Phèdre.[32] Here Hughes gives himself free rein, and such details as the sea 'a solid wall of thunder', the monster 'like a giant octopus of water' and the 'glowing figure of a naked god' urging Hippolytus's horses on, are vivid elaborations of the Racine (*P* 82–3). An example of Hughes removing the 'hauteur' to good effect is Oenone's lines to Phèdre,

> Pouvez-vous d'un superbe oublier le mépris?
> Avec quels yeux cruels sa rigueur obstinée
> Vous laissait à ses pieds peu s'en faut prosternée![33]

which Hughes vigorously renders as

> What about that spoiled brat's contempt?
> Can you forget that face? That baleful blank.
> That stone, hewn block. He hardly saw you
> While you writhed at his feet.
> (*P* 43)

Conversely, the loss of 'resonance' along with the Alexandrine can be felt when Phèdre's immortal lines,

> Ce n'est plus une ardeur dans mes veines cachée:
> C'est Vénus tout entière à sa proie attachée

(the epitome of being thrust by passion on to the 'mythic plane'!) become the rhythmically limp

> No longer a fever in my veins,
> Venus has fastened on me like a tiger.
> (*P* 18)

Ironically, Sylvia Plath was working on an essay on 'Passion as Destiny in Racine' when she met Hughes, and these lines must have influenced the poem she wrote the day after the meeting, 'Pursuit', which captures the resonance better than his translation:

> There is a panther stalks me down:
> One day I'll have my death of him.[34]

Of all the works Hughes translated whole, none has such towering canonical status as the *Oresteia*. In its dramatisation of the supplanting of what Tony Harrison in his translation called 'bloodgrudge'[35] by civic justice, it is a monument not only of European literature but of European civilisation. Hughes said he thought his translation was the best thing he had ever written,[36] and the distinguished classical scholar and critic Michael Silk has called it the best translation of Aeschylus in the twentieth century.[37] But Hughes must have felt some resistance to Aeschylus's patriarchal justice. One can only wonder what the author of 'Crow and Mama' and 'Revenge Fable' felt when wrote the lines with which Apollo defends Orestes for the murder of his mother:

> But she is not the real parent.
> She is the nurse. ...
> The mother is incidental.
>                    (*O* 177)

Or the words of Athene, the goddess who was born without a mother, casting her vote in favour of Orestes:

> The death of a woman who killed her husband
> Weighs nothing
> Against the death of her victim.
>                    (*O* 181)

This, for Hughes, is one of the key moments in the fall of Western civilisation. At the very least, from his point of view, the *Oresteia* dramatises the cost of transcending 'bloodgrudge'. Hughes does not take liberties with such an awe-inspiring text as this, but there is one moment at which he can perhaps be detected shifting the balance in favour of the feminine. The 'bloodgrudge' of this trilogy goes back a generation earlier than the oldest protagonists, to Atreus murdering his brother Thyestes's children and feeding them to their father. The immediate sequence of the trilogy, however, is Agamemnon's sacrifice of his daughter Iphigenia for a good wind to Troy; Clytemnestra's murder of her husband in revenge for this; Orestes's murder of Clytemnestra to avenge his father; and the persecution of Orestes by the Furies, the avengers of murdered 'blood kin' (*O* 174). The judgement of Athene privileges Agamemnon as victim over the women. The Furies protest to Apollo,

> Are you saying
> That Clytemnestra, remembering Iphigenia,
> Had no case, when she murdered Agamemnon?
> (*O* 175)

In none of the other three translations I have consulted[38] is the death of Iphigenia explicitly mentioned here. Hughes recalls for the audience the terrible words of the Chorus in the *Agamemnon*, when Iphigenia screams 'Daddy!' while men acting on her father's orders are 'cramming a gag into her mouth ... like a horse's bit' (*O* 15).

With the exception of Pilinszky, all the translations discussed so far – and also *Spring Awakening* and *Blood Wedding* – were commissioned. The impetus to Hughes's last major translation, *Alcestis*, however, seems to have come from within. He began it in 1993, was distracted by commissioned work, and completed it in the last year of his life, when he offered it to Barrie Rutter's Northern Broadsides company. Northern Broadsides is based in Halifax, a few miles from Hughes's birthplace, and all parts in their productions are spoken with broad Yorkshire accents. Hughes told Rutter that his 'tuning fork had always been in the Calder Valley'.[39]

King Admetos, 'a remarkable man / A saviour of his people' (*A* 2) is doomed to die young, but by the intercession of Apollo, Fate accepts a substitute, someone related to him. His aged parents refuse; the only person willing to sacrifice herself is his wife Alcestis. During the mourning for Alcestis, Admetos's friend Heracles arrives. The ethic of hospitality makes Admetos welcome Heracles without revealing Alcestis's death, as a result of which Heracles scandalises the household by carousing. Appalled to learn of his sacrilegious behaviour, Heracles atones by bringing back Alcestis from the Underworld. Tony Harrison has described Euripides's play as 'category-disturbing', because the 'satyr', in the shape of Heracles, is introduced 'into the very body of the tragedy',[40] and Keith Sagar has compared it to Shakespeare's late romances, especially *The Winter's Tale* and *Pericles* in which a wife is lost, thought to be dead, and restored.[41]

The autobiographical resonances of this story are obvious, and have not gone unnoticed. After Sylvia Plath's death Hughes is reported by Elaine Feinstein to have said, 'it was either her or me'.[42] Feinstein's informant is someone to whom Hughes was later bitterly hostile; nevertheless, *Alcestis* comes closer than any of the *Birthday Letters* poems to acknowledging, indirectly, that Hughes was in some way responsible for Plath's death.

One of the most powerful scenes in the play, greatly enhanced by Hughes, is the quarrel between Admetos and his father Pheres about the latter's refusal to sacrifice himself. Admetos tells his father he could 'only screech, a rat pinned with a stick', to which Pheres pithily answers, 'A rat's life is all a rat has.' When Admetos has left the stage, however, it is he whom the Chorus compares to a rat:

> The Admetos that brought Alcestis to the grave
> Is like the body of a rat
> Trapped with bones and sinews in the trap.
> He is trying to chew it off – the whole body.
> Admetos is trying to gnaw himself
> Free from Admetos
>
> (*A* 46–7)

As Keith Sagar has pointed out, this imagery echoes 'Song of a Rat', the poem Hughes wrote immediately after Plath's death:

> The rat is in the trap, it is in the trap,
> And attacking heaven and earth with a mouthful of screeches,
>     like torn tin.

The rat figures with profound subtlety both as the indomitable will to live, and as the horrifying self-division of ultimate anguish and guilt. Admetos recalls his wedding:

> So much confidence. So Many blessings.
> So much time!
> So many decades ahead of us
>
> (*A* 68)

This echoes a theme in *Birthday Letters*, especially 'Daffodils': 'Our lives were still a raid on our own good luck. We knew we'd live for ever.'

Admetos's father taunts him: 'She met the death that you dodged,' echoing the accusation of the protagonist's victim in *Cave Birds*: 'As you dodged / I received in full', and aligning Admetos with Hughes's other guilty male personae. Hughes himself, however, dodges what must for him have been the most painful lines of the play, when he omits Pheres's repeated jeer: 'you have hit on a way never to die at all – get each successive wife to die for you! ... Marry wife after wife, let them all die for you!'[43]

Hughes's most significant adaptation, however, is his considerable expansion of the scenes featuring Heracles. As Harrison has said, these scenes are like the incorporation of the satyr play into the tragedy. In Hughes's version Heracles is described as a 'wild man of the woods' (*A* 49) – a wodwo. As the phallic satyr he recalls the 'immortal enterprise of the sperm' of the Hughesian Trickster (*WP* 240) and the 'standing cock' of which the Phallus sings in Hughes's unpublished Epilogue to *Oedipus*.[44] Biographically, Admetos's hospitality to his friend while mourning for his wife may echo the tension between Hughes's love for Plath and loyalty to his male friendship group in Cambridge. Hughes has Heracles drunkenly act out his labours, drawing on Euripides's *Heracles*, and incorporates a scene in which the hero saves Prometheus from the Vulture, giving Hughes an opportunity to reiterate his view of the Prometheus story, when God, making his least ironised appearance in the whole of Hughes's oeuvre, accuses Prometheus of having separated man

From the illumination of heaven,
From the wisdom and certainty of heaven.

But perhaps the most interesting moment in Hughes's additions to the Heracles scenes occurs between the labours and Prometheus, when Heracles has a vision in which he murders his wife. His attendant Iolaus tells him he is remembering a dream that was turned into a play, and 'getting your dream mixed up with what will happen.' The attendants change the subject to the freeing of Prometheus to distract Heracles from this horror. (*A* 55–6). The play is, again, Euripides's *Heracles*. It is notable that in Euripides's play, and most versions of this story, in which Heracles is struck with madness by Juno, the main emphasis is on the murder of his *children*. In some versions of the story, such as the one told in the Blackwell *Dictionary of Classical Mythology* and the main version given by Robert Graves, he does not kill his wife.[45] By taking such pains to remind the audience that the hero who saves Alcestis was guilty of an even more terrible marital tragedy, Hughes both darkens the play and gives a salutary reminder to the spectator who may be too easily consoled by his play's last words, 'Let this give man hope' (*A* 83).

Hughes's *Alcestis* is most memorable, finally, not for its elements of vicarious autobiography, but for its sympathetic yet unflinching humanity. Hughes has often written well about death, but perhaps never better than in the lines he adds to the sardonically gleeful person-ification who steals the first scene from Apollo:

> Don't you know how paltry and precarious
> Life is? I am not a god.
> I am the magnet of the cosmos.
> What you call death
> Is simply my natural power,
> The pull of my gravity. And life
> Is a brief weightlessness – an aberration
> From the status quo – which is me.
> I am the very body of Admetos. ...
> And now I am awake, look at me, awake
> In the body of Alcestis
>
> (*A* 5–6)

And Hughes has perhaps written no more moving lines than those in which Alcestis imagines Admetos taking another wife:

> 'She will not even know what I looked like.'
> Alcestis wept
> As if her whole unlived life
> Had turned into weeping.
>
> (*A* 13)

This is so powerful because of the way a simple, all-too-human observation launches a breathtakingly bold, hyperbolic but entirely convincing metaphor.

Two years before his death Hughes complained, not for the first time, of how much time had elapsed since he had written any original verse: 'Translations got me off my own rails – with a feeling of going somewhere. But they went on too long.'[46] But it is hard to imagine how, in his last four or five years, he could have produced such a compelling body of work, or so incontrovertibly enhanced his reputation, as he did with these translations.

# 15
## Poet of Mourning: *Birthday Letters*

The publication of *Birthday Letters* in January 1998 was the last and most sensational event of Hughes's literary life. Hughes submitted the book to Faber in the summer of 1997, and insisted that there should be no advance publicity. *Birthday Letters* burst upon the world on the Saturday before its publication date, when *The Times* began a five-day serialisation. On the first day, it was the main headline story on the front page. The same issue contained an article by Andrew Motion, who was destined the following year to succeed Hughes as Poet Laureate, and an editorial. Motion's article set the tone for much of the sentimental exaggeration that was to follow: 'reading it is like being hit by a thunderbolt. Its power is massive and instant. There is nothing like it in literature ... . Hughes is one of the most important poets of the century, and this is his greatest book.'[1] The editorial took its cue from Motion, with the subtitle 'The greatest book by our greatest living writer.'[2] The front page of the following Monday's edition carried quotations from the responses of the Sunday papers. In general this was a publishing event that figured as much on the news and even editorial pages as in the review sections. The general tone was epitomised by the headline of the *Independent on Sunday* editorial: 'Now we know he loved Sylvia'.[3] Among a minority of more judicious voices, John Carey remarked that the expectation that all the antagonism against Hughes would be set aside might prove optimistic, noting the emphasis in the book on Plath's instability and the minimal reference to Hughes's affair with Assia Wevill as potential points of contestation.[4]

*Birthday Letters* not only aroused much more journalistic interest than anything Hughes had previously published, but provoked a fundamental rethink of his poetics and a new perspective on everything he had written since Plath's death. True, he had published two of the poems,

'You Hated Spain' and 'The Earthenware Head', as early as 1979/80, and six more in the *New Selected Poems* of 1994, (together with several comparably intimate poems addressed to Assia Wevill) but these precursors had gone largely unnoticed. *Birthday Letters* changed for ever the narrative of Hughes and Plath's personal and literary relationship, and presented Hughes himself as the exponent of a confessional mode of poetry that he had previously disdained.

The reality was of course less dramatic than it seemed, and *Birthday Letters* had many precursors, not only in the previously published poems about Plath. As early as 1978 Hughes had published *Moortown Elegies*, the first collection of farming poems, which are straightforwardly autobiographical, and written with a similar apparent unconcern for poetic effect as *Birthday Letters*, though largely without introspection. In *Wolfwatching* (1989) he published several poems about his family which, in their preoccupation with the sources of his own emotional and imaginative life, were a more emphatic anticipation. But Hughes's own utterances at the time of publication make it clear that *Birthday Letters* was an epoch for the author as well as for his readers.

He wrote to Keith Sagar that when poets such as W.D. Snodgrass, Robert Lowell and Anne Sexton 'deal with the episode directly, as material for an artistic work' he had 'despised it'. He had believed 'it would have to emerge obliquely, through a symbol, inadvertently'. Now, however, he had come to believe that this 'high-minded principal [sic] was simply wrong – for my own psychological & physical health. It was stupid.' He wondered if 'an all-out attempt to complete a full account, in the manner of those B[irthday] L[etters], of that part of my life, would not have liberated me to deal with it on deeper, more creative levels', implying that not having done so had caused a central creative failure. The preparation of *Birthday Letters* and the writing of the last few poems gave him 'free energy I hadn't known since Crow' which went into the translations of his last years.[5]

The exact chronology of the poems cannot be established at present because no manuscript material is in the public realm. In a notebook otherwise containing draft material of the late 1960s, at the back and turned over, are a few lines of verse addressed to Plath, referring to her 1953 suicide attempt.[6] The phrase 'Overexposed like an x-ray' could qualify this as an early draft of 'The Tender Place', but one can't be sure that it is contemporary with the other material in the notebook. The poem 'Visit' situates itself ten years after Plath's death, which is not in itself reliable evidence for the date of composition. However, there is evidence that Hughes began as early as 1973. In 1976, responding to the publication of Edward Butscher's biography, Peter Redgrove and Penelope Shuttle wrote urging Hughes to 'write your story. ... We are afraid there will be many such books as Butscher's unless you act, and the effect of them will gradually become permanent. On the contrary, to tell your story would be a noble action, however harrowing or even shameful you might consider the truth to be.'[7] This was very perspicacious, as was Redgrove's insight into the possible effect of Hughes's silence on his poetry. In 1979 Redgrove wrote to me that 'a *direct* account of [Hughes's] life including its tragedies would stretch him to the uttermost and perhaps procure in him a true maturity. I do not believe it is any use disguising the matter in pregnant images any longer. I believe myself that the chief error in the later poetry is in doing this'.[8] This chimes intriguingly with Hughes's own remarks about being liberated to deal with his experience on 'deeper, more creative levels'. An undated letter from Hughes in the Redgrove papers is very likely a reply to the one quoted above: 'What you say about writing my own story about S, strengthens a growing horrified realisation that I have to do it – for my own sake, if only for my own eyes.' He tells Redgrove that 'about 3 years ago' he had written a passage of verse about Plath each day for about two weeks, and began having 'the most extraordinary dreams'. For some reason he stopped the writing and the dreams stopped.[9] This dating is consistent with the internal evidence that 'Visit' was written in 1973.

A letter to Daniel Weissbort written in 1975 or 1976 compliments Weissbort on having written poems with 'the quality of being very true searchings out of genuine painful things, with no eye to anything but the truth and justness of their words'.[10] This strongly anticipates what Hughes wrote to Sagar after the publication of *Birthday Letters*: that these poems were something he had 'always thought unthinkable – so raw, so vulnerable, so naïve, so self-exposing and unguarded, so without any of the niceties that any poetry workshop student could have helped me to'.[11] Hughes goes on in the Weissbort letter to contrast his friend's poems with the confessional writings of Lowell, which he considers 'ersatz' and 'stage performance, even the careless, slovenly, loose shuffling off of imperfect approximations'. This is a revealing contemporary instance of the resistance to the confessional, that Hughes later regretted: we can see that it is grounded in a fear, or conviction, that direct sincerity is impossible. Yet, unless he is merely flattering his friend, he has the counter-example of Weissbort's poems which are 'to me, infinitely valuable.'

There is no mention in this letter of anything that was to develop into *Birthday Letters*, but Hughes goes on to complain about the effect on him of the exposure resulting from the publication of *Letters Home*: 'I might have solved it all for myself in writing, but now a straight public amputation is compulsory.' This suggests that he had given up hope of building on the start he had made in 1973, but the 'infinitely valuable' example of Weissbort's poems may have helped him whenever he did start again.

In May 1989 Hughes wrote to Ben Sonnenberg that he had recently been 'piecing together bits and scraps of my life with Sylvia',[12] and in the same year he told the American translator Carolyn Wright that he had been 'writing out my own version of events', which would be 'published posthumously'.[13] Two years later Thom Gunn wrote to Hughes commiserating with him on not having written any poetry for eighteen months (he was working on *Shakespeare and the Goddess of Complete Being*), and encouraging him 'to print whatever you have written about S.P.' and to 'add to these pieces anything needed to make the story complete'.[14] This suggests a series of fitful starts to the project, in the early 1970s and again in the late 1980s. Following this, there is a series of references to the project in letters to Sonnenberg, Janos Csokits, Daniel Weissbort and Keith Sagar, which suggest more sustained work on it in the early 1990s, perhaps after the completion of *Shakespeare and the Goddess of Complete Being* (1992).[15]

One particularly intriguing aspect of Hughes's psychological reaction to *Birthday Letters* is that the publication seems to have been as significant as the writing. Or, rather, there are two different narratives that he seems to have entertained at the same time. One is, as we might expect from a writer of Hughes's temper, that the *writing* of the poems is what matters: as he wrote to Redgrove, 'for my own sake, if only for my own eyes'. Yet, if he began writing the poems in the 1970s, this is incompatible with his later feeling that 'never having "dealt" with that, as they say, in some verbal way, had actually blocked my way as a writer'.[16] After publication he wrote to Sagar that not only the writing of the poems but their preparation for publication had given him 'free energy I hadn't known since Crow'. He had certainly been thinking about publication for a long time before 1998. As early as 1992 he told Sonnenberg that he was 'gathering a big collection' of what he called 'my own view (for a change) of my own drama with the dead', but two years later he wrote to the same correspondent that publishing them would 'drag the heavens down on the rest of my life' and those of his family.[17]

Hughes's hesitation about publishing, and his feeling of liberation at having done so, are opposite sides of the same coin. Behind *Birthday Letters*, of course, is not only the private tragedy of Hughes's and Plath's marriage, but the very public sequels that I discussed in Chapter 7. The composition of the poems may well have been largely a matter of Hughes's private communion with his dead wife, but their publication was an intervention in that harsh arena of public discourse that, he felt, had made him unable to 'deal with it naturally and creatively',[18] and one which would change that discourse, in one way or another, for ever. The book itself is therefore, inevitably, Janus-faced. Hughes may have had to tell himself that the poems were not for publication, in order to be able to write them. Not surprisingly, it elicited strong and conflicting reactions, but these did not divide, as one might have predicted, according to the critics' allegiance to Hughes or Plath. Jacqueline Rose, one of Hughes's most formidable antagonists, wrote a remarkably measured and appreciative review. By contrast Linda Wagner-Martin, in the second edition of *Sylvia Plath: A Literary Life*, complained of the 'Usurpation of Sylvia Plath's Narrative'. In her view 'There was little question that the book felt like an affront'. She particularly objected to Hughes's allusions to Plath's writing and wrote, with some exaggeration, that his poems 'nearly erased her voice'.[19] Tracy Brain, on the other hand, in *The Other Sylvia Plath*, emphasises the degree to which, far from usurping Plath's writing, 'Hughes himself is self-conscious about his own narrative fallibility.'[20] Critics' own judgements of the book seem to colour their perception of its reception: Wagner-Martin writes that 'Most of the reviews ... were negative',[21] whereas Brain says that '*Birthday Letters* has been applauded by critics', though often without 'evaluating Hughes's poems as *art*',[22] alluding to the often sentimental and sensational nature of journalistic commentary. Leonard M. Scigaj, one of Hughes's most appreciative commentators, was highly critical of the determinism of the book, its relentless emphasis on Plath's father-fixation, and its neglect of socially-specific, and gender-specific, influences on Plath's state of mind.[23] Keith Sagar, while refraining from explicit condemnation, also comments on the determinism, and contrasts the poems with Hughes's prose accounts of Plath's development, which 'take for granted a world in which the actors have a measure of freedom and control'; Sagar also notes that in Hughes's essays on Plath 'the substance of her poetry and the very substance of her survival are the same' (*WP* 184), whereas in *Birthday Letters* 'they are mutually exclusive'.[24]

In this chapter I shall be considering *Birthday Letters* as poems of explanation, self-justification and mourning. I shall be arguing that the first two of these categories are unstable and inadequate, but that they play an inevitable part in shaping a reader's response to the book. The third category, mourning, accounts for what I judge to be strongest in *Birthday Letters*. First, however, I want to comment on the most striking formal or generic characteristic of the volume. All but four of the poems are directly addressed to Plath. They are apostrophic elegies. The peculiar characteristic of apostrophe as a poetic device is that someone who is absent is addressed as if she were present. (I am excluding here apostrophes to inanimate addressees such as the 'Ode to the West Wind' which conventionalise an equally absurd form of address.) The addressee is usually dead or has deserted the speaker: hence apostrophe is particularly associated with funeral elegy and love poetry. Jonathan Culler has written that in apostrophic poetry 'something once present has been lost or attenuated', and that apostrophes 'replace this irreversible structure by removing the opposition between presence and absence from empirical time and locating it in discursive time'.[25] This shift from the empirical to the discursive tends to bring about a sublimation of the addressee: she is stripped of empirical characteristics. We see this in Hughes's previous major use of the device, in the *Gaudete* epilogue, where Hughes by his own account draws on real women that he has known, but sublimates them into the figure of the Goddess. For example, he declared in a letter that the *Gaudete* epilogue poem 'I know well' was about someone he had known who died of Hodgkins' disease.[26]

I suggest that this information inevitably influences the way one reads the poem and construes its addressivity. The Bakhtin school espoused a concept of addressivity that is essentially dialogic. According to V.N. Voloshinov the word, or discourse, is *'the product of the reciprocal relationship between the speaker and listener, addresser and addressee ... . I give myself verbal shape from another's point of view.'*[27] In traditional apostrophic poetry, such as the *Gaudete* epilogue, where the addressee is sublimated, this dialogism is – not indeed cancelled, but – considerably reduced in force. In *Birthday Letters*, by contrast, which centres on a highly circumstantial relationship with an addressee who exists not only in the private world of the poet, but in a public world of ideological discourse, whose own words are constantly quoted in the text, and who is surrounded by other discourses that are often hostile to the speaker, the dialogism is intense. Moreover, the shift from empirical to discursive time, distinctive of apostrophic poetry, is highly unstable in *Birthday Letters*:

> But then I sat, stilled,
> Unable to fathom what stilled you
> As I looked at you, as I am stilled
> Permanently now, permanently
> Bending so briefly at your open coffin.
>                        ('The Blue Flannel Suit')

As in this case, such instances are often the most memorable expressions of mourning in the book.

*Birthday Letters* drew most hostile comment for that aspect of it that purports, or seems, to offer an explanation for the tragedy of the marriage. For Linda Wagner-Martin, the book was an 'affront' because in it Hughes 'had argued with the narrative her poems had created; he had set himself the task of correcting the story her writing had told.'[28] This seems dangerously close to erecting Plath's work as a sacred text. It does however show the peculiar vulnerability of such intensely dialogic apostrophic poems. Nobody considers it an affront for Shakespeare to tell his story in the sonnets, or even Hardy in 'Poems of 1912–13'. The intimate, exclusive address that Hughes strives for in these poems is a source of much of their power, but it is constantly broken into by other discourses.

Scigaj accuses Hughes of trying to 'reduce his former wife's behaviour to one deterministic cause, and in so doing deflect attention from his actions as well as reaffirm for one last time his male control of her actions.'[29] Like Sagar, Scigaj argues that the poems contradict Hughes's prose writings about Plath: in this case, the central emphasis of *Birthday Letters* on the father-figure contradicts Hughes's identification in a 1982 essay of 'the deathly woman at the heart of everything she now closed in on' (*WP* 187), which Scigaj interprets as 'a tug-of –war with her maternal role, with her mother as model.'[30] These contradictions raise intriguing questions about the *explanatory* status of *Birthday Letters*. In Chapter 7 I discussed Hughes's double relationship to the events of his own life: inside and private, outside and public. I commented on Hughes's distrust of rational discursive prose, which was the public arena in which his life was discussed: 'My formal prose seems to exclude everything I want to say, as if some dalek had pushed me aside and taken my pen, and I loathe it.'[31] When writing prose, he would have felt that he had a different relationship to those events than when writing verse: a difference most extremely marked, as Janet Malcolm and Diane Middlebrook have noted, by his reference to himself in the third person as 'her husband' in his notes to Plath's *Collected Poems*.

Let us consider, as a notable and central instance, the contradictions in the way Hughes writes about Plath's poetry. In his 1982 introduction to Plath's *Journals*, as elsewhere in his prose, the main narrative is the birth of a 'new self' (*WP* 186). In this narrative the role of her poetry, and above all of the poems of 1962, is entirely positive: 'she had overcome, by a stunning display of power, the bogies in her life … . And indeed it was blazingly clear that she had come through, in Lawrence's sense, and that she was triumphant' (*WP* 188). In *Birthday Letters* the linked motifs, poetry and the search for the true self, appear in sinister opposition to the possibility of happiness, most clearly in 'Flounders' and 'Fishing Bridge'. There is something pathetically affecting about the way these poems begin, respectively, 'Was that a happy day?' and 'Nearly happy.' 'Flounders' narrates an adventure in the sea off Boston and concludes that it was:

> A slight ordeal of all that might be,
> And a small thrill-breath of what many live by,
> And a small prize, a toy miniature
> Of the life that might have bonded us
> Into a single animal, a single soul –
> It was a visit from the goddess, the beauty
> Who was poetry's sister – she had come
> To tell poetry she was spoiling us.
> Poetry listened, maybe, but we heard nothing
> And poetry did not tell us. And we
> Only did what poetry told us to do.

'Fishing Bridge' narrates another moment of 'infinite endowment', at Yellowstone Park, from which the couple's attention is diverted by a voice that urges them to 'Find your true selves.' This leads to a search in a labyrinth, at the centre of which is 'Your dead face.'

In his prose writings about Plath, Hughes is addressing the reading public. These are essays that presuppose publication, and engagement in the arena of rational prose discourse. But for the public occasions that prompt them, they would not have been written. They are addressed to readers whose legitimate interest is in Plath's poetry, and in her inner life only insofar as is necessary for the elucidation of the poetry. These are also readers who are not necessarily interested in Hughes except as an adjunct to Plath, and many of whom he knows to be hostile to him.

The addressivity of the poems is, of course, complicated by the fact of publication. The apostrophic address is always to some degree a fiction, because the addressee is by definition dead or absent. Nevertheless, we should allow some weight to Hughes's assertion that 'They are not really pieces for public consumption – rather for private (my) health.'[32] It may be that his indecisiveness about publication was a necessary strategy to preserve the inward, intimate addressivity, away from the polemical battlefield into which publication would inevitably draw him. It is further complicated by the arrangement of the poems in a chronological sequence. This, we can safely assume, is not the sequence of their composition – not, in other words, the sequence of Hughes's communion with Plath. This arrangement belongs to the public pole of the volume's addressivity: the chronology aligns the volume structurally with the already existing biographical accounts and therefore with the poems' polemical context. The chronology also gestures at a narrative, and therefore at the unfolding understanding of events that narrative usually offers. But actually there is no narrative. There is no continuity between the recollected moments in individual poems. Even more notably, in the later part of the book even chronological sequence dissolves. After 'Dream Life', the poem about Assia Wevill's fateful visit to Devon, there is only one poem, 'The Inscription', which narrates an incident between Hughes and Plath (and this poem, intriguingly, is one of the few not addressed to her). The later poems are mostly general reflections on Plath's life and death, and in a number of cases a fabular mode is substituted for autobiography.

This is bound to seem evasive. In the polemical context into which *Birthday Letters* was launched, Hughes's 'desertion' (to use Marjorie Perloff's word) of Plath is the central fact. Beyond linking his falling in love with Assia to her telling him a dream she had had, *Birthday Letters* does not account for this 'desertion'. It does not link the affair with Assia to difficulties in the marriage, or give any circumstantial detail of the breakdown of the marriage after May 1962. However, the expectation that *Birthday Letters* should do any of these things is based on a number of not necessarily appropriate assumptions: that it should speak to the public perception of events; that it should be 'confessional' in the way a Catholic is when seeking absolution; and, most fundamentally, that it should attempt to explain the events that it reflects on.

The matter is made more problematic by the fact that, as Scigaj and Sagar note, the book *seems* to offer an explanation for the failure of the marriage and Plath's death: a deterministic one that traces everything to Plath's father-fixation. It is quite true that Otto Plath looms large in poems such as 'The Table', 'The Shot', 'Black Coat' and 'The Minotaur', and that Hughes frequently represents himself with figures of passivity and unconsciousness, such as a puppet, a dog, and most frequently a sleepwalker. This is all of course relevant to the question of personal responsibility in *Birthday Letters*, and to whether the volume can be construed as self-justification.

One of the most intriguing things about the book is that Hughes does attach blame to himself, but not for the reasons that might be expected by a reader approaching it as a conventional story of adultery and desertion. One episode on which Hughes looks back with a particularly strong sense of failure occurred before his relationship with Plath had properly begun. After the notorious meeting at the *St Botolph's Review* party, Hughes visited Cambridge but without seeing Plath. She knew of this, and her knowledge caused her considerable anguish, of which Hughes was unaware until he read her journal after her death.[33] He devotes two poems to this incident: 'Visit' and 'The Machine'. I think they are two of the finest poems in *Birthday Letters*, and I shall be returning to consider them as poems of mourning. In 'The Machine' Hughes portrays his own passivity in a particularly unflattering way:

> When you tried
> To will me up the stair, this terror
> Arrived instead. While I
> Most likely was just sitting,
> Maybe with Lucas, no more purpose in me
> Than in my own dog
> That I did not have.

Here Hughes resembles the protagonist of *Cave Birds*, in the poem 'Something Was Happening', who is similarly affectlessly unaware of the female victim's suffering:

> As I hung up my coat and went through Into the kitchen
> And peeled a flake off the turkey's hulk, and stood vacantly
>     munching
> Her sister got the call from the hospital
> And gasped out the screech.
>
> And all the time
> I was scrubbing at my nails and staring through the window
> She was burning.

Unusually for the poems that narrate a specific incident, 'Visit' and 'The Machine' are both placed out of chronological order. Both poems chronologically belong between 'St Botolph's' (their meeting) and '18 Rugby Street' (their first night together); but 'Visit' is printed before both these poems, and 'The Machine' after both. If we can attach any significance to the ordering, it would seem to be an implicit questioning of causal explanation. The poems might be considered proleptic, in that they place Hughes's failure of Plath at a time when nothing could reasonably have been expected of him, but they could also be construed to mean that he had always already failed her, simply by being the person he was.

Another, even more striking, example of what seems like displaced self-blame is the poem 'Epiphany'. This poem refers to the period when, having returned from America, and their first child Frieda recently born, Hughes and Plath were living in a small flat in London. In the street Hughes is offered a fox-cub for a pound by a young man, and refuses it. This is an odd but plausible incident; however it is made to seem dream-like by the poem's extraordinary conclusion:

> If I had paid that pound and turned back
> To you, with that armful of fox –
> If I had grasped that whatever comes with a fox
> Is what tests a marriage and proves it a marriage –
> I would not have failed the test. Would you have failed it?
> But I failed. Our marriage had failed.

Earlier in the poem Hughes has rehearsed all the reasons against taking a fox-cub to live in a small London flat with a new baby. These reasons seem incontrovertible, and it is difficult to make sense of Hughes's self-judgement on any realistic grounds. It would be absurd to interpret the poem literally; after all, the move to a large house in Devon, where a fox might plausibly have been kept, was also, according to the title of the poem about it, an 'Error'. Keith Sagar remarks that Hughes 'identifies the fox with his own inner meaning, his authenticity, the ultimate truth of his being, the god or luminous spirit in him ...'[34] As I suggested in Chapter 1, the image of the fox reaches back to 'The Thought-Fox', Hughes's Cambridge dream of the burnt fox, and the childhood experience fictionalised in 'The Deadfall', all texts that are concerned with his sense of his poetic vocation as shamanistic. We might interpret 'Epiphany' to mean that, whatever shamanistic powers Hughes may have felt he possessed, he failed to exercise them in his marriage. The shaman is above all a healer. In another poem of failure, 'The Shot', Hughes imagines that 'the right witchdoctor' might have helped Plath; he evidently was not that person. I shall be discussing later the temporality of mourning in *Birthday Letters*. Note here that 'Our marriage *had* failed': the failure to buy the fox is not a cause but a sign of what was already the case.

Hughes cuts a far from heroic figure in *Birthday Letters*. Apart from comparing himself to a dog, a sleepwalker and a puppet, he frequently repeats locutions such as 'I did not know ...' and 'I had no idea ...' This might be seen as a strategy of self-exculpation, the verbal equivalent of helplessly holding up his hands; but it undermines the authority that the sequence otherwise claims by situating Hughes as the unique witness. This undermining of Hughes as witness is reinforced, as Tracy Brain has argued, by his self-consciousness about 'his own narrative fallibility', often beginning a poem with an unanswered question.[35] It is perhaps most striking in a number of poems that *appear* to assert his superiority over Plath, but actually dramatise his imaginative failure. 'Your Paris' begins with Hughes appearing to preen himself on the contrast between his awareness of Paris as 'a post-war utility survivor', and Plath the cultural tourist, to whom the city is 'frame after frame, / Street after street, of Impressionist paintings'. Central to the poem, however, is his failure of understanding, the 'conjectural, hopelessly wrong meanings' that he attributed to her behaviour, unaware that 'What walked beside me was flayed' by the memory of her recent anguished visit in search of the vanished Richard Sassoon, who metonymically represents the 'torturer' embedded in her psyche. The metaphor of Hughes as dog performs an ironic reversal in this poem: at first he is 'dog-nosed' in his sensitivity to the traces of the occupation; by the end he is a 'mere dog' who 'yawned and dozed'. 'You Hated Spain' opens with another prejudicial contrast between Hughes who 'felt at home' in the 'blood-raw light' and 'African / Black edges' of Spain, and Plath as a 'bobby-sox American' who recoils in panic. But the poem proceeds to attribute this superficial recoil to a far more profound response than his own: 'Spain was what you tried to wake up from / And could not.' 'Wuthering Heights' is structured round a contrast between Plath and Emily Brontë. Plath 'had all the liberties, having life. / The future had invested in you', whereas Emily 'had stared / As a dying prisoner.' The poem asks, 'What would stern / Dour Emily have made of your frisky glances / And your huge hope.' She would, the poem suggests, have burned with envy; this poem's reversal comes only in the final line, where Emily's envy is 'quenched in understanding'. 'The 59th Bear', which narrates the incident on which Plath's story of the same name was based, has Hughes enjoying the sight of the 'Awesome, fluid, / Unpredictable, dodging swiftness' of the bears, while Plath 'panicked into the tent and pleaded'. In this poem Hughes appears to assume an heroic role when he gets up in the night to see off a bear that is ransacking their car in a Yellowstone Park campground. He imagines that 'A few shock-shouts / ... a close-up assault of human abuse' would frighten the bear off. But he is 'Pitifully unimaginative / ... Your terrors / Were more intelligent, with their vision'. He does not, after all, go out, and in the morning they hear of a man who had tackled a bear, perhaps the same one, and been killed.

I have tried to demonstrate that the poems undermine their own gestures at explanation or self-justification. Anne Whitehead, in one of the earliest and best extended essays on *Birthday Letters,* argues against the widely held view that Hughes is attempting to possess his own past, and instead reads the book in the light of Cathy Caruth's trauma theory in *Unclaimed Experience,* and Lacan's exploration of the 'strange temporality' of loss.[36] Using as a template the Orpheus legend (which was of profound importance to Hughes, and which he resisted after Plath's death as 'too obvious an attempt to exploit my situation'[37]), Whitehead asserts that 'The moment of traumatic loss is irrecoverable, because it was not fully experienced at the time at which it occurred. The act of remembrance is an act of repetition – a losing over again – with a representation of the loved one as its object.'[38] It is a representation because the loved one is irrecoverably lost – in the words that Hughes attributes to Pluto in the Orpheus legend, 'No, of course you can't have her back. She's dead, you idiot.'[39] The direct line often drawn, in the poems, between a remembered moment of their life together and Plath's death is, from this point of view, not deterministic but the consequence of traumatic fixation.

I want to conclude this chapter by discussing a group of poems in which the 'strange temporality' of *Birthday Letters* explicitly superimposes the past on the present of writing, in which the mourning subject is directly glimpsed. These seem to me the most affecting moments in the sequence. I have already mentioned 'Visit' and 'The Machine', in which Hughes recollects his failure to see Plath in Cambridge, an episode that seems to mark him as the one who will go on failing her. 'Visit' locates itself at a moment ten years after Plath's death in which Hughes, reading her journal, experiences 'The shock of your joy' on learning that he was in Cambridge. The journal entry is described as 'Your actual words, as they floated / Out through your throat and tongue and onto your page' – a powerful phonocentric transformation of the written record (which normally presupposes absence) into the lost one's physical presence. This effect is reinforced by a logically inconsequential but emotionally compelling link ('Just as when ...') with another moment when the child Frieda (called 'your daughter' here) suddenly asked, 'Daddy, where's Mummy?' The link is an emotionally complex one. Hughes was 'there' both literally and supportively for his child, which he was not for Plath either at the moment of her journal entry or at her death, and the daughter's voice is a literal memory, whereas Plath's is an illusion, or in Whitehead's word a 'representation', created by the processes of mourning. The poem shifts back confusingly to the night in 1956 when Hughes threw soil at, as it turned out, the wrong Newnham College window: 'The freezing soil / Of the garden, as I clawed it'. This is the first mention of freezing in connection with that night, whereas it is a well-known motif of the time of Plath's death (referred to later in 'Robbing Myself', where Hughes digs up potatoes in freezing soil). In the soil of the college garden Hughes senses 'Our future trying to happen', and at this moment the poem returns to the present of the mourning subject:

> I look up – as if to meet your voice
> With all its urgent future
> That has burst in on me. Then look back
> At the book of the printed words.
> You are ten years dead. It is only a story.
> Your story. My story.

This poem has woven together, and almost superimposed, five moments: that of his failed visit and her journal; her death; the child's question; his reading the journal; and the poem's own present. This 'strange temporality' produces the effect of repetition – or rather, of a second chance, in which he is 'there' to meet her voice – an effect intensely registered by the gesture, in the poem's present, of looking up. The word 'future' movingly migrates from 'Our future trying to happen', the determinate, tragic future that is actually past, to 'all its urgent future', open-ended with possibility. Finally, however, the real significance of the 'printed words' asserts itself: what Hughes has encountered has all been representation, 'only a story.' The poem enacts, in Whitehead's words, 'a losing over again'.

'The Machine' is the poem from which I earlier quoted Hughes's unflattering description of himself sitting in the pub while Plath suffered. Hughes imagines that, as he sat there, the 'Juggernaut' of his future (rather like the 'Ghost Crabs' of an earlier poem) ground through the wall of the pub and consumed him along with his Guinness. This is one of the sequence's deterministic-seeming moments, but its real bearings are apparent when, again, the poem concludes in the present:

>                                        my life
> Forever trying to climb the steps now stone
> Towards the door now red
> Which you, in your own likeness, would open,
> With still time to talk.

Again, the mourning subject is doomed to repeat the past, even as he tries to repair it. The steps are at one level those of Plath's Cambridge lodgings, Hughes's failure to climb which is the paradigm of his general failure. They have become, as 'stone' and 'red' obviously signify, the unclimbable steps of death; but again there is an implied glance at the time when she died: at the steps of her flat up which Hughes did not climb on that morning when, as he has written elsewhere, he wrongly believed that they had 'still time to talk': 'We ran out of time – by days, I think.'[40] Here the phrase 'in your own likeness' is again a recognition that the Plath he imagines opening the door is a representation.

'Drawing' dramatises a moment ('Here it is') in which Hughes is looking at a sketch Plath made on honeymoon in Benidorm, and recollecting the time and place, and himself sitting beside her 'scribbling something'. This is the only moment in the whole of *Birthday Letters* in which Hughes states affirmatively that they were happy. The drawing preserves the village as it 'still slept / In the Middle Ages', before it disappeared under modern tourist development. By an analogy only explicable by the process of mourning the poem continues, 'As your hand / Went under Heptonstall to be held / By endless darkness', and draws both these moments together with the present by continuing (within the same grammatical structure though divided by full stops):

> While my pen travels on
> Only two hundred miles from your hand,
> Holding this memory ...
> And the contemplative calm
> I drank from your concentrated quiet,
> In this contemplative calm
> Now I drink from your stillness that neither
> Of us can disturb or escape.

The repetition almost fuses the moment of past happiness and the one of present grief, and the pen that is imagined continuously moving from then to now is also trapped in the stillness of her death, a superbly apt figure for the condition of mourning, and of elegiac poetry.

Another, even more memorable figure of the 'strange temporality' of mourning concludes 'The Blue Flannel Suit', a poem that recalls Plath's terror before teaching at her old college. Again the moment of being 'stilled' in her 'stilled' presence is superimposed on the time of mourning in which Hughes is

stilled

Permanently now, permanently
Bending so briefly at your open coffin.

Hughes said more than once that he was not striving for literary effect in *Birthday Letters*: that they were written 'without aesthetic exploitation' and that poetical effects are 'incidental'.[41] In so doing he ran the risk of exposing himself to the criticism he levelled at Lowell, that the 'careless, slovenly' writing was 'stage performance'. He also ran the special risk of inviting comparison with the poems of *Ariel*, which manage almost miraculously to combine a highly wrought density with an appearance of utter spontaneity. This is especially the case when, as in 'The Rabbit Catcher', he virtually invites us to read Plath's poem alongside his own. The 'flat and literal' voice that Hughes adopts for most of this poem – and, to some extent, for nearly all the poems in *Birthday Letters* – contributes to the 'affront' that Linda Wagner-Martin feels on reading the poems. A more generous view might be that Hughes is not entering into competition with his dead wife. It would need a very partial critic to assert that any of the poems in *Birthday Letters* use language as memorably as the best of Plath's work. If, as Hughes claimed, poetical effects in *Birthday Letters* are 'incidental', the danger is that the poems will be read purely for voyeuristic reasons, or as polemical interventions in Plath biography. There is no intrinsic merit in writing 'flat and literal' poetry. However, while I would not wish to accuse Hughes, as he accuses Lowell, of 'stage effects', such language does have a rhetorical function. It creates what might be called a sincerity effect. This may condition the way we read the poems, encouraging us to accept the possibly fictive device of the poet communing privately with his dead wife, and enhance the effect of passages such as the ones I have just discussed, where Hughes's language rises to a (for this book) uncharacteristic intensity, as it articulates the strange temporality of mourning. This *is* a rhetorical effect: it can be no accident that these passages are all the conclusions of poems that begin in a much more 'flat and literal' style. The intensity of the language is enhanced by contrast, and the 'sincerity effect' carries over into it, making us less likely to attribute it to a professional poetic facility. Although there is much undistinguished writing in *Birthday Letters*, I can think of no instances of what I called, in relation to *Remains of Elmet*, 'Parnassian' poetry. Despite Hughes's own discouragement, we are not condemned, as one reviewer felt, to refrain from critical commentary as 'sacrilegious'.[42]

# Epilogue

Ted Hughes died on 28 October 1998, of a heart attack following treatment for bowel cancer. He had kept the seriousness of his medical condition secret even from close friends: a last manifestation of his passion for privacy. The last public photograph of him, ten days before his death, shows him with the Queen receiving the Order of Merit, one of the highest honours that a British citizen can receive, limited to twenty-four honorees at any time.

Hughes was obituarised as a man who, in the words of a *Times* editorial marking his death, had been able to 'make peace' at the end of his life.[1] There was also a sense of the public realm, which he had always perceived as his enemy, making peace with him. The publications of his final years, especially *Tales from Ovid* and *Birthday Letters*, had restored his reputation to the extent that he was memorialised as an unambiguously great writer, though there were still few commentators who saw his work whole, especially the experiments of his middle period.

Since his death, the revival of Hughes's reputation has been consolidated. *The Oresteia* and *Alcestis* were posthumously produced, and were favourably received not only by theatre audiences but by classical scholars. The 2003 publication of *Collected Poems* for the first time made virtually the whole of Hughes's poetic output available, albeit in unwieldy form, to a wide readership. Volumes of his collected children's poetry and collected translations are also planned.

Before his death Hughes sold his vast personal archive to Emory University in Atlanta, and the availability of this material, together with letters deposited at Emory and the British Library by close friends and relatives, has been a huge stimulus to scholarly activity. During Hughes's lifetime there were only two academic conferences devoted to his work, both organised by his indefatigable champion Keith Sagar in

213

Manchester. Since his death there have been international conferences in Lyon (2000), Atlanta (2005) and Edinburgh (2005). Two biographies have appeared, both broadly sympathetic and one, Diane Middlebrook's *Her Husband*, the most balanced account yet of Hughes's relationship with Plath.

At about the same time as the present book, Hughes's *Selected Letters* will be published by Faber. I have quoted only brief extracts from the letters, which can give no sense of what Janet Malcolm has called 'their peculiar power' to arouse 'a feeling of intense sympathy and affection for the writer.' Malcolm looked forward to the day when the letters will be published and critics will wrestle with the question of what makes them 'so deeply, mysteriously moving'.[2] From his sometimes hilarious, sometimes attentively pedagogical letters to his daughter, to the revealing accounts of his own work to a sympathetic critic such as Keith Sagar, Hughes was a great letter-writer: his published letters will stand comparison with those of Byron or D.H. Lawrence.

So Hughes's literary life continues after the death of the man, if not as dramatically as his wife's did. His published *oeuvre* is not yet complete, and many aspects of it will continue to be contested. But his work is so many-sided, and reaches such a wide and various audience, that there can be little doubt he will be, to use one of his own terms of approbation, a 'permanent' writer.

# Notes

## Introduction

1. Diane Middlebrook, *Her Husband: Hughes and Plath—A Marriage*, New York, Viking, 2003, p. 8.
2. Letter to Ann Skea, 10.11.82, Ann Skea, *Ted Hughes: The Poetic Quest*, Armidale NSW, University of New England Press, 1994, p. 200.

## 1  Paradise Lost: Formation and Juvenilia

1. The version quoted is from *Elmet* (1994). It is revised from the original version published in *Remains of Elmet* (1979). For the differences between these books see Chapter 10.
2. 'Ted Hughes: The Art of Poetry LXXI', interview with Drue Heinz, *Paris Review* 134, Spring 1995, p. 59.
3. Skea, *Ted Hughes: The Poetic Quest*, p. 200.
4. Keith Sagar, *The Laughter of Foxes: A Study of Ted Hughes*, Liverpool, Liverpool University Press, 2000, p. 104.
5. Diane Middlebrook, *Her Husband: Hughes and Plath—A Marriage*, New York and London, Viking Penguin, 2003, p. 70 and note p. 305.
6. TH to Keith Sagar, 18 June 1998, BL Add.78761, f. 26.
7. Ibid., f. 30, quoted in *The Laughter of Foxes*, p. 41.
8. TH to Gerald Hughes, 1971, Emory Mss 854, Box 1, ff. 20, quoted in Elaine Feinstein, *Ted Hughes: The Life of a Poet*, London, Weidenfeld and Nicholson, 2001, p. 183.
9. Sagar, *The Laughter of Foxes*, p. 43.
10. Emory Mss 854, Box 1, ff. 40–2.
11. For example, letters to Gerald 22 March 1955 and 10 October 1955, Emory Mss 854, Box 1, ff. 4; also Middlebrook, *Her Husband*, pp. 3–4.
12. For example, 7 July 1956, Emory Mss 854 Box 1, ff. 5; Christmas 1958, ff. 7; 22 July 1963, ff. 12; 1970, ff. 19; 6 July 1975, ff. 24.
13. TH to Daniel Weissbort, 12 April 1985, Emory Mss 894, Box 1, ff. 1.
14. TH to Gerald Hughes, 21 December 1979, Emory Mss 854, Box 1, ff. 28.
15. TH to Keith Sagar, 18.6.98, BL Add.78761, ff. 28–9.
16. Sagar, *The Laughter of Foxes*, p. 41.
17. 'Ted Hughes: The Art of Poetry LXXI', p. 61.
18. TH to Gerald Hughes, Jan–May 1958?, Emory Mss 854, Box 1, ff. 7.
19. TH to Gerald Hughes, Christmas 1958, Emory Mss 854, Box 1, ff. 7.
20. *Crow*, Claddagh CCT9–10, 1973.
21. 'Orghast', Interview with Tom Stoppard, *Times Literary Supplement*, 1 October 1971, p. 1174.
22. TH to Peter Redgrove, nd, Emory Mss 867, ff. 3.
23. *Ted Hughes: The Life of a Poet*, p. 237.

24. Emory Mss 644, Subseries 2.4b, Box 111, ff. 6.
25. TH to Gerald Hughes, 27 October 1969, Emory Mss 854, Box 1, ff. 18.
26. Ted Hughes, 'The Rock', *The Listener*, 70, pp.421–3, 19 September 1963.
27. 'Ted Hughes and *Crow*', Ekbert Faas, *Ted Hughes: The Unaccommodated Universe*, Santa Barbara, Black Sparrow Press, 1980, p. 202.
28. TH to Lucas Myers, 9.6.59, Emory Mss865, Box 1, ff. 5.
29. www.zeta.org.au/~annskea/ABC2AF.htm.
30. Emory Mss 644, Box 83 ff. 90.
31. Emory Mss 854, Box 1, ff. 46.
32. This poem has an epigraph from a long poem entitled 'Unstilled Assegais', which is either apocryphal or an example of the 'sagas of involved warfare among African tribes' of which he spoke to Ekbert Faas (*Ted Hughes: The Unaccommodated Universe*, p. 203).
33. TH to Terry Gifford and Neil Roberts, 1977.
34. Robert Graves, *The White Goddess: A Historical Grammar of Poetic Myth*, 1948, amended and enlarged edition, 1966, New York, Farrar, Straus and Giroux, 1966, p. 12.
35. Graves, *The White Goddess*, pp. 446–7.
36. Graves, *The White Goddess*, p. 449.
37. Graves, *The White Goddess*, p. 110.
38. According to Olwyn Hughes, however, her brother did not have a copy of the poem in 1956 and 'was able to recapture it' by memory. This should make us wary of considering it entirely the work of an eighteen year old. Ann Skea, email, 23 October 2005, quoting Olwyn Hughes.
39. The book was a gift on matriculating to Cambridge in 1951, two years after the composition of the poem. See Diane Middlebrook's discussion of 'Song' and *The White Goddess* in *Her Husband*, pp. 30–5.

## 2   'The Thought-Fox': Hughes and Cambridge

1. Drue Heinz, 'Ted Hughes: The Art of Poetry LXXI', pp. 77, 85.
2. TH to Keith Sagar, 16 July 1979, quoted Elaine Feinstein, *Ted Hughes: The Life of a Poet*, London, Weidenfeld and Nicholson, 2001, p. 24.
3. Brian Cox, 'Ted Hughes (1930–1998): A Personal Retrospect', *The Hudson Review*, Spring 1999, Vol.52, no.1, p. 31.
4. Elaine Feinstein, *Ted Hughes: The Life of a Poet*, p. 34.
5. TH to Olwyn Hughes, undated, Emory Mss 980, Box 1 ff. 2. I date this letter soon after February 1952 because it refers to the death of the King.
6. This was by no means an unusual move, or necessarily one that signalled disenchantment with English. F.R. Leavis was in the habit of encouraging his own students to take Archaeology and Anthropology part II.
7. Brian Cox, 'Ted Hughes (1930–1998): A Personal Retrospect', p. 34.
8. TH to Lucas Myers, 9 December 1958, Emory Mss 865, Box 1, ff. 4.
9. TH to Keith Sagar, 18 June 1998, BL Add.78761, f. 21.
10. TH to Lucas Myers, April/May 1958, Emory Mss 865, ff. 4.
11. TH to Leonard Scigaj, 28 July 1989, Emory Mss 644, Box 53, ff. 3.
12. At the time of the Eliade review in 1964 Hughes wrote to Myers about the subject in a way that suggests that he knew little about it beforehand (Emory

Mss 865, Box 1, ff. 10). It may be significant that it is in 1964 that Hughes wrote the first version of *Gaudete*, as a film scenario, in which Lumb is described as drumming on a Siberian shaman's drum (Emory Mss 644, Subseries 2.2, Box 68, ff. 2).

13. Hughes uses the male pronoun though he says that shamanism is 'not exclusively male' (*WP* 58).
14. 'Ted Hughes: The Art of Poetry LXXI', p. 61.
15. 'Ted Hughes: The Art of Poetry LXXI', p. 85. In a letter to Keith Sagar in 1983, Hughes wrote that his first poem after the gap was 'The Little Boys and the Seasons', which was published in *Chequer* in June 1954 (25 March, 1983, BL Add.78757). He did not collect this poem, and therefore might not have considered it to have been 'saved'. However, he published 'The Jaguar' and 'The Casualty' in November of 1954, and 'The Thought-Fox' not until 1957: it seems unlikely that he would have held back such an important poem for so long. Although there are numerous drafts of *Hawk in the Rain* poems in the Emory archive (Mss 644, Subseries 2.1, Box 57, ff. 2), they are impossible to date, and there are none of 'The Thought-Fox'.
16. Ibid.
17. T.S. Eliot, 'Philip Massinger', *Selected Essays*, London, Faber, 1951, p. 209.
18. 'Ted Hughes and *Crow*' (an interview) in Ekbert Faas, *Ted Hughes: The Unaccommodated Universe*, Santa Barbara, Black Sparrow Press, 1980, p. 200.
19. D.D. Bradley, 'Ted Hughes 1930–1998', *Pembroke College Cambridge Society Annual Gazette* 73, September 1999, p. 23.
20. TH to Gerald Hughes, 10 August 1953, Emory Mss 854, Box 1, ff. 2.
21. William Shakespeare, *Macbeth*, 1.7.21–25, ed. A.R. Braunmuller, The New Cambridge Shakespeare, Cambridge, Cambridge University Press, 1997, pp. 132–3.
22. Feinstein, *Ted Hughes: The Life of a Poet*, p. 69.
23. F.R. Leavis, 'Imagery and Movement', *The Living Principle: 'English' as a Discipline of Thought*, London, Chatto and Windus, 1975, p. 97. Although this is one of Leavis's latest books, this essay is based on work that he did in the 1940s.
24. Ibid., p. 103.
25. Bradley, 'Ted Hughes 1930–1998', p. 22.
26. Sagar, *The Laughter of Foxes*, p. 52.
27. TH to Lucas Myers, 9 June 1959, Emory Mss 865, ff. 5.
28. Antony Easthope, *Poetry as Discourse*, London, Methuen, 1983, p. 65..
29. Elmer Andrews, *The Poetry of Seamus Heaney: All the Realms of Whisper*, Basingstoke and London, Macmillan, 1988, p. 56.
30. 'Ted Hughes: The Art of Poetry LXXI', p. 61.
31. Rainer Maria Rilke, 'Die Erste Elegie', *Duino Elegies*, tr. Stephen Cohn, Manchester, Carcanet, 1989, p. 20.
32. Rainer Maria Rilke, 'The Panther', *New Poems [1907]*, tr. Edgar Snow, San Francisco, North Point Press, 1984, p. 73.
33. Ted Hughes, 'The Jaguar', Karl Miller, ed., *Poetry From Cambridge 1952–54*, Cambridge, Fantasy Press, 1955, p. 29.
34. T.S. Eliot, 'Hamlet', *Selected Essays*, p. 145.
35. Bradley, 'Ted Hughes 1930–1998', p. 23.

## 3    The Encounter with Sylvia Plath

1. TH to Gerald Hughes, 10 October 1955, Emory Mss 854, Box 1, ff. 4.
2. Hughes's habit of writing on the verso of used paper has preserved a record of this activity. Several pages of his notes for the anthology *Five American Poets* are written on the back of pages of synopses. These include the first page of a synopsis of 'A Small Victory' by Bryan Forbes, dated 2 December 1955. Hughes's comment on the story, about 400 words, has also survived: this comment is thoughtful and critical, showing that Hughes took this work seriously. This film does not seem to have been made. Emory Mss 644, Subseries 2.4c, Box 112, ff. 13.
3. Feinstein, *Ted Hughes: The Life of a Poet*, p. 39. This information, in a letter written in 1999 based on a memory of having 'met Hughes in the street … some time in 1954–55', should perhaps not be treated as 100 per cent reliable.
4. Philip Hobsbaum, 'Ted Hughes at Cambridge', *The Dark Horse*, 8, Autumn 1999, pp. 6–12.
5. 'Ted Hughes: The Art of Poetry LXXI', p. 68.
6. Daniel, chapter1, verse 17.
7. Daniel, chapter2, verses 8–11.
8. *Chequer* 9, Winter 1956, pp. 2–3. 'Epitaph in Three Parts' is also in Sylvia Plath, *Collected Poems*, London, Faber, 1981, pp. 337–8. 'Three Caryatids without a Portico' is quoted in full in Keith Sagar, *The Laughter of Foxes*, p. 49. Plath quotes from Hughes poems in both magazines in her journal entry about the meeting, so it is likely that she had read all six of the poems mentioned here; Hughes's poem 'Caryatids (I)' indicates that he had read this poem of hers (and therefore presumably both of them) before he met her. It is curious that although he thought 'Three Caryatids without a Portico' important enough to write two poems of his own about it, he did not include it even in the 'Juvenilia' section of *Collected Poems*.
9. In *The Hawk in the Rain* this poem has the title 'Soliloquy of a Misanthrope'. It is interesting that Hughes subsequently dropped this distancing device.
10. Sylvia Plath, *The Journals of Sylvia Plath 1950–1962*, ed. Karen V. Kukil, London, Faber, 2000, p. 211.
11. Quoted in Keith Sagar, *The Laughter of Foxes*, p. 48–9. I have not seen the original, but Keith Sagar informs me that this is the whole of Huws's comment on Plath's poems.
12. *The Journals of Sylvia Plath*, p. 196.
13. *The Journals of Sylvia Plath*, p. 211.
14. Ibid.
15. Jacqueline Rose, *The Haunting of Sylvia Plath*, London, Virago, 1991, p. 73.
16. *The Journals of Sylvia Plath*, pp. 207–8.
17. Seamus Heaney, 'The Fire i'the Flint: Reflections on the Poetry of Gerard Manley Hopkins', *Preoccupations*, London, Faber, 1980, p. 88.
18. *The Journals of Sylvia Plath*, p. 173.
19. *Chequer* 7, November 1954, p. 16.
20. *The Journals of Sylvia Plath*, p. 212.
21. Sylvia Plath, 'Ode for Ted', *Collected Poems*, p. 29.
22. Sylvia Plath, *Letters Home: Correspondence 1950–1963*, ed. Aurelia Schober Plath, London, Faber, 1975, p. 222.

23. *The Journals of Sylvia Plath*, p. 214.
24. Alfred Tennyson, 'In Memoriam A.H.H.' lvi, 15, Christopher Ricks, ed., *Tennyson: A Selected Edition*, Harlow, Longman, 1969, p. 399.
25. Sylvia Plath, 'Pursuit', *Collected Poems*, p. 22.
26. Margaret Dickie Uroff, *Sylvia Plath and Ted Hughes*, Chicago, University of Illinois, 1979, p. 70.
27. Diane Middlebrook, *Her Husband*, p. 22.
28. *The Journals of Sylvia Plath*, p. 233.
29. Sylvia Plath, *Letters Home*, p. 270.
30. Linda Wagner-Martin, *Sylvia Plath: A Biography* (1988), London, Cardinal, 1990, p. 12.
31. Sagar, *The Laughter of Foxes*, p. 53.
32. Hobsbaum, 'Ted Hughes at Cambridge', p. 6.
33. Lucas Myers, 'Ah, Youth ... Ted Hughes and Sylvia Plath at Cambridge and After', Appendix I of Anne Stevenson, *Bitter Fame: A Life of Sylvia Plath* (1989) Harmondsworth, Penguin, 1990, p. 314.
34. *Ted Hughes: The Life of a Poet*, p. 68.
35. Myers, 'Ah, Youth ... ', p. 314.
36. Middlebrook, *Her Husband*, p. 26.
37. TH to Gerald Hughes, 1958, Emory Mss 854, Box 1, ff. 7.
38. *New York Times Book Review*, 6 October 1957, p. 43.
39. *Times*, 23 January 1958; *Manchester Guardian*, 4 October 1957; *Sunday Times*, 3 November 1957, p. 7; *New Statesman*, 28 September 1957, p. 392.
40. *Observer*, 6 October 1957, p. 12.
41. TH to Gerald Hughes, 1958, Emory Mss 854, Box 1, ff. 7.

## 4  Dreaming from America: *Lupercal*

1. Stevenson, *Bitter Fame*, p. 161.
2. Hughes wrote to Lucas Myers that apart from 'Thrushes', everything in *Lupercal* was written in America (9 December 1959. Emory Mss 865, Box 1, ff. 5). Myers mistakenly refers to this poem as 'Thistle' (*Crow Steered, Bergs Appeared: A Memoir of Ted Hughes and Sylvia Plath*, Sewanee, Proctor's Hall, 2001, p. 86). Elaine Feinstein asserts that 'View of a Pig' was also written in Cambridge (*Ted Hughes: The Life of a Poet*, p. 70), but gives no source.
3. In the Emory archive there is a draft of one poem about arriving at Manhattan, but Hughes seems to have abandoned it (Emory Mss 644, Subseries 2.1, Box 57, ff. 2); also eight lines of a satirical poem about American suburban life titled 'Massachussetts' (Emory Mss 644, Subseries 2.2, Box 60, ff. 20).
4. TH to Gerald Hughes, August 1958, Emory Mss 854, Box 1, ff. 7; to Lucas Myers, 22 July 1957, Emory Mss 865, ff. 3; to Daniel Weissbort, March 1959, Emory Mss 894, ff. 1.
5. TH to Lucas Myers, Autumn 1957, Emory Mss 865, Box 1, ff. 3.
6. Ekbert Faas, *Ted Hughes; The Unaccommodated Universe*, p. 208.
7. Elaine Feinstein, *Ted Hughes: The Life of a Poet*, p. 91.
8. Faas, *Ted Hughes; The Unaccommodated Universe*, p. 202.
9. J.R.R. Tolkien and E.V. Gordon, eds, *Sir Gawain and the Green Knight*, Oxford, Clarendon Press, 1925, p. 7.

10. Faas, *Ted Hughes; The Unaccommodated Universe*, p. 199.
11. TH to Olwyn Hughes, Emory Mss 980, Box 1 ff. 9, undated but written from America, probably 1959.
12. 'Ted Hughes: The Art of Poetry LXXI', pp. 66–7. Again, there are no drafts in the Emory archive.
13. Sagar, *The Laughter of Foxes*, pp. 87–103. Sagar analyses a later poem, 'The Dove Came', written in the 1970s. There are very few drafts of *Lupercal* poems in the archive, but there is evidence from *Hawk in the Rain* material that Hughes habitually wrote many drafts of his earlier poems as well: Emory has fourteen drafts of 'The Hawk in the Rain', for example (Emory Mss 644, Subseries 2.1, Box 57, ff. 2).
14. Graham Bradshaw, 'From *Wodwo* to *Crow*' (unpublished).
15. At a conference on Leeds poetry in 2003, a former student of Hill's asserted that in the 1960s Hill was 'haunted' by Hughes's poetry, particularly *Lupercal*. These lines might be an example of what haunted him. Another is 'My skull burrows among antennae and fronds' ('Fire-eater'), which might be mistaken for a quotation from *Mercian Hymns*.
16. Ekbert Faas, *Ted Hughes; The Unaccommodated Universe*, p. 199.
17. TH to Keith Sagar, 18 June 1998, BL Add.78761, ff. 23–4.
18. See A. Alvarez, *Observer*, 27.3.60, p. 22; Kenneth Young, *Daily Telegraph*, 14.4.60, p. 17; Austin Clarke, *Irish Times*, 9.4.60, p. 8; *Times Literary Supplement*, 15.4.60, p. 238.
19. Alvarez, op.cit.
20. Young, op.cit.; Norman McCaig, *Spectator*, 22.4.60, p. 582.
21. 'Desk Poet', *Guardian*, 23.3.65.
22. TH to Lucas Myers, Winter/Spring 1961, Emory Mss 865, ff. 7.

## 5   *Wodwo*: the 'single adventure' and the death of Sylvia Plath

1. TH to Ben Sonnenberg, 10 October 196,1Emory Mss 924, Box 1, ff. 1.
2. Part I of 'The House of Aries' was published in *Audience* 8, Spring 1961, p. 77–105. 'The Wound' was published in *Wodwo*. 'Difficulties of a Bridegroom' and 'Dogs: a Scherzo' were unpublished, but there is a complete ts of 'Difficulties of a Bridegroom' in the Alvarez papers in the BL. Another play, *Eat Crow*, was not broadcast but published as a limited edition, London, Rainbow Press, 1971. 'The Calm' was not published but fragments of ts survive in the BL and Emory, on the verso of drafts of poems. Later in the 1960s Hughes turned to radio plays for children, most of which were published as *The Coming of the Kings and Other Plays*, London, Faber, 1970.
3. Middlebrook, *Her Husband*, pp. 138–9, citing letter to Hughes from Peter Hall in the Emory archive.
4. TH to Lucas Myers, Winter/Spring 1961, Emory Mss 865, Box 1, ff. 7.
5. TH to Janos Csokits, 12 June 1961, Emory Mss 895, Box 1, ff. 4.
6. TH to Lucas Myers, March 1966, Emory Mss 865, Box 1, ff. 12.
7. TH to Leonard Scigaj, 14 June 1981, Emory Mss 644, Subseries 1.5, Box 53. Hughes subsequently revised the poem, removing the reference to Plath's death, and published it as 'The Angel' in *Remains of Elmet*.

8. TH to Janos Csokits, 6 August 1967, Emory Mss 895, Box 1, ff. 8; and to Ben Sonnenberg, 11 August 1967, Emory Mss 924, Box 1, ff. 1.
9. Daniel Hoffman, 'Talking Beasts: The "Single Adventure" in the Poems of Ted Hughes', Leonard M. Scigaj, ed., *Critical Essays on Ted Hughes*, New York, G.K. Hall & Co., 1992, pp. 143–52; originally published in *Shenandoah* 19, Summer 1968, pp. 49–68. The parallel between 'The Wound' and the *Bardo Thödol* is confirmed by Hughes in his letter to Ben Sonnenberg (note 8) and in the Foreword to *DB* (p. viii).
10. Emory Mss 644, Subseries 2.2, Box 68, ff. 2, pp. 39–45. The date 1964–65 derives from this typescript. In the Introduction to *DB* Hughes states, almost certainly erroneously, that the scenario was written in 1962–63. In a letter to Terry Gifford and myself (1977) he dated the 'first written-out idea' to 1962 and the scenario to 1964.
11. TH to Janos Csokits, 6 August 1967, Emory Mss 895, Box 1, ff. 8.
12. Faas, *Ted Hughes: The Unaccommodated Universe*, p. 86; Diane Middlebrook, *Her Husband*, p. 158. As well as 'The Wound' and all the stories, the following poems were certainly written and published or broadcast before Plath's death: 'Thistles', 'Still Life', 'Her Husband', 'Public Bar T.V.', 'A Vegetarian', 'Sugar Loaf', 'Bowled Over', 'Wino', 'The Rescue', 'The Green Wolf', 'Theology', 'Gog' Part I, 'Out', 'New Moon in January', 'The Warriors of the North', 'Mountains', 'Pibroch', 'Full Moon and Little Frieda', 'Wodwo'. 'Song of a Rat' and 'The Howling of Wolves' were certainly written within a few weeks of Plath's death, and 'Skylarks' in 1965 or 1966. It isn't possible to be so certain about other poems, but there are drafts in a notebook that also contains 'Skylarks' and *Crow* poems of the following, suggesting that they were at least significantly revised at a late date: 'Fern', 'Logos', 'Gnat-Psalm', 'Reveille', 'Wings', 'A Wind Flashes the Grass', 'Karma', 'Second Glance at a Jaguar', 'The Bear', 'Ballad from a Fairy Tale', 'Cadenza'.
13. TH to Keith Sr, aga18 June 1998, BL Add.78761, f. 23.
14. Hoffman, 'Talking Beasts', p. 147.
15. TH to Janos Csokits, 6 August 1967, Emory Mss 895, Box 1, ff. 8. Hughes talked at length about 'The Wound' on Australian radio in 1976. Ann Skea's transcription can be found at www.zeta.org.au/annskea/ABC2AF.htm.
16. Nick Gammage, ed., *The Epic Poise: A Celebration of Ted Hughes*, London, Faber, 1999.
17. This might be another instance of Graves's influence. Graves wrote that a collection of poems should 'form a sequence of the intenser moments of the poet's spiritual autobiography', which would not however 'keep chronological step with its historical counterpart: often a poetic event anticipates or succeeds the corresponding physical event by years', 'Foreword' to *Poems and Satires 1951*, reprinted in *Complete Poems* vol.2, ed. Beryl Graves and Dunstan Ward, Manchester, Carcanet, 1997, pp. 345–6. I am grateful to Fran Brearton for bringing this to my attention.
18. William Anderson, *Green Man: The Archetype of our Oneness with the Earth*, London and San Francisco, Harper Collins, 1990.
19. TH to A.Alvarez, undated , BL 8878 C1.3.
20. *Irish Times*, 20.5.67, p. 8.
21. Keith Sagar, *The Art of Ted Hughes* (1975), 2nd edition, Cambridge, Cambridge University Press, 1978, p. 98.

22. Samuel Beckett, *Molloy, Malone Dies, The Unnameable*, London, Calder, 1959, p. 418.
23. 'The Green Wolf' and 'The Bear' are not about real animals. 'Skylarks' certainly and 'Gnat-Psalm' probably were written later than 'Song of a Rat' and 'The Howling of Wolves'.
24. TH to Keith Sagar, 18 June, 1998, BL Add.78761, f. 23.
25. Middlebrook, *Her Husband*, pp. 227–8.
26. Lynda K. Bundtzen, 'Poetic Arson and Sylvia Plath's "Burning the Letters" ', *Contemporary Literature* 39.3, 1998, p. 437.
27. See Stevenson, *Bitter Fame*, pp. 250–1.
28. Susan R. Van Dyne, *Revising a Life: Sylvia Plath's Ariel Poems*, Chapel Hill and London, University of North Carolina Press, 1993, p. 33.
29. Bundtzen, 'Poetic Arson and Sylvia Plath's "Burning the Letters" ', pp. 442–3.
30. Van Dyne, *Revising a Life*, pp. 40–1.
31. Bundtzen, 'Poetic Arson and Sylvia Plath's "Burning the Letters" ', p. 443.
32. Emory Mss 644, Subseries 2.2, Box 60, ff. 13.
33. Hughes has consistently affirmed that he wrote 'Skylarks' in 1965–66. In his 18.6.98 letter to Keith Sagar he is uncertain about the date of 'Gnat-Psalm', stating that it might have been completed at the same time at 'Song of a Rat' and 'The Howling of Wolves', or earlier, or much later. BL Add.78761, f. 23. Drafts of the poem in notebooks also containing *Crow* poems and drafts of 'Skylarks', however, suggest that Hughes was at least revising it at a late stage. Emory Mss 644, Subseries 2.1, Box 57, ff. 6, ff. 8.
34. Hoffman, 'Talking Beasts', p. 151.
35. Emory Mss 644: Subseries 2.1, Box 57, ff. 1, ff. 8; Subseries 2.2, Box 59, ff. 53; Box 60, ff. 11; Box 61, ff. 1.
36. The version published in all the selected editions and the *Collected Poems* has two sections, IV and VIII, that are not in *Wodwo*.
37. Dylan Evans, *An Introductory Dictionary of Lacanian Psychoanalysis*, London and New York, Routledge, 1996, p. 159.
38. *Crow*, Claddagh CCT9–10, 1973.
39. A.C.H. Smith, *Orghast at Persepolis*, London, Eyre Methuen, 1972, p. 45.
40. *Irish Times*, 20.5.67, p. 8; *Spectator*, 27.7.67, pp. 105–6, *Books and Bookmen*, Nov. 67, pp. 40–1 *TLS*, 6.7.67, p. 601.

## 6   The Making of *Crow*

1. Faas, *Ted Hughes: The Unaccommodated Universe*, p. 208.
2. *Irish Times*, 31.10.70, p. 10; *Encounter*, 86.3, March 71, p. 68; *The Times*, 17.12.70, p. 15; *TLS*, 8.1.71, p. 30.
3. TH to Gerald Hughes, 27 October 1969, Emory Mss854, Box 1, ff.18.
4. TH to Keith Sagar, 1973/4(?), BL Add.78756, f. 16.
5. TH to Leonard Baskin, 16 July 1969, BL Deposit 10200.
6. See for example TH to Gerald Hughes, Sept (?) 1971, Emory Mss 854, Box 1, ff. 20.
7. TH to 'Nick' (unidentified), 17 May 93, Emory Mss 644, Box 54 ff.1.
8. Sagar, *The Laughter of Foxes*, p. xii.
9. TH to Keith Sagar, 1973/4(?), BL Add.78756, f. 16.
10. TH to Leonard Baskin 16 July 1969, BL Deposit 10200.

11. TH to Ben Sonnenberg, Emory Mss 924, 13 November 69, Box 1 ff. 1, 23 March 1970, ff. 2.
12. TH to Leonard Baskin, 15 August 1984, BL Deposit 10200.
13. TH to 'Nick' (unidentified), 17 May 93, Emory Mss 644, Box 54 ff. 1.
14. All the ones Hughes published are in *Collected Poems*. However, one exasperating feature of this indispensable volume is that when poems were published in a limited edition before they appeared in *Crow*, they are printed under that edition, thus undermining the integrity of *Crow*. For the record, all the poems in *Four Crow Poems* and *A Few Crows*, with the exception of 'Carnival', belong to the 1970 edition of *Crow*. 'The Contender' in *Crow Wakes* was added with six other poems to the 1972 edition. In 1997 Hughes recorded an 'unabridged' version of *Crow* with narrative links. This recording includes 'Tiger-Psalm' (*M*) , 'The Lovepet' (*M*) and 'Bride and Groom Lie Hidden for Three Days' (*CB*), none of which were in the British edition. Despite its description, this recording also omits six poems from the published version (*Crow*, Penguin Audiobooks, Harmondsworth, Penguin, 1997). In 1970–71 Hughes was discussing with Leonard Baskin a limited edition to be published by Baskin's Gehenna Press, that would have included nearly 40 extra poems, including nearly all that were published and some that were, in the event, never published at all. TH to Leonard Baskin, 17 June 1970, 20 September 1970, BL Deposit 10200.
15. Sagar, *The Laughter of Foxes*, pp. 170–80. This is similar to the linking commentary in Hughes's recording.
16. Faas, *Ted Hughes: the Unaccommodated Universe*, p. 206.
17. TH to A. Alvarez, undated, BL 8878 (In this letter he asks for advice about publishing *Crow*, which suggests a date of 1969).
18. TH to Ben Sonnenberg, 23 March 1970, Emory Mss 924, Box 1, ff. 2.
19. Sagar, *The Laughter of Foxes*, p. 171.
20. For a more detailed commentary on this poem, see Terry Gifford and Neil Roberts, *Ted Hughes: A Critical Study*, London, Faber, 1981, pp. 108–10.
21. Sagar, *The Laughter of Foxes*, p. 176.
22. Sagar, *The Laughter of Foxes*, p. 178. See Gifford and Roberts, *Ted Hughes: A Critical Study*, p. 256.
23. TH to Keith Sagar, 23 May 1974, BL Add.78576, f. 20.
24. The American edition included seven poems not in the first British publication, including 'The Lovepet'. The augmented sixth printing of the first British edition also included seven additional poems, but substituted 'Crowcolour' for 'The Lovepet', which in Britain was collected in *Moortown*. Three further poems, again not including 'The Lovepet', were added to the limited edition published by Faber in 1973.
25. TH to Keith Sagar, 17 March 1975, BL Add.78756, f. 29.
26. Sagar, *The Laughter of Foxes*, p. 180.
27. Sagar, *The Laughter of Foxes*, p. 171.
28. *Crow*, Penguin Audiobooks, Harmondsworth, Penguin, 1997.
29. Emory Mss 644, Subseries 2.2, Box 61, ff. 49.
30. TH to Leonard Baskin, 16.7.69, BL 10200.
31. Emory Mss 644, Subseries 2.2, Box 61, ff. 60. Hughes's unpublished writings are often strikingly prophetic. In a story probably written in 1956, 'The Callum-Makers', he anticipates Reality TV. Emory Mss 644, Subseries 2.4b, Box 111, ff. 2.

32. Emory Mss 644, Subseries 2.2, Box 61, ff. 52; Samuel Beckett, *Endgame*, London, Faber, 1958, p. 11.
33. See Paul Radin, *The Trickster*, Routledge, London, 1956.
34. Emory Mss 644, Series 2.2, Box 61, ff. 55.
35. See for example Sagar, *The Art of Ted Hughes*, 2nd edition, p. 101. This is confirmed by a letter from Baskin to Hughes, 9 May 1968, Emory Mss 644, Subseries 1.1, Box 1, ff. 10, and by Hughes in the essay 'Crow on the Beach', *WP* 243.
36. Feinstein, *Ted Hughes: The Life of a Poet*, p. 160.TH to Leonard Baskin, Oct. 65, BL Deposit 10200.
37. 'X', *Encounter*, 25.20–1, July 1965. The first actual *Crow* poems did not begin to appear until the summer of 1967, when Hughes published the first of 'Two Legends' (*Journal of Creative Behaviour*, 1.3, July 1967), 'A Disaster' (*The Scotsman*. 22 July 1967, p. 3) and 'Lineage' (Ted Hughes, *Animal Poems*, Bow, Crediton, Devon, Richard Gilbertson, 1967).
38. Emory Mss 644, Subseries 2.2, Box 68, ff. 2, p. 2.
39. TH to Leonard Baskin, 2 March 1968, BL Deposit 10200.
40. Neil Roberts, *Narrative and Voice in Postwar Poetry*, Harlow, Longman, 1999, pp. 36–48.
41. TH to Gerald Hughes, 27 October 1969, Emory Mss854, Box 1, ff. 18.
42. Miroslav Holub, *Selected Poems*, tr. Ian Milner and George Theiner, Harmondsworth, Penguin, 1967, p. 40.
43. Michael Parker, 'Hughes and the Poets of Eastern Europe', Keith Sagar, ed., *The Achievement of Ted Hughes*, Manchester, Manchester University Press, 1983, p. 38.
44. John Carpenter and Bogdana Carpenter, 'Introduction to Zbigniew Herbert, *Selected Poems*, tr. John Carpenter and Bogdana Carpenter, Oxford, Oxford University Press, 1977, p. xii.
45. TH to Keith Sagar, 1973/4? BL Add.78756, f. 13. Quoted in Sagar, *The Art of Ted Hughes*, p. 107.
46. Vasko Popa, *Collected Poems 1943–1976*, tr. Anne Pennington with an introduction by Ted Hughes, Manchester, Carcanet, 1978, pp. 67–71.

# 7 The 'Plath Wars'

1. TH to Jacqueline Rose (undated) quoted in Janet Malcolm, *The Silent Woman: Sylvia Plath and Ted Hughes/Ted Hughes and Sylvia Plath*, (1993) London and Basingstoke, Macmillan, 1995, pp. 46–7. (The order of the names is reversed on the jacket and the title page of Malcolm's book.)
2. TH to Keith Sagar, 18 June 1998, BL Add.78757, ff. 19–23.
3. Ibid., ff. 22–3.
4. TH to Janos Csokits, 1998, Emory Mss 895, Box 1, ff. 50.
5. TH to Keith Sagar, 23 May 1974 BL Add.78756, f. 18.
6. TH to Keith Sagar,1973?, BL Add.78756, f. 7.
7. TH to Lucas Myers, April/May 1958, Emory Mss 865, ff. 4.
8. TH to Leonard Scigaj, 28 July 1989, Emory Mss 644, Subseries 1.5, Box 53.
9. For example, Butscher quotes from a conversation between Plath and Peter Davison 'after a strenuous bout of lovemaking' (Edward Butscher, *Sylvia Plath: Method and Madness*, New York, Seabury Press, 1976 p. 310), which is enough

to explain Hughes's comment, 'Her boy-friends do not fail to gambol and half-strip' (TH to Lucas Myers, 1 September 1975, Emory Mss 865, Box 1, ff. 17.)

10. Mikhail Bakhtin, *Problems of Dostoevsky's Poetics*, ed. and tr. Caryl Emerson, Minneapolis, University of Minnesota Press, 1984, p. 196.
11. Malcolm, *The Silent Woman*, p. 167.
12. Butscher, *Sylvia Plath: Method and Madness*, p. 280. Butscher incorrectly assigns this incident to Christmas 1961, making Plath eight months pregnant in the process, a typical instance of the inaccuracy of his book.
13. Ted Hughes, 'Sylvia Plath: The Facts of her Life and the Desecration of her Grave', *The Independent*, 22.4.89, p. 19. This letter is a response to an article by Ronald Hayman, 'The Poet and the Unquiet Grave', *The Independent*, 19.4.89, p. 19.
14. Anne Stevenson, *Bitter Fame*, p. 204.
15. *Letters Home*, 1 January 1961, p. 404.
16. Malcolm, *The Silent Woman*, p. 50.
17. Malcolm, *The Silent Woman*, pp. 74–5.
18. Paul Alexander, *Rough Magic: A Biography of Sylvia Plath*, Harmondsworth, Viking, 1991, p. 262; *Bitter Fame*, pp. 339–40.
19. Alexander, *Rough Magic*, p. 194.
20. Robin Morgan, 'Arraignment' in *Monster*, New York, Random House, 1972.
21. Ronald Hayman, *The Death and Life of Sylvia Plath*, London, Heinemann, 1991, p. 15.
22. Marjorie Perloff, 'The Two *Ariels*: The (Re)Making of the Sylvia Plath Canon', Neil Fraistat, ed., *Poems in their Place: The Intertextuality and Order of Poetic Collections*, Chapel Hill and London, University of North Carolina Press, 1986, pp. 313–14.
23. See my argument for the variety of Plath's last poems in *Narrative and Voice in Postwar Poetry*, pp. 31–3.
24. Middlebrook, *Her Husband*, pp. 163–74.
25. Perloff, 'The Two *Ariels*', p. 312. It is true that the dates and details were not in the public realm when Perloff published her article. My point is not that she is wilfully ignoring the evidence but that her argument *needs* the poems from 'Elm' onwards to be drawn into the narrative of Hughes's infidelity.
26. Alvarez archive, BL 8878 C1.3 Alvarez's letter is dated 15.11.71; Hughes's letters are undated but obviously immediately precede and succeed this date. Extensive extracts from this correspondence are quoted in Malcolm, *The Silent Woman*, pp. 124–30.
27. A. Alvarez, *The Savage God: A Study of Suicide* (1971), London, Bloomsbury, 2002, p. 52.
28. Malcolm, *The Silent Woman*, p. 130.
29. TH to Janet Malcolm, *The Silent Woman*, p. 210.
30. Middlebrook, *Her Husband*, p. 229.
31. TH to Gerald Hughes, 25 November 1974, Emory Mss 854, Box 1, ff. 23.
32. TH to Daniel Weissbort, 1975/76, Emory Mss 894, Box 1, ff. 1.
33. TH to Gerald Hughes, 1975 and December 1976 (incorrectly dated 77) Emory Mss 854, Box 1, ff. 24–5.
34. Sylvia Plath, *The Journals of Sylvia Plath*, ed. Frances McCullough and Ted Hughes, New York, Dial, 1982. This book was only published in the United States. See Middlebrook, *Her Husband*, pp. 257–61.

35. The essay quoted, which was first published in *Grand Street*, I.3, Spring 1982, is a revised version of the Introduction to the *Journals*.
36. Plath, *The Journals of Sylvia Plath 1950–1962*, ed. Karen V. Kukil, pp. 211–12. The review referred to is a contemptuous comment on Plath's poems by Hughes's friend Daniel Huws in the magazine *Broadsheet*. See Chapter 3.
37. Plath, *The Journals of Sylvia Plath*, ed. Frances McCullough and Ted Hughes, pp. 111–12.
38. This was a particularly clumsy instance of editing, because it occurred, as Jacqueline Rose says, 'between the galleys sent out to reviewers and the final publication of the text.' Rose, *The Haunting of Sylvia Plath*, p. 88.
39. I would like to put on record, from the point of a Hughes scholar, that when Terry Gifford and I were writing *Ted Hughes: A Critical Study*, Olwyn was extremely co-operative and generous, sending us proofs of Rainbow Press editions before they were published.
40. Hughes, 'Sylvia Plath: The Facts of her Life and the Desecration of her Grave'.
41. Rose, *The Haunting of Sylvia Plath*, pp. 66–7.
42. Hayman, 'The poet and the unquiet grave'.
43. Alexander, *Rough Magic*, pp. 197–8.
44. Julia Parnaby and Rachel Wingfield, 'In memory of Sylvia Plath', *The Guardian*, 7.4.89, p. 39.
45. 'Problems strewn on the path to Sylvia Plath's grave', *The Guardian*, 11.4.89, p. 18.
46. Wagner-Martin, *Sylvia Plath: A Biography*, p. 238.
47. Malcolm, *The Silent Woman*, p. 142.

# 8   The Shaman-Poet and Masculine Guilt: *Gaudete* and *Cave Birds*

1. Diane Middlebrook, *Her Husband*, p. 234. The significance of Hughes's mother's death is clear in a letter to Gerald in which he couples it with Assia's: 'From the age of about 16–17 my life has been quite false' (1971, Emory Mss 854, Box 1, ff. 20). Elaine Feinstein says that 'the key to this letter is in a sentence that is scratched out so vehemently as to be illegible' (Feinstein, *Ted Hughes: The Life of a Poet*, p. 183), but in fact the deleted phrase is decipherable as 'Ma and Assia dying'.
2. Interview with Tom Stoppard, *Times Literary Supplement*, 1.10.71, quoted in A.C.H. Smith, *Orghast at Persepolis*, p. 46.
3. Smith, *Orghast at Persepolis*, p. 45.
4. Letter to Ben Sonnenberg, 29.10.72, Emory Mss 924, Box 1 ff. 2.
5. Smith, *Orghast at Persepolis*, pp. 93–7.
6. Smith, *Orghast at Persepolis*, p. 92.
7. 'Baboons and Neanderthals: A Rereading of *The Inheritors*, John Carey, ed., *William Golding, The Man and his Books: A Tribute on his 75th Birthday*, London, Faber, 1986.
8. Emory Mss 644, Subseries 2.1, Box 57, ff. 11, p. 22. This poem alludes to reading *Parsifal*, which supplies one of the epigraphs to *Gaudete*.
9. TH to Keith Sagar, 18 June 1998, BL Add.78761, f. 20.
10. As *Spring, Summer, Autumn, Winter*, Rainbow Press, 1974.

11. As *Moortown Elegies*, Rainbow Press, 1978. This sequence is titled 'Moortown' in the compendium volume *Moortown*, Faber and Harper & Row, 1979, and *Moortown Diary* when reprinted separately, with notes, in 1989.
12. *CP* (p. 1263) gives the date of composition of the *Gaudete* narrative as 1971–72, but in letters to me and Terry Gifford, and to Keith Sagar, both written in 1977, Hughes dated the whole work to 1973–75 and 1973–76 respectively. I have elsewhere been sceptical about Hughes's dating but it seems unlikely that he would be mistaken about such a major work so soon after the event.
13. *Orts* is a collection of 63 poems, many of them rejects from the 'Epilogue' to *Gaudete*, published by Rainbow Press in 1978. Fourteen of these poems are included in the 'Orts' section of *Moortown*, which also includes other poems. 'Caprichos' is a sequence of 16 or more poems that were never published as such. In *Collected Poems* 4 are printed under that title, 6 are numbers 2–7 of 'Seven Dungeon Songs' (one of these a variant of one of the previous 4), 2 are in *Monomaki* as 'Halfway Head' and 'Restless Head', one is in *A Primer of Birds* as 'For Leonard and Lisa', and 4 are unpublished. The dating of these works is based on letters to Keith Sagar, 30.5.77, BL Add.78757, f. 1, and to Neil Roberts and Terry Gifford, 1977, as well as to manuscript evidence. There is a typescript in the Leonard Baskin papers, BL Deposit 10200.
14. TH to Keith Sagar, 18 June 1998, BL Add.78761, ff. 22–3.
15. TH to Lucas Myers, 10 November 1982, Emory Mss 865, Box 1, ff. 19.
16. Sagar, *The Art of Ted Hughes*, p. 187.
17. Gifford and Roberts, *Ted Hughes: A Critical Study*, p. 199; Graham Bradshaw, 'Creative Mythology in *Cave Birds*', Sagar, ed., *The Achievement of Ted Hughes*, p. 238.
18. TH to Gerald Hughes, 12 April 1977, Emory Mss 854, Box 1, ff. 26.
19. TH to Keith Sagar, 30 May 1977, BL Add.78757, f. 1.
20. *TES*, 10.6.77 p. 18; *TLS* 1.7.77 p. 800; *Observer* 22.5.77; *Guardian*, 19.5.77.
21. *New York Times Book Review*, 25.12.77, p. 4.
22. See Sagar, *The Art of Ted Hughes*, pp. 188–9.
23. Hughes is here drawing on a well-known piece of Dartmoor folklore. See Craig Robinson, *Ted Hughes as Shepherd of Being*, Basingstoke, Macmillan, 1989, p. 76 and www.ashburton.org/myths.htm.
24. TH to Neil Roberts and Terry Gifford, 1979.
25. Emory Mss 644, Box 68, ff. 2.
26. Emory Mss 644, Box 64, ff. 2.
27. Inteview with Ekbert Faas, 1977, *Ted Hughes: The Unaccommodated Universe*, p. 214.
28. TH to Neil Roberts and Terry Gifford, 1979.
29. Plath, *Collected Poems*, p. 35.
30. Emory Mss 644, Box 65, ff. 45.
31. TH to Neil Roberts and Terry Gifford, 1979.
32. TH to Janos Csokits, 6 August 1967, Emory Mss 895, Box 1, ff. 8.
33. Emory Mss 644, Box 65, ff. 45.
34. Emory Mss 644, Box 68, ff. 2, pp. 39–45.
35. Emory Mss 644, Box 65, ff. 45.
36. Sagar, *The Art of Ted Hughes*, p. 203, quoting John Sharkey, *Celtic Mysteries*, London, Thames and Hudson, 1975, p. 12.

37. Gifford and Roberts, *Ted Hughes: A Critical Study*, p. 175, quoting Joseph Campbell, *The Masks of God: Primitive Mythology*, London, Secker and Warburg, 1960, p. 265.
38. Emory Mss 644, Box 64 ff. 6 and Box 65 ff. 45.
39. See A.K. Ramanujan, tr., *Speaking of Siva*, Harmondsworth, Penguin, 1973.
40. Rand Brandes, 'The Economy of Flesh in Ted Hughes's *Gaudete*', Leonard M. Scigaj, ed., *Critical Essays on Ted Hughes*, New York, G.K. Hall, 1972, p. 172.
41. Emory Mss 644, Box 65, ff. 45.
42. Stuart Hirschberg, *Myth in the Poetry of Ted Hughes*, Dublin, Wolfhound Press, 1981, p. 197.
43. Bradshaw, 'Creative Mythology in *Cave Birds*', p. 212.
44. Brandes, 'The Economy of Flesh in Ted Hughes's *Gaudete*', p. 173.
45. Terry Eagleton, 'Recent Poetry', *Stand*, Vol.19, no.2, 1978, p. 78.
46. TH to Neil Roberts and Terry Gifford, 1979.
47. Hirschberg, *Myth in the Poetry of Ted Hughes*, p. 211.
48. Although a few were written much earlier, the Epilogue poems as a group originate in a notebook containing a sequence of poems each of which is explicitly addressed to a 'lady of the hills'. Some of these are in *Orts*, with that phrase omitted. Poems eventually published in the Epilogue begin to appear late in the sequence, and at this point Hughes drops the 'lady of the hills'. It is in these 'lady of the hills' poems that Hughes directly imitates Dravidian *vacanas*, an often cited source for the Epilogue, which are addressed to Siva as 'lord of the meeting rivers', 'lord white as jasmine' and 'Lord of the Caves'. (Ramanujan, tr., *Speaking of Siva*; Emory Mss 644, Subseries 2.1, Box 57, ff. 17). Hughes told Ekbert Faas that he began writing these poems as 'little prayers' when he feared that he had throat cancer (Faas, *Ted Hughes: The Unaccommodated Universe*, p. 138). One of them is quoted complete in Sagar, *The Achievement of Ted Hughes*, pp. 309–10.
49. Jonathan Culler, 'Apostrophe', *The Pursuit of Signs*, London, Routledge and Kegan Paul, 1981, pp. 149–50.
50. Hirschberg, *Myth in the Poetry of Ted Hughes*, p. 209.
51. TH to Neil Roberts and Terry Gifford, 1979.
52. Brandes, 'The Economy of Flesh in *Gaudete*', p. 184 and n. Hughes makes this disavowal in a letter to Leonard Scigaj, 28 July 1989, Emory Mss 644, Box 53.
53. TH to Keith Sagar, 18 June 1998, BL Add.78761, f. 21.
54. BL Deposit 10200, 1975.
55. TH to Keith Sagar, 1977, BL Add. 78757, f. 7.
56. TH to Keith Sagar, 20 March 1975, BL Add. 78756, f. 32; 30 May 1977, BL Add.78757, ff. 1, 3, 7. The groups were: 1. 'The Summoner', 'The Advocate'*, 'The Interrogator', 'The Judge', 'The Plaintiff', 'The Executioner', 'The Accused', 'The Risen' and 'Finale'; 2. 'The Knight', 'The Gatekeeper', 'A Flayed Crow in the Hall of Judgement', 'The Baptist', 'A Green Mother', 'A Riddle', 'The Scapegoat', 'The Guide', 'Walking Bare' and 'The Owl Flower'; 3. 'The Scream', 'After the First Fright', 'She Seemed So Considerate', Your Mother's Bones Wanted to Speak'*, 'In These Fading Moments I Wanted to Say', 'First, the Doubtful Charts of Skin', 'Something was Happening', 'Only a Little Sleep, a Little Slumber', As I Came I Saw a Wood', 'After There was Nothing There was a Woman'#. 'His Legs Ran About' and 'Bride and Groom Lie Hidden for Three Days'. * These poems were never collected. They are

published in Sagar, ed., *The Achievement of Ted Hughes*, pp. 346, 348. Along with four other previously unpublished poems included in this book (including two *Crow* poems and another dropped from *Cave Birds*) they are not in *Collected Poems*. # 'After There was Nothing Came a Woman' in *Collected Poems*.

57. TH to Keith Sagar, 20 October 1982, BL Add.78757, f. 78.
58. TH to Neil Roberts and Terry Gifford, 29 October 1978.
59. It was published with this title in *London Magazine*, 16, April/May 1976, pp. 5–7.
60. Plato, 'Phaedo' 118, Hugh Tredennick, tr., *The Last Days of Socrates*, Harmondsworth, Penguin, 1954, p. 157.
61. TH to Neil Roberts and Terry Gifford, 29 October 1978.
62. Graves, *The White Goddess*, p. 12.
63. Exeter University EUL Mss 58, Sequence A, 'The Advocate'.
64. Bradshaw, 'Creative Mythology in *Cave Birds*', p. 217.
65. Robinson, , *Ted Hughes as Shepherd of Being*, p. 112.
66. Typesript of *Howls and Whispers* (titled *Cries and Whispers*), BL deposit 10200.
67. Sagar, *The Art of Ted Hughes*, p. 183.

# 9 Farmer Hughes: *Moortown Diary* and *Season Songs*

1. TH to Janos Csokits, May 1976, Emory Mss 895, Box 1, ff. 24.
2. TH to Daniel Weissbort, 17.4.85, Emory Mss 894, Box 1, ff. 1.
3. TH to Gerald Hughes, 1973, Emory Mss 854, Box 1, ff. 22.
4. Richard Murphy, in a compendious review (*New York Review of Books* 10.6.82, p. 39) of several books by Hughes, including *Moortown* and *Cave Birds*, concentrated almost entirely on the farming poems and had almost nothing to say about the latter. Martin Dodsworth's review of *Season Songs* (*Guardian* 20.5.76 p. 14), which he finds 'utterly original in an un-Victorian, un-Edwardian way, even without their wholly unsentimental acceptance of pain and stress' contrasts markedly with his review the following year of *Gaudete*, quoted in my last chapter.
5. Emory Mss 644, Subseries 2.2, Box 68 ff. 71–7, Box 69, ff. 1–23.
6. 'Ted Hughes: The Art of Poetry LXXI', p. 66.
7. TH to Keith Sagar, 18.6.98, BL Add.78761, ff. 23–4.
8. Emory Mss 644, Box 69, ff. 12–13.
9. Craig Robinson, 'The Good Shepherd: *Moortown Elegies*', Sagar, ed., *The Achievement of Ted Hughes*, p. 278.
10. Emory Mss 644, Box 69, ff. 3.
11. Feinstein, *Ted Hughes: The Life of a Poet*, p. 195.
12. TH to Keith Sagar, 21.4.77, BL Add.78756, f. 69.
13. Martin Dodsworth, review of *Season Songs*, *Guardian*, 20.5.76, p. 14.

# 10 Return to the Calder Valley: *Remains of Elmet*, *Wolfwatching* and *Elmet*

1. Fay Godwin, 'Ted Hughes and *Elmet*', Gammage, ed., *The Epic Poise*; Emory Mss 644, Box 3 ff. 4.

2. Keith Sagar, personal conversation, July 2005.
3. Fay Godwin to TH, Emory Mss 644, Box 3 ff. 4.
4. TH to Leonard Baskin, BL Deposit 10200, 15 August 1984.
5. TH to Keith Sagar, 14 October 1998, BL Add. 78759, f. 66.
6. See Godwin, 'Ted Hughes and *Elmet*', p. 106, and Terry Gifford, 'Interview with Fay Godwin on the Making, with Ted Hughes, of *Remains of Elmet* (1979) and *Elmet* (1994)', *Thumbscrew* 18, 2001, pp. 114–17.
7. Ted Hughes, 'Ted Hughes on Wolfwatching', *The Poetry Book Society Bulletin*, 142, Autumn 1989, pp. 1–3.
8. Fay Godwin to TH, Emory Mss 644, Box 3 ff. 4.
9. Gifford, 'Interview with Fay Godwin'.
10. Gerard Manley Hopkins, W.H.Garner, ed., *Poems and prose of Gerard Manley Hopkins*, Penguin, 1953, pp. 154–5.
11. Feinstein, *Ted Hughes: The Life of a Poet*, p. 7.
12. Emory Mss 644, Box 71 ff. 22.
13. Patricia Boyle Haberstroh, 'Historical Landscape in Ted Hughes's *Remains of Elmet*, Scigaj, ed., *Critical Essays on Ted Hughes*, p. 210. (reprinted from *Clio* 14, Winter 1985, pp. 137–54.)
14. Ann Skea, *Ted Hughes: The Poetic Quest*, p. 176.
15. 'Ted Hughes on Wolfwatching', p. 3.
16. Diane Middlebrook, *Her Husband*, p. 255.
17. TH to Keith Sagar, 14 October 1998, BL Add. 78759, f. 66.
18. TH to Leonard M. Scigaj, 14 June 1981, Emory Mss 644, Box 53.
19. There are also five uncollected poems about Hughes's mother—'Edith', 'Anniversary', 'Black Hair', 'Comics' and 'Mother-Tongue'—and one about his father, 'The Last of the 1st/15th Lancashire Fusiliers'. The poem 'The Stone', collected in *Moortown*, is about the death of an unnamed woman, but its subsequent publication under the title, 'The Beacon', the name of his parents' later home in Heptonstall, suggests that it is about his mother.
20. TH to Keith Sagar, 18 June 1998, BL Add.78761, f. 19.
21. William Wordsworth, *The Prelude* [1850], Book I, l.340.
22. TH to Leonard Baskin, 15 August 1984, BL Deposit 10200.
23. TH to Keith Sagar, 14 October 1998, BL Add. 78759, f. 66.

## 11   Fisherman Hughes: *River*

1. Peter Redgrove, 'Windings and Conchings', *TLS*, 11 November 1983, p. 1238
2. TH to Gerald Hughes, 26 August 1980, Emory Mss 854, ff. 29.
3. 'So Quickly It's Over', interview with Thomas Pero, *Wild Steelhead and Salmon*, Vol.5 no.2, Winter 1999, p. 56; abridged version in *The Guardian Saturday Review*, 9 January 1999, pp. 1–2. See also Terry Gifford, '"Go Fishing": An Ecocentric or Egocentric Imperative?', Joanny Moulin, ed., *Lire Ted Hughes: New Selected Poems 1957–1994*, Paris, Editions du Temps, 1999, pp. 145–56, which quotes extensively from a long letter by Hughes.
4. Sagar, *The Laughter of Foxes*, pp. 147–8.
5. Joanny Moulin, 'Ted Hughes's Anti–Mythic Method', in Joanny Moulin, ed., *Ted Hughes: Alternative Horizons*, London, Routledge, 2004, pp. 98–9.

6. Mircea Eliade, *Patterns in Comparative Religion*, tr. Rosemary Sheed, London, Sheed and Ward, 1958, p. 216.
7. Terry Gifford, 'Gods of Mud: Hughes and Post-Pastoral', Keith Sagar, ed., *The Challenge of Ted Hughes*, Basingstoke and London, Macmillan, 1994, p. 138.
8. Leonard M. Scigaj, *The Poetry of Ted Hughes: Form and Imagination*, University of Iowa Press, 1986, pp. 288–315; Ann Skea, *Ted Hughes: The Poetic Quest*, Armidale NSW, University of New England Press, 1994, pp. 208–34; Bo Gustavsson, 'Ted Hughes's Quest for a Hierophany: A Reading of *River*', Leonard M. Scigaj, ed., *Critical Essays on Ted Hughes*, pp. 230–40.
9. Sagar, *The Laughter of Foxes*, p. 165.
10. The superb poem 'Stealing Trout on a May Morning', added in *Three Books*, was written in the early 1960s and first published in the 1966 volume *Recklings*.
11. TH to Gerald Hughes, 7 August 1980, Emory Mss 854, ff. 29.
12. TH to Gerald Hughes, August 1976, Emory Mss 854, ff. 26; TH to Daniel Weissbort, 23 October 1983, Emory Mss 894, ff. 1.
13. See Chapter 2, p. 25.
14. TH to Leonard Scigaj, 14 June 1981, Emory Mss 644, Box 53, ff. 1. See my discussion of this poem in Chapter 1, pp. 5–8.
15. T.S. Eliot, 'East Coker', *Collected Poems*, London, Faber, 1962
16. Jules Laforgue (1860–87): French poet whose self-conscious and ironic manner influenced the early Eliot, most notably 'The Love-Song of J. Alfred Prufrock'.

## 12  The Poet Laureate

1. Nick Russel, *Poets by Appointment: Britain's Laureates*, Poole, Blandford Press, 1981, p. 4.
2. Kenneth Hopkins, *The Poets Laureate*, London, Bodley Head, 1954, p. 109.
3. Edmund Kemper Broadus, *The Laureateship: A Study of the Office of Poet Laureate in England, with some Account of the Poets*, Oxford, Clarendon Press, 1921, p. 164.
4. *Guardian* 5.8.95.
5. Seamus Heaney, 'The New Poet Laureate', Scigaj, ed., *Critical Essays on Ted Hughes*, pp. 45–6. First published in *Belfast Review* 10, March/May 1985.
6. TH, draft letter to Grey Gowrie, 16 February 1985, Emory Mss 644, Box 53
7. TH to Joan Hughes, n.d. (1953?), Emory Mss 854, ff. 38.
8. TH to Frieda Hughes, 14 February 1975, Emory Mss 1014, Box 1 ff. 53.
9. Emory Mss 870, Box 1, ff. 8. Hughes wrote facetiously flirtatious letters to Edna, who was three or four years older than him, when he was in the R.A.F., and disapproved of her marriage to 'a chap that couldn't shoot and didn't know how to fish' (Edna Wholey Chilton, 'Ted and Crookhill', Emory Mss 870, Box 1, ff. 1; TH's letters ff. 2–7). How serious Hughes's feelings for Edna were is not clear either from his letters or from her memoir.
10. Emory Mss 854, Box 1, ff. 41.
11. Emory Mss 854, Box 1, ff. 40.
12. It was originally intended for the collection *River*. Letter to Keith Sagar, 21 January 1985, BL Add. 78757, f. 150.

13. Neil Roberts, 'Ted Hughes and the Laureateship', *Critical Quarterly*, 27, 2, 1985, p. 5.
14. Letters from Charles Monteith to TH, 3 May 1977 and 16 May 1977, Emory Mss 644, Box 12.
15. Philip Larkin, letter to Kingsley Amis, 3 June 1967, *Selected Letters of Philip Larkin, 1940–1985*, ed. Anthony Thwaite, London, Faber, 1992, p. 396.
16. TH to Keith Sagar, 19 January 1986, BL Add.78757, f. 158.
17. TH to Janos Csokits, Emory Mss 895, n.d., Box 1, ff. 37.
18. TH to Philip Larkin, 21 November 1985 and Monica Jones, 8 December 1985, Emory Mss 644, Box 53.
19. TH to Daniel Weissbort, 21 November 1983 and 25 November 1983, Emory Mss 894, Box 1, ff. 1.
20. TH, draft letter to Alan Bold, 15 March 1988, Emory Mss 644, Box 53.
21. TH to Daniel Weissbort, 18 December 1992, Emory Mss 894, Box 1, ff. 1.
22. Philip Larkin, *Collected Poems*, ed. Anthony Thwaite, London, Faber, 1988, p. 210.
23. Philip Larkin, *Selected Letters*, p. 557.
24. C.G. Jung, *The Collected Works of C.G. Jung*,Volume 12, *Psychology and Alchemy*,tr. R.F.C. Hull, London, Routledge, 1953, 2nd edition 1968, pp. 95–223.
25. W.B. Yeats, *Collected Poems*, London, Macmillan, 1963, pp. 210–11.
26. In this poem Tennyson originally wrote, and published in successive editions from 1853 to 1862, 'Thank Him who isled us here, and roughly set/ His Saxon in blown seas and storming showers.' He later corrected 'Saxon' to 'Briton'. See Christopher Ricks, ed., *Tennyson: A Selected Edition*, Harlow, Longman, 1969, p. 494.
27. Peter Reading, 'Turning on the water works' (review of *Rain-Charm for the Duchy and Other Laureate Poems*), *Sunday Times*, 28.6.92, p. 13.
28. Emory Mss 644, Subseries 2,2, Box 78, ff. 3.
29. *Tennyson: A Selected Edition*,pp. 494–5.
30. It should be acknowledged that in the notion of 'a people's voice' and in Tennyson's poem itself, there is something faintly bullying and, to a modern reader, potentially totalitarian. Something of this was felt by people who didn't share the national orgy of sentimentality at the death of Princess Diana. Hughes himself admitted that in writing the poem '6 September 1997' to mark Diana's funeral he was 'grabbed by the mob current undertow'. TH to Keith Sagar, 10 November 1997, BL Add 78760.
31. Valerie Pitt, *Tennyson Laureate*, London, Barrie and Rockliff, 1962, pp. 194–5.
32. Matthew Campbell, 'Memorials of the Tennysons', Matthew Campbell, Jacqueline Labbe and Sally Shuttleworth, ed., *Memory and Memorials, 1789–1914*, London, Routledge, 2000, p. 176.

## 13  Writing for Children

1. Drafts from 1956 in the Emory archive show that the stories Hughes was writing then are early versions of *How the Whale Became*, from which many phrases and whole sentences survive into the published version. Emory Mss 644, Box 7 ff. 4.
2. Middlebrook, *Her Husband*, p. 97.

3. Emory Mss 1014, passim.
4. Letter to Keith Sagar, 21 April 1977, BL Add.78756, f. 69. In this letter Hughes says that 'Amulet' and 'The Grizzly Bear' in *Under the North Star* were also originally Crow poems (the latter under the title 'I See a Bear').
5. www.zeta.org.au/~annskea/Adelaide.htm.
6. Lissa Paul, 'The Children's Ted Hughes', Joanny Moulin, ed., *Lire Ted Hughes: New Selected Poems 1957–1994*, Paris, Editions du Temps, 1999, p. 47.
7. TH to unknown correspondent, 20 March 1995, Emory Mss 644, Box 54 ff. 3.
8. Ibid.
9. Keith Cushman, 'Hughes' Poetry for Children', Keith Sagar, ed., *The Achievement of Ted Hughes*, p. 242.
10. About thirteen. In the later moon poems he envisaged readers of about fifteen. TH to unknown correspondent, 20 March 1995, Emory Mss 644, Box 54 ff. 3.
11. TH to Gerald Hughes, 27 August.1957, Emory Mss 854, Box 1, ff. 6.
12. Rudyard Kipling, 'The Elephant's Child', *Just So Stories* (1902), London, Puffin Books, 1987, p. 55.
13. One programme, 'Creatures of the Air', broadcast in June 1962, was not included in the book. The final chapter, 'Writing and Experience', was broadcast in 1967 in the 'Religion in its Contemporary Context' series.
14. TH to Keith Sagar, 8 September 1998, BL Add.78761 f. 27.
15. TH to Janos Csokits, 8 June 1967 Emory Mss 895, Box 1 ff. 8.
16. 'Myth and Education', *Children's Literature in Education*, 1, March 1970, p. 63.
17. 'Myth and Education', pp. 66–7.
18. 'Myth and Education', p. 68.
19. Blake Morrison, 'Man of Mettle', *The Independent on Sunday*, 5 September 1993, p. 32.
20. TH to Keith Sagar, 21 April 1977, BL Add.78756 f. 69.
21. TH to unknown correspondent, 20 March 95, Emory Mss 644, Box 54 ff. 3.
22. Hughes's companion in this poem is his brother Gerald, on a visit to England, their first meeting after eighteen years. For an account of the background to the poem see Sagar, *The Laughter of Foxes*, pp. 148–50.
23. TH to unknown correspondent, 20 March 1995, Emory Mss 644, Box 54 ff. 3.
24. Morrison, 'Man of Mettle', p. 32.
25. In a paper delivered at the Fifth International Ted Hughes conference, Atlanta, October 2005.
26. Morrison, 'Man of Mettle', p. 34.
27. Morrison, 'Man of Mettle', p. 32.

## 14   Hughes as Translator

1. TH, 'Introduction' to Daniel Weissbort, ed., *Modern Poetry in Translation: 1983, An Annual Survey*, pp. 9–10.
2. Yehuda Amichai, *Selected Poems*, translated by Assia Gutmann, Cape Goliard, 1968. Although only Assia is credited, Sagar and Tabor assert that Hughes collaborated on the translation (Keith Sagar and Stephen Tabor, *Ted Hughes: A Bibliography 1946–1995*, London, Mansell, 1998, p. 201).
3. TH to Leonard Baskin, 28 December 1995, BL Deposit 10200.
4. TH, prose account of the *Oedipus* project, Emory Mss.644, Box 131, ff. 13.

5. Turner's version is published in Robert W. Corrigan, ed., *Classical Tragedy Greek and Roman: Eight Plays*, New York, Applause, 1990. Perusal of it confirms that Hughes's translation owes little if anything to it.
6. TH, prose account of the *Oedipus* project, Emory Mss.644, Box 131, ff. 13.
7. Ronald Bryden, *Observer*, 24 March 1968, p. 31.
8. David Williams, ed., *Peter Brook: A Theatrical Casebook*, London, Methuen, 1991, p. 116.
9. Albert Hunt and Geoffrey Reeves, *Peter Brook*, Cambridge, Cambridge University Press, 1995, p. 128.
10. Martin Esslin, review of *Oedipus, Peter Brook: A Theatrical Casebook*, p. 121.
11. *Oedipus* 1.514: *Seneca VIII Tragedies I*, tr. Frank Justus Miller, Loeb Classical Library, London, Heinemann, 1917, pp. 470–1.
12. *Seneca* 11. 978–9, p. 514.
13. TH to Gerald Hughes, 15 March 1968, Emory Mss.854, Box 1 ff. 17.
14. TH to A. Alvarez, undated, BL Deposit 8878.
15. David Williams, *Peter Brook: A Theatrical Casebook*, p. 116.
16. TH to Neil Roberts and Terry Gifford, October 1979.
17. *Peter Brook*, p. 131.
18. Charles Marowitz, review of *Oedipus, Peter Brook: A Theatrical Casebook*, p. 124.
19. Hunt and Reeves, *Peter Brook*, p. 131.
20. TH to Gerald Hughes, 15 March 1968, Emory Mss. 854, Box 1 ff. 17.
21. Theodor Adorno, 'Cultural Criticism and Society' (1949), *Prisms*, tr. Samuel and Shierry Weber, Cambridge MA, MIT Press. 1981, p. 34.
22. Daniel Weissbort to Neil Roberts, email, 23 October 2005.
23. Emory Mss.644, Box 131 ff. 32.
24. Emory Mss.644, Box 131 ff. 21.
25. Emory Mss.644, Box 131 ff. 30.
26. Emory Mss.644, Box 131 ff. 24, 45.
27. TH to Leonard Baskin, 23 May and 28 December 1995, BL Deposit 10200.
28. Ovid, *Metamorphoses* Book IV, ll.285, 386, tr. Frank Justus Miller, Loeb edition, London, Heinemann, 1916, Vol.1, pp. 198–205.
29. *Metamorphoses*, Loeb, Vol.1, p. 3.
30. *Metamorphoses*, l.127, Loeb, Vol.1, pp. 10–11; Penguin, p. 32.
31. TH to Ben Sonnenberg, 9 September 1998, Emory Mss. 924, Box 1.
32. Hughes mixes French and Latin versions of names. Curiously, he renders 'Aricie', who is Racine's invention, as 'Aricia'.
33. Racine, *Phèdre*,Act III Scene I, *Tragédies Choisies de Racine*, New York, Doubleday, 1962, p. 295.
34. Plath, *Journals*,pp. 214, 225; *Collected Poems*, p. 22.
35. Tony Harrison, *The Oresteia*, London, Rex Collings, 1981, p. 16 and *passim*.
36. Conversation with Ann Skea, Sagar, *The Laughter of Foxes*, p. xxxi.
37. At the 'Ted Hughes and the Classics' conference, Edinburgh University, November 2005.
38. Harrison, op.cit.; Aeschylus, *The Oresteian Trilogy*, tr. Philip Vellacott, Harmondsworth, Penguin, 1956; Aeschylus, *The Oresteia*, tr. Robert Fagles, Harmondsworth, Penguin, 1977.
39. Barrie Rutter, quoted by Keith Sagar in programme note for Northern Broadsides production of *Alcestis*, 2000; also on the 'Earth-Moon' website, http://www.earth-moon.org, visited 1.12.05.

40. Tony Harrison, *The Trackers of Oxyrhybchus*, London, Faber, 1990, p. xii.
41. Keith Sagar, programme note for Northern Broadsides production of *Alcestis*.
42. *Ted Hughes: The Life of a Poet*, p. 145.
43. Euripides, *Alcestis and Other Plays*, tr. Philip Vellacott, Harmondsworth, Penguin, 1953, p. 143.
44. Emory Mss.644, Box 131 ff. 14.
45. Pierre Grimal, *The Dictionary of Classical Mythology*, Oxford, Blackwell, 1986, p. 195; Robert Graves, *The Greek Myths*, 1955, revised edition, Harmondsworth, Penguin, 1960, Vol. 2, pp. 100–1.
46. TH to Leonard Baskin, 13 October 1996, BL Deposit 10200.

# 15  Poet of Mourning: *Birthday Letters*

1. Andrew Motion, *The Times*, 17 January 1968, p. 22.
2. *The Times*, 17 January 1968, p. 23.
3. *Independent on Sunday*, 18 January 1998, Section 2 p. 4.
4. John Carey, review of *Birthday Letters*, *Sunday Times* Books section, 25 January 98, pp. 1–2.
5. TH to Keith Sagar, 18 June 1998, BL Add. 78761, ff. 19–23.
6. Emory Mss 644, Box 57, ff. 8, p. 97 verso.
7. Peter Redgrove to TH, 30.10.76, Emory Mss 644, Box 6, ff. 1.
8. Peter Redgrove, letter to Neil Roberts, 26 October 1979, Peter Redgrove archive, University of Sheffield, uncatalogued.
9. TH to Peter Redgrove and Penelope Shuttle, undated, Peter Redgrove archive, uncatalogued.
10. TH to Daniel Weissbort, 1975/6, Emory Mss 894, Box 1, ff. 1.
11. TH to Keith Sagar, 18 June 1998, BL Add. 78761, ff. 21–2.
12. TH to Ben Sonnenberg, 23 May 1989, Emory Mss 924, Box 1, ff. 3.
13. Carolyn Wright, 'What Happens in the Heart', *Poetry Review*, Vol.89 no.3, Autumn 1999, p. 9.
14. Thom Gunn to TH, April 14 1991, Emory Mss 644, Box 3 ff. 7.
15. 19 May 1994, Emory Mss 924, Box 1, ff. 4; 18 June 1997, Emory Mss 895, Box 1, ff. 49; 29 August 1997 Emory Mss 894, Box 1, ff. 1; 15 August 1997,BL Add.78760, f. 194.
16. TH to Janos Csokits, 18 June 1997, Emory Mss 895, Box 1, ff. 49.
17. TH to Ben Sonnenberg,, 17 June 1992, 19 May 1994, Emory Mss 921, Box 1, ff. 4. Of the additional poems that Hughes mentions in his 1994 letter to Sonnenberg, eleven are published in the 1998 limited edition, *Howls and Whispers* and in *Collected Poems*.
18. TH to Keith Sagar, 18 June 1998, BL Add. 78761, f. 21.
19. Linda Wagner-Martin, *Sylvia Plath: A Literary Life*, second edition, Basingstoke and New York, Palgrave Macmillan, 2003, pp. 148–9.
20. Tracy Brain, *The Other Sylvia Plath*, Harlow, Longman, 2001, p. 181.
21. Wagner-Martin, *Sylvia Plath: A Literary Life*, p. 152.
22. Brain, *The Other Sylvia Plath*, p. 189.
23. Leonard M. Scigaj, 'The Deterministic Ghost in the Machine of *Birthday Letters*', Moulin, ed., *Ted Hughes: Alternative Horizons*, London and New York, Routledge, 2004, pp. 1–15.
24. Sagar, *The Laughter of Foxes*, p. 71.

25. Jonathan Culler, 'Apostrophe', *The Pursuit of Signs*, London, Routledge and Kegan Paul, 1981, pp. 149–50.
26. TH to Neil Roberts and Terry Gifford, October 1978.
27. V.N.Voloshinov, *Marxism and the Philosophy of Language*, tr. Ladislav Matejka and I.R.Titunik, 1973, Cambridge MA and London, Harvard University Press, 1986, p. 86.
28. Wagner-Martin, *Sylvia Plath: A Literary Life*, p. 148.
29. Scigaj, 'The Deterministic Ghost in the Machine of *Birthday Letters*', p. 5.
30. Scigaj, 'The Deterministic Ghost in the Machine of *Birthday Letters*', p. 10.
31. TH to Ben Sonnenberg, 17 May 1992, Emory Mss 924, Box 1, ff. 4.
32. THto Janos Csokits, 18 June 1997, Emory Mss 895, Box 1, ff. 50.
33. Plath, *Journals*, pp. 233–5.
34. Sagar, *The Laughter of Foxes*, p. 61.
35. Brain, *The Other Sylvia Plath*, p. 181.
36. Jacques Lacan, *The Four Fundamental Concepts of Psychoanalysis*, ed. Jacques-Alain Miller, tr. Alan Sheridan, Harmondsworth, Penguin, 1979, p. 25.
37. TH to Keith Sagar, 18 June 1998, BL Add. 78761, f27. Critics have commented on the omission of the Orpheus legend from *Tales from Ovid*.This is not surprising, however, when one considers that Hughes would have had to render, or conspicuously omit, the lines, 'Eurydice, dying now a second time, uttered no complaint against her husband. What was there to complain of, but that she had been loved?' (Ovid, *Metamorphoses*, tr. Mary Innes, Harmondsworth, Penguin, 1955, p. 226.)
38. Anne Whitehead, 'Refiguring Orpheus: The Possession of the Past in Ted Hughes's *Birthday Letters*', *Textual Practice*, 13 (2), 1999, p. 232.
39. TH to Keith Sagar, 18 June 1998, BL Add. 78761, f. 27.
40. See Middlebrook, *Her Husband*, pp. 208–9, citing letters written between 1963 and 1981
41. TH to Keith Sagar, 15 August 1997, BL Add.78760, f. 194.
42. Heather Neill, 'The Fire That Still Burns After Sylvia', *Times Educational Supplement*, 30.1.98, p. 12, cited in Brain, *The Other Sylvia Plath*, p. 190.

# 16  Epilogue

1. *The Times* editorial, 30 October 1998.
2. Malcolm, *The Silent Woman*, p. 104.

# Bibliography

## Works by Ted Hughes

### I. Major books, including translations

*The Hawk in the Rain*, London, Faber, 1957.
*Lupercal*, London, Faber, 1960.
*Meet My Folks*, London, Faber, 1961.
*The Earth-Owl and Other Moon-People*, London, Faber, 1963.
*How the Whale Became*, London, Faber, 1963.
*Nessie the Mannerless Monster*, London, Faber, 1964.
*Recklings*, London, Turret Books, 1966.
*Poetry in the Making*, London, Faber, 1967.
*Wodwo*, London, Faber, 1967.
*The Iron Man*, London, Faber, 1968.
*Seneca's Oedipus*, London, Faber, 1969.
*Crow: From the Life and Songs of the Crow*, London, Faber, 1970.
*Earth-Moon*, London, Rainbow Press, 1976.
*Moon-Whales and Other Moon Poems*, New York, Viking, 1976.
*Season Songs*, London, Faber, 1976.
*Gaudete*, London, Faber, 1977.
*Cave Birds*, London, Faber, 1978.
*Moon-Bells and Other Poems*, London, Chato and Windus, 1978.
*Orts*, London, Rainbow Press, 1978.
*Moortown*, London, Faber, 1979.
*Remains of Elmet*, London, Faber, 1979.
*A Primer of Birds*, Devon, Gehenna Press, 1981.
*Under the North Star*, London, Faber, 1981.
*River*, London, Faber, 1983.
*What is the Truth?*, London, Faber, 1984.
*Ffangs the Vampire Bat and the Kiss of Truth*, London, Faber, 1986.
*Flowers and Insects*, London, Faber, 1986.
*The Cat and the Cuckoo*, Devon, Sustone Press, 1987.
*Tales of the Early World*, London, Faber, 1988.
*Moortown Diary*, London, Faber, 1989.
*Wolfwatching*, London, Faber, 1989.
*Capriccio*, Devon, Gehenna Press, 1990.
*A Dancer to God*, London, Faber, 1992.
*Rain-Charm for the Duchy*, London, Faber, 1992.
*Shakespeare and the Goddess of Complete Being*, London, Faber, 1992.
*The Mermaid's Purse*, Devon, Sunstone Press, 1993.
*The Iron Woman*, London, Faber, 1993.
*Three Books (Cave Birds, Remains of Elmet, River)*, London, Faber, 1993.
*Difficulties of a Bridegroom*, London, Faber, 1994.

*Elmet*, London, Faber, 1994.
*Winter Pollen*, London, Faber, 1994.
*The Dreamfighter and Other Creation Tales*, London, Faber, 1995.
*Spring Awakening*, London, Faber, 1995.
*Blood Wedding*, London, Faber, 1996.
*Tales from Ovid*, London, Faber, 1997.
*Birthday Letters*, London, Faber, 1998.
*Howls and Whispers*, Devon, Gehenna Press, 1998.
*Phèdre*, London, Faber, 1998.
*Alcestis*, London, Faber, 1999.
*The Oresteia*, London, Faber, 1999.
*Collected Plays for Children*, London, Faber, 2001.
*Collected Poems*, London, Faber, 2003.
*Selected Translations*, ed. Daniel Weissbort, 2006

## II   Other Works by Ted Hughes mentioned in the text

### i   Interviews

'Desk Poet', interview with John Horder, *Guardian*, 23 March 1965.
'Orghast', Interview with Tom Stoppard, *Times Literary Supplement*, 1 October 1971, p. 1174.
'Ted Hughes: *The Wound*', transcript of the interview with Ted Hughes from the A Adelaide Festival, March 1976, www.zeta.org.au/~annskea/ABC2AF.htm.
'Ted Hughes: The Art of Poetry LXXI', interview with Drue Heinz, *Paris Review* 134, Spring 1995.
'So Quickly It's Over', interview with Thomas Pero, *Wild Steelhead and Salmon*, Vol.5 no.2, Winter 1999, pp. 50 7; abridged version in *The Guardian Saturday Review*, 9 January 1999, pp. 1–2.

### ii   Readings

*Crow*, Claddagh CCT 9–10, 1973.
Transcription of Hughes reading at Adelaide, March 1976, www.zeta.org.au/~annskea/Adelaide.htm.
*Crow*, Penguin Audiobooks, Harmondsworth, Penguin, 1997.

### iii   Contributions to books and periodicals

'X', *Encounter*, 25.20–1, July 1965.
'Myth and Education', *Children's Literature in Education*, 1, March 1970, pp. 55–70.
'Introduction' to Daniel Weissbort, ed., *Modern Poetry in Translation: 1983, An Annual Survey*.
'Baboons and Neanderthals: A Rereading of *The Inheritors*', John Carey, ed., *William Golding, The Man and his Books: A Tribute on his 75th Birthday*, London, Faber, 1986, pp. 161–88.
'Sylvia Plath: the facts of her life and the desecration of her grave', *The Independent*, 22.4.89, p. 19.

### iv   Edited anthologies

(With Seamus Heaney) *The Rattle Bag*, London, Faber, 1982.
(With Seamus Heaney) *The School Bag*, London, Faber, 1997.

*v Archives*

The Ted Hughes Papers, Mss.644, Woodruff Library, Emory University, Atlanta
Other archives held at the Woodruff Library:
Letters to Gerald Hughes, Mss.854.
Letters to Lucas Myers, Mss.865.
Letters to Peter Redgrove, Mss.867.
Letters to Edna Wholey, Mss.870.
Daniel Weissbort Papers, Mss.894.
Letters to Janos Csokits, Mss.895.
Letters to Ben Sonnenberg, Mss.924.
Olwyn Hughes Papers, Mss.980.
Letters to Frieda Hughes, Mss.1014.

Letters to Keith Sagar, Add. 78756–78761, British Library.
A.Alvarez Deposit, Deposit 8878, British Library.
Baskin/Hughes Papers, Deposit 10200, British Library.
Redgrove Papers, Mss.171, University of Sheffield Library.
*Cave Birds* papers, Mss.58, Exeter University Library.
Letters to Terry Gifford and Neil Roberts, private collection.

**III Other works cited**

Adorno, Theodor, 'Cultural Criticism and Society' (1949), *Prisms*, tr. Samuel and Shierry Weber, Cambridge MA, MIT Press. 1981.
Aeschylus, *The Oresteian Trilogy*, tr. Philip Vellacott, Harmondsworth, Penguin, 1956.
Aeschylus, *The Oresteia*, tr. Robert Fagles, Harmondsworth, Penguin, 1977.
Alexander, Paul, *Rough Magic: A Biography of Sylvia Plath*, Harmondsworth, Viking, 1991.
Alvarez, A., *The Savage God: A Study of Suicide* (1971), London, Bloomsbury, 2002.
Anderson, William, *Green Man: The Archetype of our Oneness with the Earth*, London and San Francisco, Harper Collins, 1990.
Andrews, Elmer, *The Poetry of Seamus Heaney: All the Realms of Whisper*, Basingstoke and London, Macmillan, 1988.
Bakhtin, Mikhail, *Problems of Dostoevsky's Poetics*, ed. and tr. Caryl Emerson, Minneapolis, University of Minnesota Press, 1984.
Beckett, Samuel. *Endgame*, London, Faber, 1958.
Beckett, Samuel, *Molloy, Malone Dies, The Unnameable*, London, Calder, 1959.
Bradley, D.D., 'Ted Hughes 1930–1998', *Pembroke College Cambridge Society Annual Gazette* 73, September 1999, pp. 22–30.
Bradshaw, Graham, 'From *Wodwo* to *Crow*' (unpublished).
Brain, Tracy, *The Other Sylvia Plath*, Harlow, Longman, 2001.
Broadus, Edmund Kemper, *The Laureateship: A Study of the Office of Poet Laureate in England, with some Account of the Poets*, Oxford, Clarendon Press, 1921.
Bundtzen, Lynda K., 'Poetic Arson and Sylvia Plath's "Burning the Letters" ', *Contemporary Literature* 33, 1998, p. 437.
Butscher, Edward, *Sylvia Plath: Method and Madness*, New York, Seabury Press, 1976.
Campbell, Matthew, 'Memorials of the Tennysons', Matthew Campbell, Jacqueline Labbe and Sally Shuttleworth, eds., *Memory and Memorials, 1789–1914*, London, Routledge, 2000.

Cox, Brian, 'Ted Hughes (1930–1998): A Personal Retrospect', *The Hudson Review*, Spring 1999, Vol.52, no.1.

Culler, Jonathan, 'Apostrophe', *The Pursuit of Signs*, London, Routledge and Kegan Paul, 1981.

Eagleton, Terry, 'Recent Poetry', *Stand*, Vol.19 no.2, 1978, pp. 78–9.

Easthope, Antony, *Poetry as Discourse*, London, Methuen, 1983.

Eliade, Mircea, *Patterns in Comparative Religion*, tr. Rosemary Sheed, London, Sheed and Ward, 1958.

Eliade, Mircea, *Shamanism: Archaic Techniques of Ecstasy* (1964), London, Arkana, 1989.

Eliot, T.S., *Selected Essays*, London, Faber, 1951.

Eliot, T.S., *Collected Poems*, London, Faber, 1962.

Euripides, *Alcestis and Other Plays*, tr. Philip Vellacott, Harmondsworth, Penguin, 1953.

Evans, Dylan, *An Introductory Dictionary of Lacanian Psychoanalysis*, London and New York, Routledge, 1996, p. 159.

Faas, Ekbert, *Ted Hughes: the Unaccommodated Universe*, Santa Barbara, Black Sparrow Press, 1980.

Feinstein, Elaine, *Ted Hughes: The Life of a Poet*, London, Weidenfeld and Nicholson, 2001.

Fraistat, Neil, ed., *Poems in their Place: The Intertextuality and Order of Poetic Collections*, Chapel Hill and London, University of North Carolina Press, 1986.

Gammage, Nick, ed., *The Epic Poise: A Celebration of Ted Hughes*, London, Faber, 1999.

Gifford, Terry, 'Interview with Fay Godwin on the Making, with Ted Hughes, of *Remains of Elmet* (1979) and *Elmet* (1994)', *Thumbscrew* 18, pp. 114–17, 2001.

Gifford, Terry and Neil Roberts, *Ted Hughes: A Critical Study*, London, Faber, 1981.

Graves, Robert, *The Greek Myths*, 1955, revised edition, Harmondsworth, Penguin, 1960.

Graves, Robert, *The White Goddess: A Historical Grammar of Poetic Myth*, 1948, amended and enlarged edition, 1966, New York, Farrar, Straus and Giroux, 1966.

Graves, Robert, *Complete Poems* vol.2, ed. Beryl Graves and Dunstan Ward, Manchester, Carcanet, 1997.

Grimal, Pierre, *The Dictionary of Classical Mythology*, Oxford, Blackwell, 1986.

Harrison, Tony, *The Oresteia*, London, Rex Collings, 1981.

Harrison, Tony, *The Trackers of Oxyrhybchus*, London, Faber, 1990.

Hayman, Ronald, 'The Poet and the Unquiet Grave', *The Independent*, 19.4.89, p. 19.

Hayman, Ronald, *The Death and Life of Sylvia Plath*, London, Heinemann, 1991.

Hayman, Ronald, et al., 'Problems strewn on the path to Sylvia Plath's grave', *The Guardian*, 11.4.89, p. 18.

Heaney, Seamus, *Preoccupations*, London, Faber, 1980.

Herbert, Zbigniew, *Selected Poems*, tr. John Carpenter and Bogdana Carpenter, Oxford, Oxford University Press, 1977.

Hirschberg, Stuart, *Myth in the Poetry of Ted Hughes*, Dublin, Wolfhound Press, 1981.

Hobsbaum, Philip, 'Ted Hughes at Cambridge', *The Dark Horse*, 8, Autumn 1999, pp. 6–12.

Holub, Miroslav, *Selected Poems*, tr. Ian Milner and George Theiner, Harmondsworth, Penguin, 1967.

Hopkins, Gerard Manley, W.H.Garner, ed., *Poems and prose of Gerard Manley Hopkins*, Penguin, 1953.
Hopkins, Kenneth, *The Poets Laureate*, London, Bodley Head, 1954.
Hunt, Albert and Geoffrey Reeves, *Peter Brook*, Cambridge, Cambridge University Press, 1995.
Jung, C.G., *The Collected Works of C.G. Jung*, Volume 12, *Psychology and Alchemy*, tr. R.F.C. Hull, London, Routledge, 1953, 2nd edition, 1968.
Kipling, Rudyard, *Just So Stories* (1902), London, Puffin Books, 1987.
Lacan, Jacques, *The Four Fundamental Concepts of Psychoanalysis*, ed. Alain Miller, tr. Alan Sheridan, Harmondsworth, Penguin, 1979.
Larkin, Philip, *Collected Poems*, ed. Anthony Thwaite, London, Faber, 1988.
Larkin, Philip, *Selected Letters of Philip Larkin, 1940–1985*, ed. Anthony Thwaite, London, Faber, 1992.
Leavis, F.R., *The Living Principle: 'English' as a Discipline of Thought*, London, Chatto and Windus, 1975.
Malcolm, Janet, *The Silent Woman: Sylvia Plath and Ted Hughes/Ted Hughes and Sylvia Plath*, (1993) London and Basingstoke, Macmillan, 1995.
Middlebrook, Diane, *Her Husband: Hughes and Plath–A Marriage*, New York, Viking, 2003.
Miller, Karl, ed., *Poetry From Cambridge 1952–54*, Cambridge, Fantasy Press, 1955.
Morgan, Robin, *Monster*, New York, Random House, 1972.
Blake Morrison, 'Man of Mettle', *The Independent on Sunday*, 5 September 1993, pp. 32–4.
Moulin, Joanny, ed., *Lire Ted Hughes: New Selected Poems 1957–1994*, Paris, Editions du Temps, 1999.
Moulin, Joanny, ed., *Ted Hughes: Alternative Horizons*, London, Routledge, 2004.
Myers, Lucas, 'Dolphin Catch', *Chequer 7*, November 1954, p. 16.
Myers, Lucas, *Crow Steered, Bergs Appeared: A Memoir of Ted Hughes and Sylvia Plath*, Sewanee, Proctor's Hall, 2001.
Ovid, *Metamorphoses*, tr. Frank Justus Miller, Loeb edition, London, Heinemann, 1916.
Ovid, *Metamorphoses*, tr. Mary M. Innes, Harmondsworth, Penguin, 1995.
Parnaby, Julia and Rachel Wingfield, 'In memory of Sylvia Plath', *The Guardian*, 7.4.89, p. 39.
Pilinszky, János, *Selected Poems*, translated by Ted Hughes and János Csokits, Manchester, Carcanet, 1976.
Pitt, Valerie, *Tennyson Laureate*, London, Barrie and Rockliff, 1962.
Plath, Sylvia, ' "Three Caryatids without a Portico" by Hugo Robus. A Study in Sculptural Dimensions', *Chequer 9*, Winter 1956, pp. 2–3.
Plath, Sylvia, *Letters Home: Correspondence 1950–1963*, ed. Aurelia Schober Plath, London, Faber, 1975.
Plath, Sylvia, *Collected Poems*, London, Faber, 1981.
Plath, Sylvia, *The Journals of Sylvia Plath*, ed. Frances McCullough and Ted Hughes, New York, Dial, 1982.
Plath, Sylvia, *The Journals of Sylvia Plath 1950–1962*, ed. Karen V. Kukil, London, Faber, 2000.
Plato, *The Last Days of Socrates*, tr. Hugh Tredennick, Harmondsworth, Penguin, 1954.

Popa, Vasko, *Collected Poems 1943–1976*, tr. Anne Pennington with an introduction by Ted Hughes, Manchester, Carcanet, 1978.

Racine, Jean, *Tragédies Choisies de Racine*, New York, Doubleday, 1962.

Radin, Paul, *The Trickster*, Routledge, London, 1956.

Ramanujan, A.K., tr., *Speaking of Siva*, Harmondsworth, Penguin, 1973.

Redgrove, Peter, 'Windings and Conchings', *TLS*, 11 November 1983, p. 1238.

Rilke, Rainer Maria, *'New Poems [1907]*, tr. Edgar Snow, San Francisco, North Point Press, 1984.

Rilke, Rainer Maria, *Duino Elegies*, tr. Stephen Cohn, Manchester, Carcanet, 1989.

Roberts, Neil, 'Ted Hughes and the Laureateship', *Critical Quarterly*, 27, 2, 1985, pp. 3–5.

Roberts, Neil, *Narrative and Voice in Postwar Poetry*, Harlow, Longman, 1999.

Robinson, Craig, *Ted Hughes as Shepherd of Being*, Basingstoke, Macmillan, 1989.

Rose , Jacqueline, *The Haunting of Sylvia Plath*, London, Virago, 1991.

Russel, Nick, *Poets by Appointment: Britain's Laureates*, Poole, Blandford Press, 1981.

Sagar, Keith, *The Art of Ted Hughes* (1975), 2nd edition, Cambridge, Cambridge University Press, 1978.

Sagar, Keith, ed., *The Achievement of Ted Hughes*, Manchester, Manchester University Press, 1983.

Sagar, Keith, ed., *The Challenge of Ted Hughes*, Basingstoke and London, Macmillan, 1994.

Sagar, Keith, *The Laughter of Foxes: A Study of Ted Hughes*, Liverpool, Liverpool University Press, 2000.

Sagar, Keith, Programme note for Northern Broadsides production of *Alcestis*, 2000; also on the 'Earth-Moon' website, http://www.earth-moon.org.

Sagar, Keith and Stephen Tabor, *Ted Hughes: A Bibliography 1946–1995*, London, Mansell, 1998.

Scigaj, Leonard M., *The Poetry of Ted Hughes: Form and Imagination*, University of Iowa Press, 1986.

Scigaj, Leonard M., ed., *Critical Essays on Ted Hughes*, New York, G.K. Hall & Co., 1992.

Seneca, Lucius Annaeus, *Seneca VIII Tragedies I*, tr. Frank Justus Miller, Loeb Classical Library, London, Heinemann, 1917.

Shakespeare, William, *Macbeth*, ed. A.R. Braunmuller, The New Cambridge Shakespeare, Cambridge, Cambridge University Press, 1997.

*Sir Gawain and the Green Knight*, ed. J.R.R. Tolkien and E.V. Gordon, Oxford, Clarendon Press, 1925.

Skea, Ann, *Ted Hughes: The Poetic Quest*, Armidale NSW, University of New England Press, 1994.

Smith, A.C.H., *Orghast at Persepolis*, London, Eyre Methuen, 1972.

Stevenson, Anne, *Bitter Fame: A Life of Sylvia Plath* (1989) Harmondsworth, Penguin, 1990.

Tennyson, Alfred, *Tennyson: A Selected Edition*, ed. Christopher Ricks, Harlow, Longman, 1969.

Uroff, Margaret Dickie, *Sylvia Plath and Ted Hughes*, Chicago, University of Illinois, 1979.

Van Dyne, Susan R., *Revising a Life: Sylvia Plath's Ariel Poems*, Chapel Hill and London, University of North Carolina Press, 1993.

Voloshinov, V.N., *Marxism and the Philosophy of Language*, tr. Ladislav Matejka and I.R.Titunik, 1973, Cambridge Mass. and London, Harvard University Press, 1986.

Wagner-Martin, Linda, *Sylvia Plath: A Biography* (1988), London, Cardinal, 1990.

Wagner-Martin, Linda, *Sylvia Plath: A Literary Life*, second edition, Basingstoke and New York, Palgrave Macmillan, 2003.

Williams, David, ed., *Peter Brook: A Theatrical Casebook*, London, Methuen, 1991.

Wright, Carolyn, 'What Happens in the Heart', *Poetry Review*, Vol.89 no.3, Autumn 1999, pp. 3–9.

Ycats, W.B., *Collected Poems*, London, Macmillan, 1963.

# Index

Printed in the United States
112714LV00001B/66/A